W9-DCG-927

One Nation, Indivisible

One Nation, Indivisible

Seeking Liberty and Justice from the Pulpit to the Streets

EDITED BY CELENE IBRAHIM

Foreword by Jennifer Howe Peace

WIPF & STOCK · Eugene, Oregon

ONE NATION, INDIVISIBLE
Seeking Liberty and Justice from the Pulpit to the Streets

Wipf & Stock
An Imprint of Wipf and Stock Publishers
199 W. 8th Ave., Suite 3
Eugene, OR 97401

www.wipfandstock.com

PAPERBACK ISBN: 978-1-5326-4570-9
HARDCOVER ISBN: 978-1-5326-4571-6
EBOOK ISBN: 978-1-5326-4572-3

Manufactured in the U.S.A. FEBRUARY 19, 2019

To the Light of the heavens and the Earth.

Contents

List of Illustrations

Contributors

VOLUME EDITOR:

Celene Ibrahim, PhD, is the author of numerous publications in the fields of Qur'anic studies, women's and gender studies, and interreligious relations. She holds a bachelor's degree with highest honors from Princeton University, an MDiv from Harvard University, and a PhD in Arabic and Islamic civilizations from Brandeis University. Dr. Ibrahim currently serves as the Muslim chaplain for Tufts University and has taught on the faculties of Boston Islamic Seminary, Hartford Seminary, Andover Newton Theological School, Hebrew College, Episcopal Divinity School, and Merrimack College. Her monograph on women in the Qur'an is forthcoming from Oxford University Press.

CONTRIBUTORS:

Imam Taymullah Abdur-Rahman is Muslim chaplain for the Massachusetts Department of Correction and is currently pursuing a doctorate in leadership psychology from William James College and an advanced degree in Islamic scholarship at Al-Salam Institute based in London. He has previously served as a Muslim chaplain at Harvard University and Northeastern University and for several years provided Holocaust education through the nonprofit Facing History and Ourselves. He is the author of *44 Ways to Manhood* (International Islamic Publishing House, 2018) and is executive producer and host of Exconversations, a podcast on TIDAL streaming featuring reformed convicted felons. Imam Taymullah is a passionate advocate for prison-sentencing reform and urban youth intervention.

AHMAD ABUMRAIGHI is a Palestinian artist, architectural designer, and community activist. Raised in Jordan, and now based in the Washington, DC, metro area, he is training to be a humanitarian architect and is working toward more efficient approaches to refugee resettlement, rebuilding in cities following natural disasters, making schools more accessible, and improving access to clean water. Through his art and work, he hopes to counter hate and fear with beauty, peace, and a celebration of the connections that unite all people in a common humanity.

SOBIA AHMAD is an artist whose work probes how social, cultural, and political forces shape personal narratives and community experiences. By combining imagery from her own life with local-global dialogues about immigration, nationalism, persecution, and womanhood, she explores how struggles of identity and belonging can inform larger conversations about the fluidity of self, trans-nationalities, and social justice. Born and raised in Pakistan, Ahmad moved to the United States at the age of fourteen. She holds a bachelor's in studio arts and is a graduate of the Honors Art Program at the University of Maryland College Park. Her work has been included in the Sadat Art for Peace permanent collection and is displayed widely in the Washington, DC, metro area, in Los Angeles at the Craft and Folk Art Museum, and in several other cities including Chicago, Denver, Seattle, and London. Her work can be viewed online at www.sobiaahmad.com.

LUCA ALEXANDER works within and beyond the American Muslim community on themes related to gender and sexuality as a disabled, queer, and transgender writer who is passionate about raising the voices of marginalized women and LGBTQ+ individuals. Luca is the office manager at VISIONS, a Boston-based consulting team dedicated to issues of diversity and inclusion, is completing a master's degree in theological studies at Boston University, holds a bachelor's degree from Tufts University in religion and Middle Eastern studies, and has been invited to speak about Islam, gender, and sexuality at multiple institutions of higher education, including Columbia University and the Massachusetts Institute of Technology.

NANDO ÁLVAREZ is an Ecuadorian visual artist based in Washington, DC, and is a member of The Sanctuaries, a multicultural collective of local artists and community organizers who are transforming public discourses and policies surrounding race and religion by using their artistic collaborations to bring attention to pressing issues and causes.

ZAYNAB ANSARI serves as an instructor, board member, and scholar-in-residence at Tayseer Seminary in Knoxville, Tennessee, where she teaches classes on Islamic law, Qur'anic studies, early Islamic and American Muslim history, and women in Islam. She is a contributor to numerous Islamic educational portals, including SeekersHub, Lamppost Productions, and Rabata. She spent a decade studying Farsi, Arabic, and traditional Islam in the Middle East, the land of her ancestry, and graduated from Abu Nour Institute in Damascus. She also holds undergraduate degrees in history and Middle Eastern Studies from Georgia State University, and has pursued graduate coursework in world history.

MADONNA J. C. ARSENAULT, MDIV, is a certified spiritual director and director of spiritual care at Hammond Street Congregational Church in Bangor, Maine. She is also a chaplain at Northern Light Eastern Maine Medical Center and a residential counselor with Volunteers of America. Madonna was an activist and water protector at Standing Rock in North Dakota and a spiritual care provider with multiple organizations that serve Boston's chronically homeless population. She holds a masters of divinity from Andover Newton Theological School and is in the process of becoming ordained in the United Church of Christ. Madonna is the widow of Allen J. Sockabasin, the mother of four children, and the grandmother of five children who love sharing music and their creative souls.

GAYLE BRIDGET BARTLEY, MSW, LCSW, MDIV, is a licensed certified social worker who brings clinical experience with mental health disorders, trauma, and addictions. Her spiritual practice is drawn from Roman Catholicism, Taoism, and Buddhism. She is currently an educator at Boston Chong De Cultural and Educational Center in Cambridge, Massachusetts and provides pastoral care through St. Anthony's Shrine in Boston. She holds a master of divinity with honors at Andover Newton Theological School, a master of social work at Washington University, and a bachelor of science in education with highest honors from Lesley University.

REV. SUNDER JOHN BOOPALAN, PHD, earned his doctoral degree in religion and society at Princeton Theological Seminary and is ordained in the Baptist tradition. His latest book with Palgrave Macmillan is entitled *Memory, Grief, and Agency: A Political Theological Account of Wrongs and Rites*. John currently serves as minister for community life and theologian in residence at First Baptist Church in Newton Centre, Massachusetts.

SERGEANT KEVIN P. BRYANT is an affiliated Baptist minister and member of the Harvard University Police Department, where he serves as the security services coordinator, diversity and community liaison, and the Protestant chaplain. He has served the Departmentat Harvard University since 1991 and also serves as chaplain for the Newton, Massachusetts Police Department. He is a member of the National Organization of Church Security and Safety Management and serves on the board of directors for Granada House, a residential treatment facility with a proud history of helping people live free from addiction. Sergeant Bryant received a master of arts in pastoral studies from Andover Newton Theological School.

REV. LAUREN SEGANOS COHEN, MDIV, lives in southern California, where she has recently been called as pastor of the Pomona Fellowship Church of the Brethren. She is ordained in the Church of the Brethren, a church with Anabaptist roots that emphasizes community, peace, and service to others. In 2014–15 she was named a fellow in the Center for Interreligious and Communal Leadership Education (CIRCLE) and has served in both higher education and hospital chaplaincy settings.

LYNN COOPER, MDIV, serves as Catholic chaplain at Tufts University, her undergraduate alma mater, a position she has held for over a decade. She earned a master of divinity from Harvard Divinity School and is a candidate for the doctor of ministry at Boston University School of Theology. Her academic work explores how the Catholic religious imagination and sacramental living can support a campus culture that encourages reverence for the body, attentiveness to the spirit, and an orientation toward the holy. Her spouse, Andrew, is a Unitarian Universalist minister and chaplain, and together they delight in Rory, their little tyke. If becoming a mom has taught her anything, it is that spirituality can thrive in the mucky, messy, and mundane.

WIL DARCANGELO, MDIV, is the minister at First Parish Unitarian Universalist Church in Fitchburg, Massachusetts. Also a columnist and blogger, he writes a weekly column called Hopeful Thinking on spiritual optimism in the information age. Wil is active in community organizing, event production, and youth mentorship, specifically regarding individual and community empowerment through participation in the cultural economy. Married to his husband Jamie Darcangelo, RN, they live with their daughter Lavender, friends Peter and Christoph, and several beloved animals. Wil is also a vocalist, carpenter, and stained glass artist.

Rabbi Michelle Dardashti serves as the rabbi of Brown RISD Hillel and associate university chaplain for the Jewish community at Brown. Daughter of an Iranian Jewish cantor and an American folk singer, Rabbi Dardashti brings to her roles a deep understanding of global Jewry; Jewish music, practice, and culture; and a commitment to fostering pluralistic communities. She has also served as director of community engagement at Temple Beth El in Stamford, Connecticut and was the Marshall T. Meyer Rabbinic Fellow at Congregation B'nai Jeshurun in Manhattan, one of the country's most vibrant congregations. Rabbi Dardashti was ordained and received a master's degree in Jewish education from the Jewish Theological Seminary.

Tahirah Dean, Esq., is an immigration attorney in Dallas, Texas where she assists asylum seekers and those in deportation proceedings. Before moving to Texas, she was involved in interfaith work through the Islamic Society of Boston Cultural Center (ISBCC).

Gabriela De Golia is an activist, educator, and healer who became a spiritual seeker in her early childhood. The granddaughter of devout Catholics, she grew skeptical of dogmas while simultaneously being enamored with the beauty of faith. She fell in love with the teachings of Jesus in her mid-twenties thanks to Zen Master Thich Nhat Hanh during her residency at a Buddhist monastery. Gabriela is now joyfully connected to her Christian heritage and is pursuing a lifelong journey of fusing spiritual growth with social transformation.

Rev. Donna Dolham, MSW, MDiv, is an ordained minister in the Unitarian Universalist Association and holds a master's degree in social work from Boston University and an MDiv from Andover Newton Theological School with a certificate in ethics and justice. She has served as a clinical social worker in coastal Maine with a specialty working with transgender and queer persons and their families and has been involved for decades in community organizing efforts to increase access to basic rights for people living on the margins of society.

Rabbi Leonard Gordon, DMin, received his doctor of ministry at Andover Newton Theological School. He codirects Interfaith Partners for Peace and is rabbi at Temple Beth Sholom in Framingham, Massachusetts.

Linda Hartley, PhD, earned her doctoral degree in political science from the Rutgers State University of New Jersey. She holds an MDiv and a certificate in spiritual and pastoral care from Andover Newton Theological School and an undergraduate degree in government and economics from California State University, Sacramento. She is a member of the Rhode Island Conference of the United Church of Christ and taught political science at several colleges and universities in the northeast and Montana.

Kythe Heller is a poet, writer, performer, filmmaker, and scholar currently completing a doctorate at Harvard University in comparative religion and critical media studies. She is author of the poetry collections *Immolation* and *The Thunder Perfect Mind*, as well as scholarly works published in *Arvo Pärt's White Light: Media, Culture, Politics* (Cambridge University Press, 2017) and *Quo Anima: Innovation and Spirituality in Contemporary Poetry* (University of Akron Press, forthcoming). She has received grants, awards, and residencies from Harvard University, Radcliffe Institute, MacDowell Artists' Colony, Virginia Center for the Creative Arts, Portland State University, Vermont Studio Center, and elsewhere; her recent film and multimedia work has been presented in Boston, New York, and California. Currently, she is a visiting poet on the faculty of Bard College's Language and Thinking Program.

Rev. Soren M. Hessler is director of graduate academic services at Drew University and senior consultant at the Miller Center for Interreligious Learning and Leadership at Hebrew College. Soren previously served as associate director of the Miller Center and as chapel associate for leadership development at Boston University's Marsh Chapel. He is an ordained elder in full connection in the West Ohio Annual Conference of the United Methodist Church and coeditor of *Words to Live By: Sacred Sources for*

Interreligious Engagement (Orbis, 2018). He is completing a PhD in practical theology at Boston University School of Theology, concentrating in leadership and administration, and holds a BA/MA in church administration, MDiv, and EdM from Boston University.

MATTHEW BLAIR HOYT, MTS, is an ordained bishop in the Church of Jesus Christ of Latter-day Saints. He holds a master of theological studies degree from Harvard Divinity School and currently serves on the School's Alumni/ae Council. He resides in California with his family.

MIRIAM ISRAEL serves at the National Democratic Institute, a nonprofit, nonpartisan organization, where she focuses on inclusion and civic participation for minority and marginalized populations abroad. She holds a BA from Tufts University, where she studied international relations and Middle Eastern studies. She was an inaugural Boston Interfaith Leadership Initiative Fellow at the Miller Center of Hebrew College and is currently on the board of the International Association for Religious Freedom's US chapter. Hailing from the Washington, DC, area, she is passionate about language learning, interreligious exchange, vegetarian food, and connecting with people of diverse backgrounds.

YUSEF ABDUL JALEEL is a New York-based digital media artist who specializes in vector-based illustration. He has created media and apparel geared toward the Muslim experience in America and has been commissioned by Harlem Heritage Tours and other entities. Abdul Jaleel has enjoyed major exhibitions in New York and at the Art Sanctuary Gallery in Philadelphia. His art is also included in notable private collections. He is a graduate of the City College of New York where he received a bachelor of fine arts in electronic design and multimedia.

REV. KAREN G. JOHNSTON, MDIV, is an ordained Unitarian Universalist minister and is currently serving as settled minister at The Unitarian Society in East Brunswick, New Jersey. She is a graduate of the cooperative MDiv program between Hartford Seminary and Andover Newton Theological School.

HAJJAH KAMARA is completing a degree in law at Northeastern University School of Law. In addition to her legal studies, she coordinates programs and continuing education at the Boston Islamic Seminary. Before moving to Boston, she taught social studies at a private Islamic school in Tampa, Florida, spent nearly a decade working with a homeless advocacy organization called Project Downtown Tampa, and organized dental relief trips to multiple countries. Ethnically from Sierra Leone, Hajjah was born in Virginia and grew up in Florida. She graduated from the University of South Florida with a BA in international studies.

Saskia Bory Keeley is a Swiss photographer based in New York City. She was educated at Geneva University, Sotheby's Institute of Art, and the New Academy for Art Studies in London. She also received training at the International Center for Photography in New York City. Saskia partners with humanitarian organizations to bring attention to their valuable work, including Leaders' Quest in India, The END Fund/Amani Global Works in the Democratic Republic of the Congo, Roots and Taghyeer in Palestine's West Bank, the We Love Reading program in Jordan, and the Pico Union Project in Los Angeles. She also runs photography workshops in which participants unpack fear and bias through the simple acts of looking and listening.

Rev. David M. Kohlmeier, MDiv, serves as minister at the Unitarian Universalist Fellowship of Falmouth in Cape Cod, Massachusetts. He earned a master of divinity degree at Andover Newton Theological School with a certificate in interfaith leadership. His spiritual journey has taken him from his upbringing as a Jehovah's Witness in rural Appalachia through Neo-Paganism and Buddhism into Unitarian Universalism.

Rabbi Nancy Fuchs Kreimer, PhD, is associate professor of religious studies and the founding director of the Department of Multifaith Studies and Initiatives at the Reconstructionist Rabbinical College where she was ordained in 1982. She holds a master's degree from Yale Divinity School and a doctorate from Temple University. With support from the Henry Luce Foundation, she has pioneered innovative community-based learning opportunities for rabbinical students and their Christian and Muslim peers. She is a founding board member of the Interfaith Center of Philadelphia, Shoulder-to-Shoulder, and the Sisterhood of Salaam Shalom. Her many publications include a coedited volume entitled *Chapters of the Heart: Jewish Women Sharing the Torah of Our Lives* (2013) and a coauthored volume, with Kelly Clark and Aziz Abu Sarah, entitled *Strangers, Neighbors, Friends: Jewish, Christian, and Muslim Reflections* (2018), both by Wipf and Stock Publishers.

Lisa Loughlin, MDiv, earned a master of divinity, a certificate in interfaith leadership, and a certificate in spiritual and pastoral care from Andover Newton Theological School and is currently a member-in-discernment in the Metropolitan Boston Association of the Massachusetts Conference of the United Church of Christ. She was raised Roman Catholic, and her faith is influenced by an introduction to Twelve-Step philosophy in early adulthood.

Huda Lutfi, PhD, is a cultural historian whose work in the field of the visual arts translates, excavates, and makes vocal the silenced voices and marginalized spaces that cross historical and cultural contexts. Her work merges art and activism, all the while communicating a desire to liberate the human spirit and imaginary. She holds a PhD in Islamic culture and history from McGill University in Montreal, Canada.

Nancy Marks has been a community activist and visual artist for over twenty-five years—primarily as a printmaker and painter. A Boston resident, she is fascinated by urban living, with all its trials and tribulations. In her work, Nancy also explores themes of memory and grieving, as well as addiction and recovery. Her work can be viewed at nancymarksartist.com.

Marlyn Miller, PhD, earned a doctoral degree in comparative history from Brandeis University, where she studied the history of women in the Russian Orthodox Church. She continues to publish in the field as well as edit and translate related works. She graduated from Andover Newton Theological School with a master of arts in theological studies, and is currently in a process of ministerial discernment. At seminary, she was blessed to be able to approach religion with both heart and head, including the study of the Qur'an. She is grateful to be the mother of an amazing son, Elijah.

Rev. Otto O'Connor, MDiv, is the minister at the First Parish Unitarian Universalist congregation in Malden, Massachusetts. He has served as an associate chaplain at the Waysmeet Center, the United Campus Ministry to the University of New Hampshire and as the intern minister at the Unitarian Universalist Area Church at First Parish in Sherborn. He earned an MDiv and an MA in global interreligious leadership at Andover Newton Theological School.

Jennifer Howe Peace, PhD has been an interfaith educator and activist for two decades. She was the first associate professor of interfaith studies at Andover Newton Theological School where she co-founded CIRCLE, the Center for Interreligious and Communal Leadership Education. In addition, Peace co-founded the Interreligious/Interfaith Studies Program Unit at the American Academy of Religion in 2013 and the Association for Interreligious/Interfaith Studies (AIIS) in 2017. Her publications include the co-edited volumes *Interreligious/Interfaith Studies: Defining a New Field* (Beacon, 2018) and *My Neighbor's Faith: Stories of Interreligious Encounter, Growth, and Transformation* (Orbis, 2012). She resides in Cambridge, Massachusetts where she consults and writes in the area of interreligious education.

Nancy Elizabeth Reinhardt holds a master of arts in pastoral care with honors from Andover Newton Theological School and a bachelor's degree in American history with high honors from the University of Massachusetts Boston. She is currently working toward becoming a Jewish chaplain. Her areas of interest within pastoral care include end of life care and trauma care. A Reiki practitioner with experience volunteering in a hospice for five years, she is passionate about interfaith engagement as well as deepening her Jewish faith and practice.

Rev. Jerrell Riggins, MDiv, is a pastor at Messiah Baptist Church in Brockton, Massachusetts. He earned a master of divinity from Andover Newton Theological School and specializes in clergy compensation, pastoral care, and education.

Ariella Ruth is a poet whose work has appeared in *Epiphany*, *Bombay Gin*, *Yew Journal*, *The Ocean State Review*, and elsewhere. She was a finalist for the Two Sylvias Press 2017 Full-Length Poetry Manuscript Prize, and has a poem published on a sandstone monolith as part of the City of Boulder, Colorado's Downtown District and the Library and Arts Department's West Pearl Poetry Project. She works at the Center for the Study of

World Religions at Harvard Divinity School, where she assists in curating a programming thread on poetry, philosophy, and religion.

REV. STEPHANIE RUTT, DMIN, has been an interfaith minister since 2005 and serves as presiding minister of the Tree of Life Interfaith Temple in Amherst, New Hampshire. She is the founder of the Tree of Life School for Sacred Living, LLC, and creator of the Tree of Life Interfaith Seminary. Rev. Rutt has developed numerous spiritual study programs and has published four books, including most recently a work entitled *Doorway to the Sacred: Transform Your Life with Mantra Prayer* (Tree of Life Publishing, 2014). She holds a doctor of ministry from Andover Newton Theological School with honors.

ARIZ SALEEM is currently pursuing his MDiv at the University of Chicago Divinity School. He has served as a community organizer for the Islamic Circle of North America's ICNA Relief, a faith-based charity organization headquartered in New York. Alongside his studies, he works for *Incomer Magazine* as a contributing writer and lives with his wife and two children in Hyde Park, Chicago.

KEVIN SINGER is codirector of Neighborly Faith, an initiative that helps encourage evangelical Christians to be active in interreligious networks. He is also a PhD student at North Carolina State studying higher education, and a research assistant for the Interfaith Diversity Experiences and Attitudes Longitudinal Survey (IDEALS), a nationwide study of college students' experiences with worldview diversity. Finally, he is an adjunct faculty member teaching religious studies at two Chicagoland-area community colleges. He lives with his wife, Brittany, and four young children in Raleigh, North Carolina.

JOHN SODERBLOM, MDIV, earned a master's degree in counseling from Cambridge College, an MDiv at Andover Newton Theological School, and a bachelor's degree in political science and history from Gordon College. He writes regularly on issues of social justice and interfaith relations, has worked in information technology, and has served on the staff for several elected officials. He is a father of four and a grandfather of three.

Cheryl Stromski, MDiv, is a music minister at the Stratham United Church of Christ and has been a professional pianist and vocal director for over forty years playing locally, nationally, and internationally. She holds an MDiv with a certificate in interfaith studies from Andover Newton Theological School and works in New England and beyond to promote interfaith cooperation around social justice issues, especially on criminal justice reform and reentry.

Rev. Sam Teitel, MDiv, is a Unitarian Universalist minister, poet, and punk rocker currently serving as the minister of The Church of the River in Memphis, Tennessee. He holds an MDiv and a master's degree in global interreligious leadership from Andover Newton Theological School. He has previously worked on the congregational staff of Unitarian Universalist churches in Boston and Wayland, Massachusetts and was a fellow at the Center for Interreligious and Communal Leadership Education, where he used poetry as a setting for dialogue between people from different faith traditions. He is the recipient of the H. Otheman Smith Community Congregational Preaching Award and is a storytelling prizewinner at the Preachers Fight Club.

Charity Terry-Lorenzo resides in San Diego, California, where the mountains, desert, and ocean converge and where she homeschools her children, which is almost as much of an education for her as it is for them.

John Torrey, MDiv, earned a degree in ministry from Andover Newton Theological School and holds a bachelor's degree from Princeton University, where he majored in religion, minored in global health and health policy, and conducted research in Tanzania. John is a dedicated environmentalist and proudly hails from Hanover, New Hampshire.

Rev. Pamela Wannie, MDiv, is the associate pastor at South Congregational Church in Centerville, Massachusetts and a spiritual care provider at Duffy Health Center on Cape Cod, where she helps to provide a path to healing and wholeness for those who are experiencing homelessness or who are at risk. For over twenty years Pamela has led a vital music ministry, teaching foundational faith values through song and sound. Through a grant from the Calvin Institute, Pamela has co-led innovative and creative worship services and offers workshops through the United Church of

Christ. She holds a master of divinity from Andover Newton Theological School.

Allyson Zacharoff is pursuing rabbinical studies at the Reconstructionist Rabbinical College. She has a passion for bringing people together from different faith traditions and has been honored as a Russell Berrie Fellow in Interreligious Studies at the Pontifical University of St. Thomas Aquinas in Rome, a Conflict Resolution Fellow at the Pardes Institute of Jewish Studies in Jerusalem, and an International Peacemaking Fellow at Hartford Seminary in Connecticut. She works on multifaith strategy at the Multifaith Alliance for Syrian Refugees and blogs at christmasandkreplach.blogspot.com.

Nora Zaki, MDiv, is the inaugural coordinator of Muslim student life at Vassar College, is a *State of Formation* fellow, and serves as an Arabic-English editor for the publishing company Fons Vitae. She was among the first Muslims to graduate from the University of Chicago's master of divinity program where she specialized in Islamic studies, Arabic language, and chaplaincy. She has served as a counselor at the American Learning Institute for Muslims (ALIM) and has lived and studied in Morocco, Jordan, and Egypt in addition to traveling in Palestine, Israel, Turkey, and Algeria.

Foreword

Jennifer Howe Peace

Celene Ibrahim began this collection during the lead-up to the 2016 US elections, and since this time we have seen an alarming rise in the rhetoric of dehumanization. This has been on vivid display in the language and assemblies of emboldened white supremacists, in sweeping mischaracterizations of people immigrating to this country as "criminal illegal aliens," and in the language of the president's executive order (13769), recently upheld by the Supreme Court, banning immigration from Muslim-majority countries under the inflammatory title "Protecting the Nation from Foreign Terrorist Entry into the United States."

Now more than ever, we need to listen to the voices included in this volume offering more faithful ways of speaking to and about each other that are rooted in a commitment to upholding the human dignity of every person. In moments of moral crisis, our showing up for one another—with our voices and with our feet—can offer hope to those who have been ostracized. Moreover, what we say about each other from the podium, the pulpit, the bimah, or the minbar matters.[1] Given the rise and persistence of anti-Islamic rhetoric, we must think about what is said or left unsaid about our Muslim brothers and sisters by our clergy and representatives. This is especially true when, given the prevalence of social media, what we say about each other transcends our parochial niches.

How can we use our various platforms to speak about each other in ways that promote understanding, compassion, and relationship-building? How can we speak in ways that interrupt stereotypes, mitigate violence,

1. A bimah is a raised platform in a Jewish synagogue, the place from where the Torah is read. Similarly, a minbar is the raised platform in a mosque from where the sermon is delivered during the Friday afternoon congregational prayer.

and promote healing across divides? How can we create room for what the late theologian Krister Stendahl termed "holy envy"—that sense of awe and gratitude we experience when discovering something unique and powerful in our neighbor's religious identity, practices, or beliefs?

This gem of a collection is a window into how innovative religious leaders are thinking about and engaging with and within Muslim communities. For those with pulpits, in particular, the volume's sermons, stories, prayers, and poems are models for inspired, informed, and compassionate preaching. It is a book full of heart, insights, and provocative questions that have emerged from deep theological and personal reflections.

The collection makes an implicit argument that our spiritual formation cannot happen in isolation. We need each other. It represents a commitment on the part of the editor, Celene Ibrahim, and all the contributors, to foster healing conversations as we live out our respective faith and civic commitments.

May it be so.

Preface

***Our Voice Our Power*, by Nando Álvarez**[1]

THIS ANTHOLOGY COMPRISES THE wisdom of preachers, poets, artists, mystics, scholars, and social changers working within movements for racial justice, immigrant justice, interfaith understanding, and on issues of socioeconomic equity. It is a conduit for the voices of professionals who are engaged in the work of healing, teaching, ministry, and civic activism, and it is a resource for people of curiosity and conviction to discover more

1. This image was originally commissioned for Dulles Justice Coalition to launch the campaign #MyMuslimBanStory and was then adapted for screen printing. The creator, Nando Álvarez, is an Ecuadorian visual artist based in Washington, DC, and is a member of The Sanctuaries, a multicultural collective of local artists and community organizers who are transforming public discourses and policies surrounding race and religion.

about the lives of American Muslims and the teachings of Islam through the reflections and personal stories of activists, rabbis, reverends, ministers, and chaplains who have built tried and true relationships with their colleagues, counterparts, and neighbors across lines of faith.

The reflections, poetry, and art found in this book are born of the longing for creative, honest, and bold thought-leadership. Whether readers are already deeply engaged in the world of anti-racism activism or anti-Islamophobia solidarity work, or possibly standing just outside this world and contemplating how to best engage, this compilation brings insight, perspective, and wisdom minted from experience. It provides encouragement for those of us who will not be intimidated by racist fearmongering, and hope for those of us who are seeking another way of being in relationship across human difference. It is a guide for those seeking deeper connections with Muslims and broader knowledge of Islam, but simultaneously, it provides sustenance for those of us who must necessarily wake up each morning and muster the chutzpah to keep challenging racism, xenophobia, and Islamophobia.

Together, the contributors and I share the conviction that robust and informed communication across our religious and philosophical differences is essential to our thriving as a multiethnic, multireligious, and multicultural society. We understand that promoting civil dialogue is crucial to the advance of democracy, and we embrace the possibility that our collective action, and our striving to promote cultural and religious literacy, will ultimately advance the dream of a united polity, a polity with liberty and justice *for all.*

Dr. Celene Ibrahim
Cambridge, Massachusetts
Muharram 1, 1440
September 11, 2018

Acknowledgments

This book would not have been possible without the dedicated and talented copy-editing of Dr. Marlyn Miller. I am especially grateful to Dr. Jennifer Howe Peace and Rabbi Or Rose for their friendship and excellent mentorship. The Reverend Soren Hessler has been a true colleague and exceptional administrator. Tahirah Dean, Sue Fendrick, Ariz Saleem, Arif Shaikh, Méli Solomon, and Nora Zaki have all been sources of generous editorial feedback. The staff of the Miller Center for Interreligious Learning and Leadership at Hebrew College, including Phoebe Oler, assisted with communications to bring the volume to press. A grant from The Henry Luce Foundation supported my joint appointment to the faculties of Andover Newton Theological School and Hebrew College between 2014 and 2017, and that role initially inspired this project.

Dr. Diana Eck and her team at the Pluralism Project at Harvard University initially propelled and supported my interests in the multireligious landscape of America. Rabbi Dr. Nancy Fuchs Kreimer has been a constant exemplar for how to bring joy to multifaith work. The Reverend Dr. Sarah Drummond and Rabbi Sharon Cohen Anisfeld have shown me how to lead institutions with wisdom and courage through changing times. My current and former colleagues at Tufts University Chaplaincy, including the Reverend Dan Bell, Walker Bristol, Alex Chiu, Zach Cole, Lynn Cooper, the Reverend Greg McGonigle, the Reverend Lambert Rahming, the Venerable Priya Sraman, the Venerable Upali Sraman, Rabbi Dr. Jeffrey Summit, and most recently Rabbi Dr. Naftali Brawer, have shown me how to serve with compassion and courage. The Ocean Park Association at Old Orchard Beach in Maine has been wonderful for interreligious dialogue and a summer respite, thanks to the hospitality and vision of Jerry Gosselin. The Morrissey family is, simply put, awesome. All praise to Whom all good comes and all good returns.

Introduction

MADE IN AMERICA

I REGULARLY GET ASKED questions about where I come from, how I ended up where I am, and why I do the work that I do, all questions that deeply inform this book's vision and origin. Truth be told, I did not know that Muslims *existed* when I was growing up. The school curriculum I was exposed to did not include anything about Islam (we were still in the 90s), and nearly every person I encountered within a fifty-mile radius of home was almost assuredly some variety of Christian and had an extremely high probability of also being of white European ancestry. In my schooling, textbooks contained overly simplified versions of American history and little pertaining to world history beyond ancient Egypt, Greece, and Rome, which were given as examples of cosmopolitanism before the dark ages. I distinctly remember that history education began with coloring pilgrims, just as my own daughter's schooling did two decades later in another small American town. Although names given by Native American and First Nation peoples dominated our knolls and streams, we barely discussed how "our" land had been appropriated, and the word "colonize" still held a positive valance for me. My whole frame of reference was Euro-American-centric.

I did receive good mentorship from dedicated individuals, but the curriculum was extremely thin on probing the significance of the twentieth-century social movements that redefined—and that continue to reconfigure—the social and civic landscape of America. We learned a scant bit about the civil rights movement and struggles for racial justice; what we did learn made it seem like all the prior glitches in the system had been worked out to satisfaction. I was tested in school on the maker of the cotton gin (Eli

Whitney), but if you asked me, I would have guessed that Malcolm X was a hip-hop artist. Martin Luther King Jr. Day meant little to my peers beyond a long-weekend ski escape. Korematsu? A variation of Italian tiramisu? I thought of "race" as something that other people had. All of my childhood friends—seemingly all of my town, and all of the adjacent towns for that matter—were descended from European ancestry. I was, quite frankly, clueless about other ways of defining the American experience.

I was mostly unconscious then of my immense socioeconomic privileges too, probably in part because my mother shopped second-hand before it was trendy. My parents owned a home with a picket fence, a pool, a golden retriever, and the perfect number of children (two, so as not to overrun them entirely). A vivid memory—overhearing a girl on my cheerleading team asking the coach to wait until the *next* Friday to pay for her uniform—still lingers in my mind as one of my early glimpses into living paycheck to paycheck. This idyllic home life sheltered me from plenty of other social dynamics too.

I definitely could not define "gender," but so long as I could win a pushup contest and outrun all the boys, whatever "gender" was, it was not holding me back. I had little realization of how much further I would have to run to get ahead as a female in the professional world. I would be hard pressed then to talk cogently about "the women's movement" beyond a few celebrated suffragettes;[1] and despite having won some landmark cases, RBG was not yet "Notorious" as a superhero.[2] I was a beneficiary of the courageous labor of generations, but I could not anticipate then all of the unfinished business still ahead. I did, however, one glorious day happen upon a rack of my mother's old bell-bottoms, including a pair of bright red, velvet "hot pants" that I suspected had something to do with an idea called "feminism."[3]

1. Some of those suffragettes were even ardent advocates *against* voting rights for African Americans, but somehow those messier details never came up in the curriculum.

2. The Ruth Bader Ginsberg action figure comes complete with wire-rimmed glasses "to see through patriarchal bullsh*t," heeled loafers "to stand tall against oppressors," and a "righteous robe," that is the "the next best thing to a cape." For details (and preorders) see, "Ruth Bader Ginsburg."

3. For the record, my mother maintains that those hot pants were not actually *hers*, but a yard-sale find for a potential Halloween costume. We'll believe her.

STRETCHING THE HORIZONS

Wikipedia describes my hometown of Kresgeville, Pennsylvania as a "climatic region"; wonderfully climatic it is, but—aside from the demolition derby at the county fair—the pace of life was hardly climactic. The world beyond the idyllic countryside beckoned, such that when my newly minted driver's license permitted escapades to Philadelphia, I seized upon a reprieve from country homogeneity. Through participation in the Hugh O'Brien Youth Organization, I was connected to the United World College movement and, thankfully, to an immense international scholarship fund sponsored by Shelby M. C. and Gale Davis.

I forfeited my senior year of high school in Pennsylvania to study at a United World College located in and around the grounds of a giant castle next to famed hot springs in Montezuma, New Mexico. There I took a two-year religion class that was taught by a Zen monk whose features matched the image of God on the Sistine Chapel—with the addition of full robes. His look alone helped me find the discipline to meditate: I could imagine that with an outstretched finger he would zap me into enlightenment when I started to doze or squirm. His laugh would echo off the rainbow-streaked walls of the Dawn Light Sanctuary and make his belly bounce like a Hallmark Santa. He was simply brilliant, and fit my definition of insanely cool. He had built a home from his own sunbaked clay bricks complete with zendo, labyrinth, library, indoor fountain (think the likes of an Alhambra Palace courtyard), with an adjacent art studio; *and* he ran an NGO supporting orphaned girls in Nepal and Central America. I began to see that there were more possibilities for living life than I had previously imagined.

The United World College curriculum most definitely did bring up world history, indigenous peoples, colonialism, religions, socioeconomic issues, and so much more. The environment was like barre class for the mind, and it gave my worldview a great stretch. I blissfully poured over shelves worth of brilliant literature—much of it from outside of a Eurocentric heritage. I had to intensely question who I was, what I stood for, and what I wanted to try to contribute to the world.

I followed these studies with a "gap year"[4] quest winding through parts of South America and then Europe, spurred on by insatiable curiosity and a global cast of friends with couches, cabins, and cottages that

4. Parents: The "gap year" is real, I assure you. Your child is not trying to escape adulthood—they are stretching their adult wings. Just let them fly and ready your safety nets.

were up for dibs in an era before Airbnb. I financed myself through occasional stints teaching English and in several nonprofit internships where I made coffee and pretended that I was making policy. In any event, the term "global South" began to mean something more than the lower half of a three-dimensional map.

By the time that I entered college, I had basically already acquired the "global perspective" promised by the liberal arts and distinctly recall being shocked by the lack of "diversity" in the student body I joined, as compared to the experiences that I had just come from. Everyone at college seemed to dress in clothing from the same three stores and carry virtually the same handbag. If these peers of mine had different worldviews and religious identities, it was not a subject of much conversation. It seemed that among my classmates two modalities for being were dominant: stressed then drunk.

I found myself craving midnight discussions of Langston Hughes, the latest policies of the IMF—I even missed conversations about cricket now that I knew it was both a bug and a sport. It took some time, but I eventually did find a cohort, mostly among *other* international students who were also trying with varying degrees of success to call Princeton home.[5] I found the campus sangha where we would do different varieties of insight meditation. I hung out around the psych labs where you could get paid to have graduate students attach electrodes to your brain.

Despite all my prior travels and exposure, before taking a class with esteemed political scientist Dr. Amaney Jamal in my first semester in college, I had not conceptualized the Middle East as having much more than sand, camels, palms, pyramids, and Bedouins. But as it turned out, there was so much more to offer, including the very last study abroad program that was accepting enrollments. So, as a sophomore, I arrived at the door of the American University in Cairo proudly knowing my first Arabic phrase: "*Shukran yā ḥabībī*!"[6] As a parting gift, my best friend at Princeton

5. Well, I was *still* an American at an American university, but by that point, I already thought of myself as a "global citizen." Little did I realize it, but I was right with the vision for the university; a few years prior to my arrival on campus, Princeton had added "and in the service of all nations" to the words of its prior motto, "in the Nation's Service," which originally harkened back to the legacy of Woodrow Wilson. Not so long ago, the motto was again updated to replace "in the service of all nations" with the words "and the service of humanity," a tribute to Princeton alumna and US Supreme Court Justice Sonia Sotomayor.

6. The expression I knew to be a term of endearment, and it proved to be my essential phrase for exiting taxis, purchasing street food, and just generally making friends with

had gifted me her copy of the *al-Kitaab* Arabic textbook. In retrospect, I now distinctly recall that Amity complained quite regularly about how the drudgery of Arabic homework was destroying her social life. I clearly did not take heed; my weekends for the next decade consisted of good times with Hans Wehr and Edward William Lane, linguists whose copious Arabic-English dictionaries are the delight of every Arabic student.[7]

PROVIDENCE

Much transpired in those next few months in Egypt, but to summarize the essential parts—as I did for my parents on a transatlantic phone line—I converted to Islam, decided to put classes at Princeton on hold to study in Egypt longer, and agreed to marry an Egyptian because I was ready for a new phase in life. That conversation put my mother on the next plane across the Atlantic, but I remember it all going much better than I could have hoped. As she hugged me with greetings, she whispered something to the effect: "oh, he'll make *such* cute kids."

Many people begin exploring Islam when they meet a Muslim life partner, but this was just partially true in my case. In my first weeks in Egypt, I had developed an affinity for the works of Persian Sufi masters through a class at the American University of Cairo taught by historian and visual artist Huda Lutfi. I gravitated toward the formidable intellectual legacy of Islam and its practices for cultivating the spirit. The legacy of the Prophet Muhammad, peace be upon him, was so vivid and brilliant; reading through thousands upon thousands of sayings passed down from him and about him awakened my desire to better understand his legacy. I began to discover so much more than what had met my cursory glance in my previous world religion classes. Islam was the most personally inspiring religious and philosophical framework that I had encountered in all of my journeyings; the more I studied the Qur'anic revelations, the more the Qur'an would reveal itself. The religion was alive in people's beings, and it

locals. Unbeknownst to me, it was not exactly a term that a twenty-something white Western woman would typically use in those contexts. I can only imagine how hilarious I sounded when topping off my broken classical Arabic with something akin to "thanks, homie."

7. To be fair, Arabic has been an actively spoken language for over two millennia, giving rise to an incredibly rich and varied vocabulary; the language has regional dialects from Mauritania to Afghanistan. When people ask me if I am fluent in Arabic, I just have to laugh.

made me alive too. Islam was an ocean, and I was thoroughly enjoying the plunge into learning.

Many of the Muslim twenty-somethings I knew were wise beyond their years, and I suspected that it had something to do with their immersion in Islamic spiritual practices. In any case, my own studies and emerging practices brought about a clarity that enabled me to see a golden-hearted person when I stumbled upon him. I was utterly lost—literally—and needing directions for how to get back to the "*bayt al-ṭulāb*," the student's house affiliated with the American University.[8] It just so happened that the person I came upon on the street corner was courteous in giving me directions back to the student house and also happened to resemble, in my grandmother's best description (her words not mine), "a model in a Macy's catalogue." As I later came to understand, he was a professional athlete, and I had managed to get lost on the street in front of his gym—thank you Providence!

We came from different cultural backgrounds, but in conversations over the course of a few weeks—conversations in an amalgamation of broken English on his part and broken Arabic on mine—we clicked over our mutual dedication to spiritual practice, our competitive but generous spirits, and our appreciation for humor and health food. It just worked. So, I did *exactly* what the staff of our study abroad orientation cautioned us against: I accepted a marriage proposal from a local. We got married at a government office a few weeks after we had met on the street. I had accepted Islam officially a week or so earlier in an office somewhere in al-Azhar, the millennia-old institution of Islamic learning. On our big day, we taxied around Cairo on a bureaucratic scavenger hunt to get all the right validation stamps for the marriage paperwork, but even when all stamps were secured, there was another hurdle: I was due a *mahr*.[9] My husband-to-be had forgotten that part, and I was not studied enough in Islamic law at that point to know that I was due a gift. The clerk behind the desk insisted we *had to have one* before he could legitimately finish the marriage contract (otherwise known as the certificate for winning our bureaucratic scavenger hunt). I gleefully received the crumpled one hundred Egyptian pounds

8. The Arabic root for *ṭulāb* are the letters corresponding in transliteration to *ṭ-l-b*, a root that carries a primary meaning of "seeking out"; hence, students are "seekers" of knowledge.

9. In Islamic law, the groom must give the bride a *mahr*, a mutually agreed upon gift, as a type of security deposit for the marriage.

Ahmed happened to have in his pocket.[10] Contract completed, the man at the desk had us stamp our inky thumbprints on the contract. The entirety of the contract was in Arabic, and I had essentially no clue at that point what it said precisely: it was a leap of faith, but it worked.

OVERCOMING THE PERCEPTION OF OPPRESSION

A headscarf is often depicted as the epitome of a Muslim women's oppression. While my Christian mother was worrying about my eternal salvation, and while my Italian-American father was worrying over how I would make proper pasta sauce without wine, my decision to wear a headscarf came without much deliberation. A headscarf was easy. Soon after I moved to wearing an Arabian-style face veil (commonly called a niqab). The head coverings were external trappings—the harder parts entailed improving character *and* waking up to pray the predawn prayer consistently (still works in progress). Initially, I had some rather pragmatic reasons for assuming the face veil: my Arabic was *finally* improving, and with a concealed face, street vendors and taxi drivers could not realize that I was foreign, and *then* I could get the prices for locals instead of for Western tourists.

Aside from allowing me literally to go undercover, I found the privacy enjoyable, and I began to consider it as a spiritual practice.[11] Much of life experience up to that point had been about gaining external forms of approval; it was refreshing to have the privacy to focus on the internal dimensions of who I was and who I was becoming. My veils came straight from Mecca—they were my request of my mother-in-law when she went on a pilgrimage trip—and to me, they epitomized sacred space. I wore a niqab for about a year in Egypt, and when we returned to the United States as a couple, I had no interest in removing it. The practice had more to teach me.

Back in the States, there were indeed a lot of lessons to be learned, both for me and for others who encountered me. The United States was in the midst of the Iraq War (we still are), and stereotypes of women in veils as silenced and oppressed were being used as a justification to "liberate

10. This sum was about twenty American dollars then; a kilo of beef now costs more than what I happily received in *mahr*. Thankfully, having a *mahr* was not a vital part of my economic security, but it can be for some women who may even write their marriage contracts so as to be entitled a "deferred *mahr*" should their husbands subsequently pursue a divorce.

11. My Catholic middle school class had voted me "most likely to become a nun"; they got the covering part right.

women" (by invading their societies, dismantling their governments, and arming militia groups). I regularly got a barrage of questions about why I would "oppress myself," but I would gladly chat about *Muslim* women's rights—right through the niqab—with anyone who cared to engage.

Once while walking with my family down a pleasant tree-lined sidewalk in Princeton, I caught a glimpse of a man scowling at me from behind the wheel of his shiny car. He was so focused on scowling at me that he did not take notice of a parked delivery truck and rear-ended it. Aside from his Mercedes, no one was hurt. The niqab also took me some trial and error to figure out back in the American context. I once attempted to water ski, and in my black "garb"—as I have heard it called—jumping in and out of the wake, I was nothing short of a water ninja until the face flap became suctioned to my face. Then, the water ninja in her abaya went down.[12] I have since acquired a "burkini," a full-body swimsuit designed especially for active Muslim women—think wetsuit with a skirt.

After a three-year commitment, I decided to no longer wear a face veil,[13] and wearing headscarves has been my practice since.[14] Still, there are mornings when I miss the wonderful degree of mobile privacy that the niqab provided. Just as many women have a practice of putting on "concealer" makeup when leaving the house, for me, the niqab was a practice too. This practice, though, enabled me to begin to unlearn what I had spent years thinking about notions of female beauty, female worth, and the entanglement between the two. Perhaps it was my inverse version of bra-burning.

12. An abaya is a piece of clothing that is long and loose-fitting except when subjected to water, or wind, or both simultaneously, at which point it turns into a giant suction cup. Take my word for it.

13. Never mind the attitudes of the grownups; seeing me in a niqab clearly confused many of the children with whom I would regularly interact as a parent. My daughter's preschool friends thought I was a "for-real" ninja, but other youngsters were clearly frightened. In some locales, I still occasionally get stares from little eyes with my scarf; but at least with a face visible, I can give my biggest smile and mostly disarm any fears. This strategy works wonderfully until the accompanying grownup get sight of me smiling with abandon at their child, and then the thought occurs to me that I might just be making the whole situation worse.

14. Ask me my age, and whether or not I dye my hair, but *do not* ask me how many scarves are in my closet.

THE URGENCY OF NOW

I am presently a scholar and chaplain in the extremely diverse and multicultural urban center that is greater Boston. Each time I hear Mayor Marty Walsh's voice blaring over the loudspeakers at Logan Airport proclaiming Boston to be the "Hub of the Universe," I am reminded of my context. Hyperbole aside, the rising generation is the most ethnically diverse America has ever seen. American Muslims are themselves the most ethnically diverse of America's faith communities, and the majority of us are under forty. Even in the face of severe anti-Muslim bias, our generation, our children's generation—and whoever comes after generation X, Y, and Z—will help shape an America that is more multicultural, multiethnic, multiracial, and multireligious than ever before.

If you are thinking this is a rather scary prospect instead of a delightful and exciting one, I am glad that you are reading this book and hope that you will continue to read. And to be clear, I still do live in a primarily rural area, which I adore, and I own a Dodge Ram pickup truck,[15] which I proudly drive wearing a headscarf. You can take the girl out of the country, but you cannot take the country out of the girl!

I actually am not an anomaly. Every so often, I return to my old neck of the Pennsylvania woods and note that—like many parts of rural America—the residents have diversified a bit with respect to religion and ethnicity. There is even a mosque a short drive from my hometown that gets packed to capacity on Fridays, and the city of Allentown, where I was born, now hosts an impressive enclave of Muslim teachers providing instruction in traditional Islamic sciences. My father, once the "foreigner" in rural Pennsylvania as an Italian fresh from the Bronx, now has a retirement job as the town constable. Italians are no longer the foreigners in this country; there are newer kids on the block who have to stand tall and face down the ridicule.

In our current hometown in rural New Hampshire, my daughter is most likely the first "hijabi" (headscarf wearing person) that the vast majority of her classmates had ever befriended. She initially got many blunt questions to the effect of: "Why are you wearing that?" The real answer: The alternative option I gave her was to brush her hair in the morning, which

15. Don't stop reading either, my dear environmentalist friends. We mostly drive a fully electric vehicle and buy organic foods with reusable bags from local farmers. If it is possible to subsist on harvesting wild blueberries and sorrel, we are nearly in the category of homesteaders.

seemed to her to be less convenient at best, and a complete waste of time at worst—basically useless (apparently in the same category as making the bed). Getting from bed to school in record time is the pragmatic angle of the hijab; the subtle angle is that she is genuinely proud to be Muslim. She is proud to be American and proud to be Egyptian too, which, she insists, makes her African American: isn't Egypt in Africa? These are integral parts of who she is and how she understands herself in the world.

For her teachers and classmates, their sustained interactions with her put a face and a personality to what might otherwise be a stereotype. Who are Muslim girls? They are softball pitchers and cat lovers; they can be precocious and—against the stereotypes—quite assertive. Rahma[16] in Arabic means "compassion" or "loving mercy"; her name harkens to both the Arabic word for the womb and one of the most prominent epithets for God in the Qur'an. However, she is better known to her friends and teachers as "Rocky," a nickname my father gave her because he could not pronounce the breathy "hhh" of the Arabic, and, apparently, because he liked the idea of his grandchild being named after a fictional boxing icon. Somehow, it fits.

Naming aside, there are immense challenges in parenting in a socio-political environment where hate, against Muslims and others, is rampant and increasingly normalized. As a parent, I am mindful of the toll the political zeitgeist has on youth. The increase in hateful rhetoric, the incidents of race-based violence, the insecurity immigrants feel, and bullying are issues we talk about regularly at home: we have to. One such conversation, in particular, is etched into my mommy-memories. The weekend after the initial signing of the legislation known widely as the "Muslim Ban," my daughter piped up at bedtime: "Mom, we are citizens, right? What's the worst they can do to us?" Oscillating for a moment between my impulse to shelter her and my urge to equip her with the knowledge she will need to navigate the world, I replied, "Anne Frank saw the worst that can happen." She understood the high stakes. I continued, "but there are a lot of people who are working tirelessly to ensure something like that never happens here." We had read the diary together when the proposal of a "Muslim list" was initially embraced with gusto by a cohort of powerful American politicians, including the current president of the United States. After a moment, she

16. This is a breathy "HAAAA" like you're generating fog to clean glass. This is *not*—Hebrew speakers take special note—a scratchy "kh" sound, which, rest assured, Arabic is not devoid of, but which should not be heard at all in "Rahma"—at least not in her presence.

inquired pensively: "Why do they want to put us on a list anyway?" We had discussed Islamophobia before, but I again went through my spiel about how some politicians win votes by depicting Muslims as a danger to society. When I had finished my piece, she launched into a monologue, the parts I remember most vividly being: "*We're* dangerous? *Seriously*? Are they going to put baby Noura on the list too, because they definitely *should*, because *she* is wicked dangerous!" Noura is a daughter of our family friends, and her name harkens to a divine epithet meaning "light." However, Rahma, equipped with her ever-sardonic sense of humor and a marked dislike for babies, continued unabashedly: "Mom, have you *smelled* her stink bombs? They're *deadly*."

I am grateful for my daughter's resilience, but I also want her to appreciate the enormous privilege of her education, her American citizenship, and the relative stability of her day-to-day life. I want her to recognize that these privileges come not only with the promise of civil protections but with the duty of civic engagement. At least, that is the point I was *trying* to make when I shared with her the news of one of my mentors, Dr. Ahmed Ragab, who had just been arrested for protesting against policies that attempted to suspend DACA.[17] This all transpired on *the very day* that Dr. Ragab had become an American citizen in Boston's Faneuil Hall, just like Rahma's own father had.[18] As I shared the story, I felt Rahma's preteen eyes glaring at me quite bemused. Arms crossed at the chest, she was peering over large-rimmed glasses poised on her nose: "So you're telling me this because you want me to get myself *arrested*?" (Cue raised preteen squint.) "Not necessarily," I said. (Cue best serious parent look.) "But I do want you to have the courage to take risks and stand up for what you believe is right." She spent the next year as a "senator" at MicroSociety Academy fighting hard to get recess back for sixth grade. She even learned some valuable lessons from the fight: some days you win, some days you lose, but by June, you will definitely win because the teachers want to get out of the building just as much as you do. Moral: everybody can win when you seek common ground.

17. DACA stands for Deferred Action for Childhood Arrivals. The program enables young people who were brought to the United States without immigration paperwork as children to secure government permission to reside and to go to school in the United States legally. If you did not know what DACA stood for before reading this footnote, this is a moment to, as the generation Z-babies would say, "check your privilege." (Do not worry; there is probably an app for that.)

18. See Ragab, "The First Thing."

We have distinct priorities and diverse causes; some causes we carry on from the generations before us, others are unique to our times. Fifty years after the watershed year of 1968 that was such a defining historical moment for movements for peace; for racial justice; for immigrant, youth, and women's rights, and many of us find ourselves engaged in similar struggles on the streets and within our civic institutions. In some moments the news seems hopeful, and in other moments we would be best advised to get the news from a late-night comedian; at least then we can cry and not be entirely sure if it is out of glee or despair. Throughout many such moments of mixed glee and despair, this volume took shape as an effort to speak out against the dangers of prejudiced ignorance and as a call for a greater recognition of our common humanity, in all its complexities and paradoxes, and in spite of all of our real and perceived differences.

In this collection, we turn to the voices of activists, ministers, rabbis, and chaplains. They approach their work in the world from a place of moral conviction—but readers need not have a particular faith background or heritage to appreciate the contribution that this book aims to make to public discourse. It is a book for those with Muslim neighbors, colleagues, and friends, for those who are Muslim or have Muslim family members, and for those who may never have had the occasion to strike up a relationship with a Muslim in the flesh, but who might seize the next opportunity. It may even be a book for those who *think* they probably dislike all Muslims but are willing to be persuaded that we have some redeemable qualities. I invite readers to enjoy the spirit of intellectual curiosity and occasional humor that animates these pages and to appreciate the willingness of the contributors to reach for meaning and connection in new ways and in unexpected places.

In order to build together, govern together, live together, we must make the effort to *know* one another. There are many entry points into this work of building inclusive polities, and many organizations and individuals doing brave and inspiring work. I have been fortunate enough to meet some of these individuals and to convince them to write a reflection for this anthology or contribute their artistic talents. Because of my identity and life experiences, my push for greater literacy and inclusion is focused on making space for Muslims, in particular, as valued participants in American civic discourse and institutions. Hence, this anthology seeks to humanize Muslims and teach about lived Islam. It is my hope that such an effort can help, in whatever small way, to foster cohesion across our often divided social and political enclaves.

Each of us can contribute toward creating a polity that is, at least, a bit stronger—or *greater*—than the one that we have inherited. This great, strong polity *cannot* tolerate bigotry in its midst. Realizing a vision for a truly pluralistic society requires all of us. I am convinced of the dire need—the obligation even—that we have, as residents of the United States, and as human beings, whoever we are, to reach beyond our social and political niches, niches that can all too easily become homogenous and confining without our conscientious efforts. Developing literacy in issues related to the religious and philosophical diversity in our midst can even be thought of as a civic duty.

Much in this spirit, the volume's contributors address themes such as anti-bigotry activism, radical hospitality, spiritually grounded efforts for socioeconomic justice, and more. Drawing upon reflections, poetry, essays, sermons, photography, and protest art, the book highlights different kinds of efforts—from the pulpit to the streets—to move American public discourse and civic institutions toward a more robust vision of pluralism.

The contributors are all individuals who are mobilizing social change and opening up new and positive horizons for fostering public discourse related to religion and civic life. As their biographies and reflections in this book reveal, some contributors are at the forefront of efforts to push for greater diversity and inclusion at the grassroots level. Others have decades of experience leading on social issues from homelessness, to international conflict resolution, to promoting the arts as spaces of spiritual sanctuary. They have each inspired me with their wit, sincerity, and presence as they model how to engage creatively with human differences and as they make space for the human beings who are all too readily pushed to the social margins, villainized, and dehumanized. Their collective wisdom attests to the richness of encounters across difference as well as to some of the real struggles and limitations.

As the volume's editor and curator, I have annotated throughout to provide further orientation on concepts that might otherwise be foreign to some readers. Apart from source citations, all footnotes are editorial contributions.[19] Throughout the book, readers will come across simplified

19. I would like to acknowledge volume contributor Nora Zaki for her work in reviewing annotations for accuracy and clarity, standardizing Qur'anic citations, and providing other editorial feedback. All potential errors are, of course, my own.

transliteration of Arabic terms. I have attempted to keep terminology to a minimum, except in places where I hope that particular terms will enter more fully into the lexicon of English speakers. I'll know that we have achieved some success in this regard when my spell checker stops converting "*minbar*" to "min*i*bar" and "*dhikr*" to "liquor."[20]

Some of the contributors use the Arabic word for God, "Allah," in their contributions. This name means "God" and is also the same word that Arabic-speaking Christians or Jews, for instance, would use to evoke God. Even if the faiths do have creedal differences in the way that God is understood, "Allah" is not typically understood to be a different deity,[21] and many English-speaking Muslims readily use the word "God" and "Allah" interchangeably.

Unless otherwise noted, the Qur'anic verses quoted in this volume are drawn from *The Study Quran: A New Translation and Commentary*.[22] This volume is, in my estimation, the best translation of the Qur'an on account of its helpful scholarly notation that aims to span the breadth of Islamic intellectual history. I have amended *The Study Quran*'s use of the term "mankind" to "humankind" in a humble attempt to persuade the authors to make that update in their next edition. As a stylistic preference, I have rendered in italics all masculine pronouns referring to God. Readers will note that English translations of the Qur'an use "He" and "Him" as referents for God, which could be misleading for those reading from within a theological framework where God is regarded as "Father" or "Son." According

20. *Minbar* is roughly the equivalent of "pulpit," and *dhikr* is a form of repetitive chanting, commonly of divine epithets and short prayers, as described in this volume by contributors Lynn Cooper and Cheryl Stromski. These are actual corrections made all the more ironic in that the Qur'an expressly prohibits the consumption of alcohol as the final word in an ongoing dialectic with the subject, a dialectic that includes other useful advice such as (I am paraphrasing): don't come to prayer drunk until you know what you're saying (Q. 4:34), and when it comes to wine, the potential for depravity can be greater than the potential for benefit (Q. 2:129). This last point is something I *did* learn from my small-town American teen experience. Let us be clear: I was not ever fond of drinking myself (waste of time and calories), but somehow, I would end up being the one called upon to help take care of intoxicated people. I suppose I was training for college chaplaincy even then.

21. The documentary *Same God* chronicles how Dr. Larycia Hawkins, the first black, female tenured professor at Wheaton College, a prominent Christian liberal arts college, drew criticism and was placed on paid administrative leave in 2015 after asserting that Christians and Muslims worship the same God. For reflection on evangelical Christian views of Muslims, see the essay by Kevin Singer in this volume.

22. Nasr et al., *The Study Quran*.

to Islamic understanding, God is in no way biologically male.[23] The Qur'an translations also employ "he" for the pronoun meaning "human being" generally. I have also italicized such uses of *he*, *him*, or *his* so that readers can pause and understand the all-gender encompassing relevance of the verse.

I hope that this anthology will both inspire and challenge, entertain and provoke. These pages offer the potential to enrich—or even to transform—the state of our spirits as we attempt to chart a course forward amid waves of rising bigotry and the tides of rising discrimination. I remain hopeful that we can live up to our highest ideals to be "indivisible," to be one nation that honors our many different origins. Rather than hide, fear, exacerbate, or suppress our differences in creed and conviction, we can acknowledge and even embrace that we have a multiplicity of conceptions of what it means to be "under God." And maybe, in the end, our ability to wholeheartedly welcome persons of different creeds and origins to this country is the epitome of being American (right up there with baseball and apple pie, folks).

We have different pulpits in different places, we have bimahs and minbars (and yes, some have min*i*bars), but I encourage all of us, wherever we find our spiritual and intellectual homes, to tap into that imagination and mystery, that wisdom and that prophetic voice, to advocate for an American polity that is "indivisible" in its quest for liberty and justice, *for all.*

REFERENCES

Midgett, Linda, dir. *Same God.* Baton Rouge, LA: Midget Productions, 2018.

Nasr, Seyyed Hossein, et al., *The Study Quran: A New Translation and Commentary.* San Francisco: HarperOne, 2015.

Ragab, Ahmed. "The First Thing I Did as a U.S. Citizen Was Get Arrested." *The Washington Post.* September 13, 2017. https://www.washingtonpost.com/news/posteverything/wp/2017/09/13/the-first-thing-i-did-as-a-u-s-citizen-was-get-arrested/?noredirect=on&utm_term=.64c2752d25c2.

"Ruth Bader Ginsburg Action Figure." Kickstarter.com. https://www.kickstarter.com/projects/fctry/ruth-bader-ginsburg-action-figure.

23. If you just gave an impulsive sigh of relief, do not worry; you are in good company. According to Islamic theology, God has no partner or likeness and is thus beyond any gender. In no place does the Qur'an use the epithet "father" to refer to God. Moreover, human beings are not referred to metaphorically as "children of God." So, despite the best-intended interfaith harmony-geared programming, we do not *all* see ourselves as "children of God"; we can, however, find plenty of other good reasons to get along.

Part I

ECLIPSING HATE

***Eclipse Viewing from Harvard Art Museums*, photograph by Anthony Trifone**

Viewing glasses flew off shelves as a complete solar eclipse swept darkness over much of the continental United States in August of 2017. Hardcore eclipse enthusiasts and casual observers alike stared into the darkened afternoon sky; many Muslims recited eclipse prayers together in mosques, homes, and workplaces. On my way home that day, my eye caught a Cambridge yard sign reading: "Eclipse Hate." My gut wrenched as I was taken—from the sweet afternoon memories of people marveling together with strangers on sidewalks, passing eclipse glasses back and forth with generous enthusiasm—to the darkness of the white nationalist, Nazi sympathizers with their Tiki torches blazing, weapons menacing, swarming the streets and green spaces of Charlottesville, Virginia.

How can we, as individuals and communities, intervene in countering this destructive hate and fear that brews beneath the surface of our polity? How can we prevent it from again instigating violence and causing havoc? What can we learn from the peace activists and clergy of all colors and cloths who amassed a counter presence with prayer and song in a testament to the resilience of the human spirit? With the rise of isolationism, nativism, rampant fearmongering, the spread of American-made weapons around the globe, and even the proposals from those in positions of power for increased militarization of our schools and workplaces, what wisdom can be derived from core texts, teachings, and traditions? How do we understand our seemingly innate capacities for monstrosity? How can we overcome our more destructive collective impulses? What can help us bridge divides, counter hate, and stand up for those whose safety and security are most threatened? What interventions does the present moment necessitate? Such questions are the heart of this section.

Dr. Jennifer Howe Peace, Nancy Elizabeth Reinhardt, the Reverend Dr. Sunder John Boopalan, and Dr. Marlyn Miller critique the discourses promoting the social exclusion of minorities and immigrants and highlight the social and moral costs of this bigotry. Jenny Peace explores how dehumanizing propaganda can readily pave the way for even more vitriolic acts. Nancy Reinhardt explains why she was not going to let the Islamophobia industry define how she related to her fellow Bostonians. Sunder John Boopalan provides a novel motivation for dismantling stereotypes, and Marlyn Miller provides a window on the past to inform our shared present. Together, their contributions shine light on the basic concept of human dignity that can be found pulsing so strongly through our wisdom traditions and our collective civic values.

The Dangers of Dehumanizing Language[1]

Jennifer Howe Peace

Between the Twitter-driven rancor of contemporary discourse and the belittling rhetoric that has come to characterize campaign cycles, it can be tempting to dismiss vitriolic speech as political spin or to tune it out because of the sheer volume of unsubstantiated claims and caricatures. Yet, the proliferation of dehumanizing language in public discourse, and particularly at the highest levels of government, deserves attention. Dehumanization is a chilling part of the process of peeling back the moral conscience that protects our most cherished values about how we are to interact with each other. Language that deprives people of human qualities, attributes, individuality, personality, or spirit is a threat to the very fabric of our civic life. As a professor of interfaith studies concerned with training future (primarily Christian) ministers and educators, I feel a particular responsibility to work with my students to identify patterns of thought, dangerous stereotypes, and problematic sources of influence—both in their own personal and theological perspectives as well as in the wider national context.

The tendency to dehumanize individuals, lumping them into groups, comparing them to diseases, infestations, monsters, or other malignant non-human threats is a tendency we are all subject to and must guard against. This tendency is not the exclusive practice of one community or one political party. For instance, in 2016 Representative Hank Johnson (D-GA) compared Jewish people living in disputed territories in Israel to

1. An earlier version of this essay was published in *Religious Studies News*, the web magazine of the American Academy of Religion. Peace, "The Dangers of Dehumanizing Language."

"termites";[2] Michael Flynn, a retired US Army lieutenant general and registered Democrat who had a short-lived appointment as national security advisor in the current Republican administration, described Islam as a cancer.[3] It is easy to slip from disagreeing with a policy or a practice to demonizing a people, but this is a line we must recognize and resist crossing.[4]

A *New York Times* article from February 1, 2017, with the headline, "A Sinister Perception of Islam Now Steers the White House," written by Scott Shane, Matthew Rosenberg, and Eric Lipton, heightened my concern about a resurgence of such language.[5] The focus of the article is on the distorted views of Islam held by many of President Trump's advisors, including Stephen Bannon and Michael Flynn. (Both of whom were still advising Trump when the article was written). The article mentions organizations and figures associated with Bannon and Flynn that share a deeply divisive "us/them" narrative about Islam and Muslims.

Among the many troubling attitudes and associates influencing Trump's policy toward Muslims, Frank Gaffney Jr. stands out. Gaffney is founder and president of the Center for Security Policy, which the Southern Poverty Law Center has designated as an anti-Muslim hate group. As reported in the article, Gaffney, a frequent guest on Bannon's Breitbart radio program, argues that a "stealth Jihad" is underway by everyday Muslims in mosques and student associations in the United States. Gaffney is quoted as saying that these Muslims, "essentially, like termites, hollow out the structure of the civil society and other institutions, for the purpose of creating conditions under which the jihad will succeed." This is where I paused my reading of the *Times* article and began thinking about my role as a citizen and a scholar. One of my ethical commitments, and a hallmark

2. Kredo, "Congressman." Representative Johnson is quoted as saying: "There has been a steady [stream], almost like termites can get into a residence and eat before you know that you've been eaten up and you fall in on yourself, there has been settlement activity that has marched forward with impunity and at an ever increasing rate to the point where it has become alarming." Johnson later apologized for these remarks.

3. Kaczynski, "Michael Flynn." Flynn, who has called Islam as a whole a "cancer" in the past, made the comments during a speech to the Ahavath Torah Congregation in Stoughton, Massachusetts. "This is Islamism, it is a vicious cancer inside the body of 1.7 billion people on this planet and it has to be excised," asserted Flynn.

4. The Qur'an makes a similar case, urging in one verse: "O you who believe! Let not one group of men deride another; it may be that the latter are better than the former. Let not a group of women deride other women; it may be that the latter are better than the former." Qur'an 49:11.

5. Shane, Rosenberg, and Lipton, "A Sinister Perception."

of interreligious/interfaith studies, is an emphasis on the importance of safeguarding the religious identity of others, particularly those from minority traditions.[6] Gaffney's comment, coupled with the possibility that this attitude is not only tolerated but is actually dominant in the ideology of Trump's advisors, is a significant threat to this value.

We know from studying history, politics, and religion, that dehumanizing language can have dire consequences. Beverly Eileen Mitchell, scholar and professor of historical theology, unmasks the systematic dehumanization at the heart of both white supremacy and anti-Semitism in her powerful book, *Plantations and Death Camps: Religion, Ideology, and Human Dignity*. Mitchell defines the "sin of dehumanization" as "defacement" and writes: "The absence of empathetic imagination—the inability to see members of the 'pariah' group as being like oneself—is the psychological foundation for participation in dehumanizing a fellow human being."[7]

A new wave of brain science is adding to our understanding of the neurological dimension of this phenomenon. Neurologist David Eagleman reports on work by Lasana Harris of the University of Leiden in Holland. Harris looks for changes in the medial prefrontal cortex (mPFC), a region of the brain that "becomes active when we're interacting with, or thinking about, other people—but it's not active when we're dealing with inanimate objects, like a coffee mug." Showing pictures of people from different social strata to volunteers while measuring their brain activity, Harris "finds that the mPFC is less active when they look at a homeless person. It's as though the person is more like an object." Considering this study and his own experiments related to the neurology of empathy, Eagleman sees a disturbing link to the history of genocide: "Genocide is only possible when dehumanization happens on a massive scale, and the perfect tool for this job is propaganda: it keys right into the neural networks that understand other people, and dials down the degree to which we empathize with them."[8]

Comparing Muslims to termites comes straight out of the propagandist's handbook. Such rhetoric was used by Nazi propagandists preparing conditions for the Holocaust when they compared Jewish people to rats or by broadcasters in Rwanda in the lead-up to the genocide there in 1994 when members of the Tutsi ethnic group were described as *inyenzi*

6. For more on my definition of interreligious/interfaith studies, see Peace, "Spiritual Other/Spiritual Self."

7. Mitchell, *Plantations and Death Camps*, 11.

8. Eagleman, *The Brain*, 154–56.

(cockroaches). Similarly, as Eagleman notes, the genocide in Srebrenica in 1995 was fueled in part by Radio Television of Serbia when it perpetuated false and negative stories about Bosnian Muslims and Croats including one "unfounded story that Muslims were feeding Serbian children to the hungry lions of the Sarajevo zoo."[9] It is much easier to incite violence and mobilize crowds when your enemy is portrayed as an unfeeling monster or a mass infestation.

In the wake of the Holocaust, the United Nations added a new crime under international law to prosecute those responsible for "direct and public incitement to commit genocide" (Article III [c] of the Genocide Convention). This was the charge leveled against Julius Streicher during the Nuremberg trials because of his role as publisher of *Der Stürmer*, an anti-Semitic German weekly. It was also the charge applied to three Rwandans—one who owned a tabloid that published vitriolic articles against the Tutsi and two who founded an incendiary radio station that demonized and called for the death of ethnic Tutsi.[10]

The language we use for and about each other can seem harmless on one level, but language reflects patterns of thinking and creates categories of us/them polarization that religious leaders have long decried. In his book, *Not in God's Name: Confronting Religious Violence*, Rabbi Jonathan Sacks calls the impulse to divide people into good or evil, "pathological dualism," a mindset that can fuel violent action.[11] Pope Francis warned against this tendency during his presentation to the US Congress in September of 2015:

> There is another temptation which we must especially guard against: the simplistic reductionism which sees only good or evil; or, if you will, the righteous and sinners. The contemporary world, with its open wounds which affect so many of our brothers and sisters, demands that we confront every form of polarization, which would divide it into these two camps. We know that in the attempt to be freed of the enemy without, we can be tempted to feed the enemy within. To imitate the hatred and violence of tyrants and

9. Ibid., 172.

10. "Incitement to Genocide." For a powerful exploration of propaganda and the tactics of dehumanization that can also be used as a resource in the classroom, there are a broad range of excellent resources on the United States Holocaust Memorial Museum's website including: https://www.ushmm.org/propaganda/.

11. Sacks, *Not in God's Name*, 44–65.

> murderers is the best way to take their place. That is something which you as a people, reject.[12]

Interreligious studies provides some tools and strategies for rejecting the temptation of this simplistic reductionism. With its emphasis on dismantling stereotypes, building authentic relationships across lines of religious difference, highlighting moments of interreligious cooperation, and sharing stories that build an appreciative understanding of diverse traditions, this burgeoning field can contribute to cultivating a national ethos that rejects polarizing rhetoric.[13] Educational models that emphasize the importance of getting to know each other across lines of difference, especially in face-to-face interactions, can counteract the "defacement" Mitchell names as the result of "the sin of dehumanization."[14]

Rejecting policies that target religious groups, such as the Trump administration's travel ban that singles out Muslim-majority countries, is an essential part of upholding and protecting the rights of religious minorities. In tandem with protests in airports, city squares, and courtrooms, it is important to think about the sources of the attitudes informing such policies. Noticing and pointing out patterns of thought and familiar tropes behind such policy moves will help us uncover and debunk the destructive ideologies they rest on. We must actively call out, protest, and reject rhetoric that reduces individuals or communities of people to insects, infestations, or any other "less-than-human" beings. This kind of language cannot be dismissed as harmless or mere figures of speech.

Dehumanizing language corrodes our capacity for empathy and helps create the conditions that fuel mass atrocities. Anytime we read or hear such language, I hope we will pause, notice it, and call it out using our various platforms and community connections.

REFERENCES

Eagleman, David. *The Brain: The Story of You*. New York: Pantheon, 2015.

"Incitement to Genocide in International Law." United States Holocaust Memorial Museum. https://www.ushmm.org/wlc/en/article.php?ModuleId=10007839.

12. For Pope Francis's full address, see *Pope Francis*.

13. For a detailed overview of interreligious studies, see Patel, Peace, and Silverman, *Interreligious/Interfaith Studies*.

14. Mitchell, *Plantations and Death Camps*, 50–54.

Kaczynski, Andrew. "Michael Flynn in August: Islamism a 'Vicious Cancer' in Body of All Muslims That Has to Be Excised." CNN Politics. November 22, 2016. http://www.cnn.com/2016/11/22/politics/kfile-michael-flynn-august-speech/index.html.

Kredo, Adam. "Congressman: Jewish Settlers Are Like Termites." *The Washington Free Beacon*. July 25, 2016. http://freebeacon.com/politics/congressman-jewish-settlers-like-termites/.

Mitchell, Beverly Eileen. *Plantations and Death Camps: Religion, Ideology, and Human Dignity*. Minneapolis, MN: Fortress, 2009.

Patel, Eboo, Jennifer Peace, and Noah Silverman, eds. *Interreligious/Interfaith Studies: Defining a New Field*. Boston: Beacon, 2018.

Peace, Jennifer Howe. "The Dangers of Dehumanizing Language: Insights from Interreligious Studies." *Religious Studies News*. August 3, 2017. http://rsn.aarweb.org/articles/dangers-dehumanizing-language-insights-interreligious-studies.

———. "Spiritual Other/Spiritual Self: Models of Transformative Interfaith Work." Surjit Singh lecture presented at the Graduate Theological Union, Berkeley, CA, 2013. https://vimeo.com/61125666.

Pope Francis Addresses Joint Session of Congress. YouTube.com. September 24, 2015. https://www.youtube.com/watch?v=oBM7DIeMsPo.

Sacks, Jonathan. *Not in God's Name: Confronting Religious Violence*. New York: Schocken, 2015.

Shane, Scott, Matthew Rosenberg, and Eric Lipton. "A Sinister Perception of Islam Now Steers the White House." *The New York Times*. February 1, 2017. Accessed under the alternate headline, "Trump Pushes Dark View of Islam to Center of U.S. Policy-Making." https://www.nytimes.com/2017/02/01/us/politics/donald-trump-islam.html?_r=0.

Countering Racialized Narratives

NANCY ELIZABETH REINHARDT

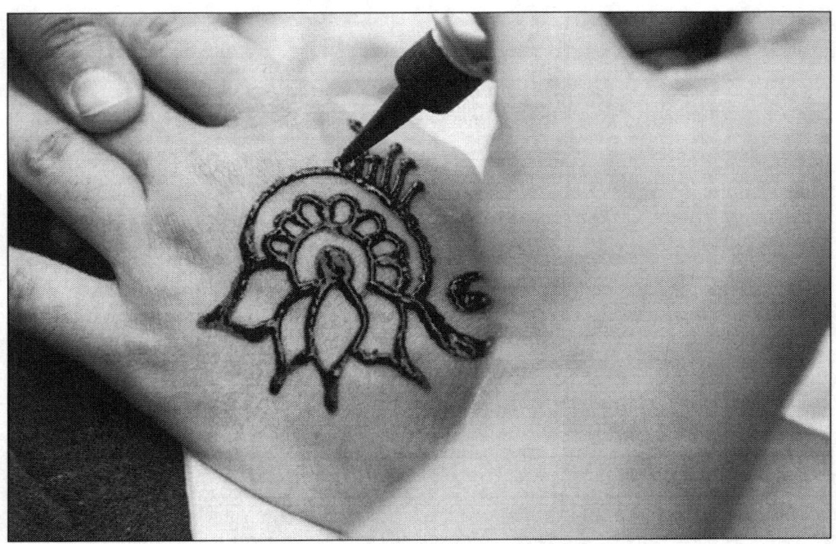

***Henna Designs at Tufts University*, photograph by Alonso Nicholas**[1]

I HAD NO SUBSTANTIAL contact with Muslims growing up, and it was not until I was older that I started to hear hateful, fear-based messaging about Muslims coming not only in the aftermath of 9/11, but also as a result of the ongoing Israeli/Palestinian conflict. Still, most of this hateful messaging

1. Two Muslim college students create henna designs for each other at a Tufts University Eid Festival in 2018. Henna is a plant-based temporary dye that allows for designs to be drawn onto the skin that last for several days. The holiday of Eid al-Fitr celebrates the end of a month-long Ramadan fast.

came from outside of my Jewish community, not from within it. For instance, once when I was organizing an interfaith event, I was warned to be careful about going to the local mosque, as everyone there would hate me.

Nonetheless, just such an opportunity for me to start a relationship came around—the religious school affiliated with the mosque was hosting a henna fundraiser one day for Eid al-Fitr. I was warmly embraced as soon as I arrived. I told them I was Jewish, but they still called me "sister," and we found common ground on the Israeli/Palestinian conflict by agreeing that people were trapped between and manipulated by their governments. I was invited to go to the Friday service and the lunch that followed. When I left that first day, a Muslim man said to me "*shalom alehem*," the Hebrew equivalent of the Arabic "*salaam alaykum*," or "peace be upon you." So much for being hated! I would go back again in order to build the relationship. One day a woman came up to me after prayers, hugged me, and said, "I know that you're not of our religion. Thank you so much for praying with us." We embraced warmly, and I told her I was happy to be with them.

Why are Muslims in America seen and depicted as an external enemy to fear, distrust, and socially exclude? One prevalent narrative is that Muslims cannot live in Western society because, as is postulated, they hate democracy and want to force Sharia law on others.[2] Such a fearmongering narrative posits that because an infinitesimally small number of Muslims are a threat to public safety and security, we should distrust all Muslims.[3]

For instance, a primarily white, ostensibly Christian elite can present America as a homogenous community, thereby causing those outside of the dominant group, such as American Muslims or other racialized minorities, to appear as disloyal threats.[4] This identity as outsider is, as the philosopher Margret Urban Walker elucidates, "a socially recognized status determining relative standing, duties, [and] prerogatives,"[5] through which human bodies acquire particular social identities.[6] In this framework, Islam is treated

2. See Ali et al., *Fear, Inc.*

3. For survey data and analysis of public views of Islam among Americans, see Ingraham, "Donald Trump." For a concise overview of US immigration policy in light of recent developments, see Scribner, "You Are Not Welcome," in particular, see 274–77 for contemporary data on Americans' views about Muslims. For analysis of how the "Global War on Terror" impacted American politics and perceptions of Muslims, see Rockmore, "On War," 81–89.

4. Lean, *The Islamophobia Industry*, 69.

5. Urban Walker, *Moral Understandings*, 168.

6. Ibid., 180.

as a race, and as a result, even people who *look* Muslim, such as those of the Sikh faith,[7] are also a target of vitriolic sentiments and abuse.[8]

The same racialized narratives that demonize Muslims often exempt persons of white, Christian identity from scrutiny. For instance, the white men of Christian backgrounds who commit mass murder are not endowed with the same ability to represent Christianity or whiteness.[9] Muslim victims of crime also suffer as a result of hesitancy to regard acts of violence and discrimination against Muslims as hate crimes, perpetuating a moral indifference to the suffering of Muslim bodies and individuals.[10] Such attitudes force Muslims—and those who are perceived to be Muslim—outside of the dominant society's "moral kin," thereby breeding apathy toward wrongs perpetrated against this marginalized group and letting discrimination fester unchecked.[11] This apathy can easily morph into violence; the normalization of Islamophobic ideas feeds into perverse desires for nationalistic dominance over Muslims in America and abroad.

My own family history has been tragically impacted by this type of "othering," and as such, I am personally committed to countering anti-Muslim bias. As allies, we can help elevate the voices of our Muslim friends and colleagues. Those who have positions of power and influence can use that influence to speak out against Islamophobia. We can invite Muslim speakers to come to our houses of worship, or, if we are educators, we can add books written by Muslim authors, for example, to our syllabi or curriculums. It is also of utmost importance that Muslims increasingly have and foster platforms to tell their own authentic stories, as supporting Muslims in attaining positions of epistemic authority helps to break down the barriers that might otherwise exclude them from platforms where their voices and narratives could gain credibility and be normalized within the public sphere.

Political platforms, news outlets, and academia are conducive to bringing about change at the level of public discourse, but on more of a microlevel, personal relationships are needed to dispel hate and ignorance. To function, Islamophobia must be perpetually normalized through politics,

7. Sikhism in a monotheistic faith with roots in the Punjab region of the Indian subcontinent.

8. See "Myths and Facts"; Basu, "15 Years after 9/11."

9. See, for instance, Ruiz-Grossman, "The Double Standard."

10. For one such horrible murder of a Muslim American teen, see "Don't Tell Me."

11. Urban Walker, *Moral Understandings*, 187.

law, and the media; however, through our collective mobilization and individual relationships, we can spawn positive change. Though it may not be possible to rid the world of all existing hateful prejudice, we can all do our small part to reduce its harmful effects.

I am surrounded by messages meant to destroy my relationship with my Muslim friends. But, if I look beyond the noise, I know the relationships I have created are real and that the people I met are not those depicted in Islamophobic stereotypes.

REFERENCES

Ali, Wajahat, Eli Clifton, Matthew Duss, Lee Fang, Scott Keyes, and Faiz Shakir. *Fear, Inc.: The Roots of the Islamophobia Network in America*. Washington, DC: Center for American Progress, 2011.

Basu, Moni. "15 Years after 9/11, Sikhs Still Victims of Anti-Muslim Hate Crimes." *CNN*. September 15, 2016. http://www.cnn.com/2016/09/15/us/sikh-hate-crime-victims/index.html.

"Don't Tell Me Nabra Hassanen's Murder Wasn't a Hate Crime." *The Cut*. June 19, 2017. https://www.thecut.com/2017/06/nabra-hassanen-murder-hate-crime-mona-eltahawy.html.

Ingraham, Christopher. "Donald Trump Is Bringing Anti-Muslim Prejudice into the Mainstream." *The Washington Post*. August 1, 2016. https://www.washingtonpost.com/news/wonk/wp/2016/08/01/donald-trump-is-bringing-anti-muslim-prejudice-into-the-mainstream/?utm_term=.0558998f43bc.

Lean, Nathan. *The Islamophobia Industry: How the Right Manufactures Fear of Muslims*. London: Pluto, 2012.

"Myths and Facts about Muslim People and Islam." Anti-Defamation League. https://www.adl.org/education/resources/tools-and-strategies/myths-and-facts-about-muslim-people-and-islam.

Rockmore, Tom. "On War, Politics, and Capitalism after 9/11." *Theoria* 53, no. 110 (2006) 74–96.

Ruiz-Grossman, Sarah. "The Double Standard in How the Media Is Portraying the Las Vegas Shooter." *The Huffington Post*. October 4, 2017. https://www.huffingtonpost.com/entry/double-standard-white-privilege-media-las-vegas-shooting_us_59d3da15e4b04b9f92058316.

Scribner, Todd. "You Are Not Welcome Here Anymore: Restoring Support for Refugee Resettlement in the Age of Trump." *Journal on Migration and Human Security* 5, no. 2 (2017) 263–84.

Urban Walker, Margaret. *Moral Understandings: A Feminist Study in Ethics*. Oxford: Oxford University Press, 2008.

Holy Proximity

Sunder John Boopalan

Five Dalitmen were lynched and murdered in broad daylight by a mob in the northern Indian state of Haryana in October 2002. The men were attending to the removal of a cow carcass at the time of the attack. "Dalit," a word with roots meaning "oppressed," "crushed," "broken," is the self-description of members of communities who were historically called and treated as "untouchables." Dalits, who are at the bottom of the caste hierarchy, are often assigned such abject work as processing the remains of dead cattle for meat and leather industries. The mob assumed that these five men were Muslims in the middle of slaughtering a cow, an animal sacred to many Hindus. It came to be known thereafter that the five men were, in fact, Hindu. The news of the murder made national headlines and the issue was debated in the Indian parliament. Some official government sources sought to rationalize the murder by saying that the mob did not know that the men were Hindu, leaving room for the problematic interpretation that the killings may have been acceptable had the men actually been Muslim.[1]

A strong current of anti-Muslim (and anti-Christian) sentiment in India is fueled by parochial religious nationalism, which stereotypes Muslims (and Christians too) as invaders and foreigners. Such stereotypes often form the backdrop of violence against Muslims in India. In the example above, the misinformed stereotype of Muslims as "beef-eating foreigners"[2] influenced the mob's violent reaction. It is easy to place the blame for anti-Muslim bias on extremist-leaning Hindus, but as an Indian Christian theo-

1. For more context, see Boopalan, *Memory, Grief, and Agency*, 50–51.

2. The consumption of meat often functions as a marker of caste whereby asserting dominant caste status involves foregoing the consumption of meat. However, many Indians, including some Hindus, eat beef. See Jha, *The Myth of the Holy Cow*.

logian now living in America, I am simultaneously aware of anti-Muslim prejudice among Christians both in India and the United States.

One idea embedded deeply in a dominant Christian theological imagination is that Muslims are inherently violent and that such violence is theologically informed.[3] Despite violence being perpetuated throughout the world by people of all different backgrounds, acts of violence committed by Muslim perpetrators are often depicted with a sinister subtext: "Well, they do that because that is *who they are*." In the minds of many Christians, a stark polarity exists between the deity that Christians worship, whom they perceive to be "the God of reason and love," and the deity that Muslims worship, whom they perceive to be "the God of arbitrary will and wrath." In the controversial Regensburg address, for instance, Pope Benedict XVI drew upon this mistaken dichotomy to suggest that violence is inherent in Islam.[4] Leaders of other Christian denominations have advanced similar rhetoric that is rooted in an unfounded idea.

As a Christian, I too was conditioned to make a big deal out of the Christian affirmation that God is *with* us, and God's immanence came to be my favorite Christian doctrine. However, it never occurred to me to be curious about what my Muslim brothers and sisters had to say about the immanence of God. I assumed—conditioned by the dominant Christian theological imagination—that the God that Muslims worshipped was a God of sheer will and abstraction, not one who is "with us." However, one of the best decisions I made during my theological training was to enroll in a course titled Muslims and the Qur'an, taught by the eminent historian Muhammad Qasim Zaman. It was only a matter of time before I discovered that the Qur'an speaks of God as being closer to us than our jugular vein. Such radical immanence in the Qur'an—"We are nearer to *him* than *his* jugular vein!"[5]—flies in the face of stereotypical conceptions of the divine in Islam.[6]

"Closer to us than our jugular vein!" I exclaimed to myself as my preconceptions and stereotypes came crashing down. Stereotypes are employed by most people in daily encounters and can help us navigate societal

3. For further discussion, see Kalin, "Islamophobia," 14.

4. Volf, *Allah*, 150.

5. In the Qur'an, the voice of God says, "We [God] created the human being, and We know what his soul whispers to him; We are nearer to him than his jugular vein." Qur'an 50:16.

6. Rahman, *Major Themes*, 4.

complexities that may otherwise be daunting. However, as people meet and interact with those who are different from them, ideally, they will gradually correct their misperceptions. Still, despite a globalized world in which people live in closer proximity and with more sophisticated degrees of interconnectedness than ever before, deep-seated prejudice and misunderstandings often go uncorrected.

Proximity does not in and of itself lead to the correction of stereotypes unless it is accompanied by deep friendship, authentic curiosity, concrete partnership, and a willingness to be surprised. As transformative as my personal experience in the course on the Qur'an was for me, I soon realized that the art of being surprised in interfaith encounters is not learned once and for all, but is rather a lifelong pursuit buttressed by interreligious friendship, learning, and unlearning.[7]

Encounters between adherents of different religions over the centuries have, of course, not always been positive. Historical antagonisms have created a climate rich in biases, and interfaith work begins with taking a hard look at cultures of hatred and prejudice that are often inherited and passed on to subsequent generations.[8] In light of often deeply seated resentments, we must examine the wider sociopolitical and theological forces in order to pave the way for constructive change. As the distinguished scholar of American and Indian religion Diana Eck argues, "terms like 'peace' and 'justice' will become nothing but the well-intentioned yet meaningless slogans of our separate tribes if they are not understood to involve a serious commitment toward working in partnership with people of other faiths."[9]

Indeed, our engagement with difference cannot just remain on a theoretical or sociological level—just as God has radical proximity with us, so too must we strive for holy proximity in our relationships and friendships across faith lines. In a world in which proximity with those that are different from us is becoming more and more common, the question, "Who are our friends?" has political significance.[10] In the face of the many forces

7. For one captivating account of such a lifelong pursuit by a second-generation Indian-American Muslim sociologist and interfaith activist, see Patel, *Acts of Faith*. For a discussion of different frameworks for dialogue, see also Cornille, *The Wiley-Blackwell Companion*.

8. For insightful analysis of these historical antagonisms in the American context, see Patel, *Sacred Ground*.

9. Eck, *Encountering God*, 202.

10. As Mona Siddiqui, a professor of Islamic and interfaith studies, notes, "there are risks involved in the cultivation of new friendships" due to our "fragmented and divided

promoting rancorous disunity, we must foster authentic curiosity and be willing to be pleasantly surprised by the holiness of our proximity *to each other*.

REFERENCES

Boopalan, Sunder John. *Memory, Grief, and Agency: A Political Theological Account of Wrongs and Rites*. New Approaches to Religion and Power. New York: Palgrave Macmillan, 2017.

Cornille, Catherine, ed. *The Wiley-Blackwell Companion to Inter-religious Dialogue*. Chichester, West Sussex: Wiley-Blackwell, 2013.

Eck, Diana L. *Encountering God: A Spiritual Journey from Bozeman to Banaras*. 2nd ed. Boston: Beacon, 2003.

Jha, D. N. *The Myth of the Holy Cow*. New York: Verso, 2002.

Kalin, Ibrahim. "Islamophobia and the Limits of Multiculturalism." In *Islamophobia: The Challenge of Pluralism in the 21st Century*, edited by John L. Esposito and Ibrahim Kalin, 3–20. New York: Oxford University Press, 2011.

Patel, Eboo. *Acts of Faith: The Story of an American Muslim, the Struggle for the Soul of a Generation*. Boston: Beacon, 2007.

———. *Sacred Ground: Pluralism, Prejudice, and the Promise of America*. Boston: Beacon, 2012.

Rahman, Fazlur. *Major Themes of the Qur'an*. Minneapolis, MN: Bibliotheca Islamica, 1980.

Siddiqui, Mona. *Hospitality and Islam: Welcoming in God's Name*. New Haven, CT: Yale University Press, 2015.

Volf, Miroslav. *Allah: A Christian Response*. San Francisco, CA: HarperOne, 2012.

communities" in the current era. See Siddiqui, *Hospitality and Islam*, 236.

Seeing the Dignity

Marlyn Miller

We have indeed dignified the Children of Adam.[1]

Elie Wiesel was interned in the Buchenwald concentration camp when he was fifteen years old, where he lost his father, brother, sister, and mother. He spent the next sixty years of his life campaigning to keep the memory of the Holocaust alive in the public consciousness. He wrote: "We must not see any person as an abstraction. Instead, we must see in every person a universe with its own secrets, with its own treasures, with its own sources of anguish, and with some measure of triumph."[2] It is particularly difficult for us humans to see people as individuals and not abstractions when faced with large-scale tragedies like the Holocaust, or what is happening today in the wars in Syria and other places. It is hard for us to comprehend the scale of such suffering, and so it is somehow easier to ignore it.

But Unitarian Universalism, too, insists that we see each person as an individual, not as an abstraction. Although Unitarian Universalists are theologically diverse, "we affirm and promote the inherent worth and dignity of every person." Every person.

Jesus, of course, demanded this, sitting with the sinners and tax collectors and prostitutes, and insisting on their share in Heaven. Most of our religious traditions share this imperative, but the fact is that we humans are very good at turning those outside our immediate circle into "others." Black, white, Republican, Democrat, Irish, Chinese, gay, straight, fat, thin,

1. Qur'an 17:70.

2. Wiesel, *The Nazi Doctors*, ix.

Yankees, Red Sox—we manage to find a million ways to wall ourselves off from each other. This begins early in our lives, on the playground, where there are those who are "worthy" of our attention and those who are not. Kids who are labeled as "different" and don't fit in are ostracized, even abused. It continues throughout high school and beyond—we find ourselves comfortable in a certain type of place, with a certain type of people, and those who fall outside that circle are suspect.

This phenomenon has been painfully obvious in our political discourse. As a historian in a past life, I am aware that this is not anything new—in the 1828 presidential election, for example, John Quincy Adams supporters accused Andrew Jackson of adultery, killing thousands of unarmed Native Americans, taking a nap among their corpses, and eating a dozen of them for breakfast, while Jackson accused Adams of serving as a pimp for the Russian tsar, and buying a billiard table for the White House on the government dime. And it has not gotten all that much better since their time.

Nevertheless, if we step back for a minute, perhaps we can remember that we are committed to affirming and promoting the inherent worth and dignity of each person. And that means, as Elie Wiesel says, that each person is a universe unto themselves. While they might be Democrats, Republicans, black, white, or anything else, they are all our brothers and sisters, however distant they might at this moment seem from us. As Albert Einstein said: "A human being is a part of the whole, called by us, 'Universe,' a part limited in time and space. He experiences himself, his thoughts and feelings as something separated from the rest—a kind of optical delusion of his consciousness. The striving to free oneself from this delusion is the one issue of true religion."[3] In other words, we need to realize that we are not in fact separate from others—we are interdependent.

All religions—from Christianity to Buddhism, from Judaism to Hinduism and Islam—all affirm the inherent worth and dignity of each person. This is evident in the call of our major religions to welcome the stranger. In the Gospel of Matthew, for example, Jesus says:

> Come, you that are blessed by my Father, inherit the kingdom prepared for you from the foundation of the world; for I was hungry and you gave me food, I was thirsty and you gave me something to drink, I was a stranger and you welcomed me, I was naked and

3. Einstein, from a letter to Robert S. Marcus of the World Jewish Congress, February 12, 1950.

> you gave me clothing, I was sick and you took care of me, I was in prison and you visited me.[4]

Those who do so to the least of those who are members of our human family, it is as if they do so for him. The Hebrew Bible also asserts: "When a stranger resides with you in your land, you shall not wrong him. The stranger shall be to you as one of your citizens; you shall love the stranger as yourself, for you were strangers in the land of Egypt."[5]

Many of us come from the stock of those who were once strangers. Given this, and given the exhortations of our faith, it is important that we find a way to embrace the "other," whether that other is of a different socioeconomic background, a different part of the country, a different race or religion, a different gender identity, or a different part of the world. Our black brothers and sisters are dying in the streets while our Latino brothers and sisters are being deported for the crime of needing to support their families. Meanwhile, our Muslim brothers and sisters are being attacked and humiliated for the crime of practicing their faith.

None of these things would or could be true if we looked at each other and saw that truly, all people have inherent worth and dignity. Non-documented immigrants so often come because they have to—they are suffering or starving or the victims of violence at home. And yet numberless men and women are treated as criminals, rounded up, kept in detention centers, deported away from their families and sent back to places where they often fear for their lives. Too often, we forget to see non-documented immigrants as individual people, for all sorts of reasons—perhaps we think they are taking our jobs, or they do not speak our language. But they are people, and as such, they have inherent worth and dignity. Deep down, we all know this.

Many of us have a similar response to Muslims, and this explains much of the terrible, Islamophobic rhetoric that has penetrated our political discourse. But Muslims around the world sit down to dinner together, test the bathwater with their fingers before bathing their children, find themselves late for work, have their hearts broken, worry about the state of the world, and struggle with questions of how best to serve God. They are us, and we are them. One of the great stumbling blocks in our ability to see this, it seems to me, is an almost pathological fear of Islam and Muslims. There are

4. Matt 25:34–8 NRSV.

5. Lev 19:33–34 JPS.

more than a billion Muslims on our planet, and, like non-Muslims, only a tiny, tiny minority of them are a danger to anyone.

Like Christian or Jewish or Buddhist or Hindu terrorists—and there have been plenty throughout history—terrorists who happen to be Muslim twist Islam into an ideology that encapsulates their anger and their hatred. For the majority of Muslims, this ideology is abhorrent. Most Muslims desire to serve their God—who, incidentally, is also our God—in peace. Many non-Muslims do not even understand that Allah, the Arabic name for God, is a synonym for the God of Abraham, Isaac, and Jacob.

While for Muslims, the Qur'an is the greatest of scriptures, Muslims also believe that the people of the book that came before were also children of God, and therefore their revelations from God were also holy. And while there are difficult and perhaps unpalatable pieces of Islamic scripture (no less than the extremely unpalatable pieces of Jewish and Christian scripture), there is also much beauty and acceptance. On other religions, for example, the Qur'an says: "Truly those who believe, and those who are Jews, and the Christians, and the Sabeans—whosoever believes in God and the Last Day and works righteousness shall have their reward with their Lord. No fear shall come upon them, nor shall they grieve."[6] The Qur'an also offers these words: "O humankind! Truly We created you from a male and a female, and We made you peoples and tribes that you may come to know one another."[7]

Writer Eudora Welty once said: "My wish, indeed my continuing passion, would be not to point the finger in judgment but to part a curtain, that invisible shadow that falls between people, the veil of indifference to each other's presence, each other's wonder, each other's human plight."[8] That veil of indifference can be hard to part. It is too easy to avoid having compassion for people we do not know. It is particularly easy to avoid thinking about unimaginable tragedy like the Syrian crisis when it is happening to people who seem unlike us. But this ability to ignore suffering is shaken at times by things like the testimony of a survivor like Elie Wiesel, or by photographs. Like the one of five-year-old Omran Daqneesh, sitting stunned and bloody, covered in dust—a child like any child—your child—my child—in his shirt with its cartoon characters and his flyaway hair—or of Aylan Kurdi, the Syrian toddler whose body washed up on the Turkish coast, captured as if

6. Qur'an 2:62.

7. Qur'an 49:13.

8. Welty, *One Time*, 12.

sleeping in his red T-shirt and blue shorts, so recently dressed with care by parents who loved him.

When we are reminded that these are real, individual people, our hearts open in compassion. These are not abstractions, not enemies; they are real people, like you and me, who are suffering. It is an imperative of our faith, whether we are Congregationalist or Unitarian Universalist or something else, to do our very best to recognize that each person we encounter has inherent worth and dignity. In the spirit of understanding our spiritual kinship, I will close today with a prayer adapted from the Qur'an:

> Praise be to the Lord of the Universe who has created us and made us into tribes and nations, that we may know each other, not that we may despise each other. If the enemy incline towards peace, do thou also incline towards peace, and trust in God, for the Lord is the one that heareth and knoweth all things. And the servants of God, Most Gracious are those who walk on the Earth in humility, and when we address them, we say "Peace!"[9]

May it be so. Amen.

REFERENCES

"A Muslim Prayer for Peace." Unitarian Universalist Association Worship Web. https://www.uua.org/worship/words/prayer/muslim-prayer-peace.

Welty, Eudora. *One Time, One Place: Mississippi in the Depression*. Jackson: University Press of Mississippi, 1996.

Wiesel, Elie. *The Nazi Doctors and the Nuremburg Code: Human Rights in Human Experimentation*. Edited by George J. Annas et al. New York: Oxford University Press, 1992.

9. "Muslim Prayer." See Qur'an 49.13 and 8.6.

The Commuting Hijabi

LUCA ALEXANDER

Imagine—you're on the train platform,
Uptown Line, heavy rail, outbound, rush hour,
Hijab tucked tight with pins.

Destination: the comfort of your bed.

Then a memory hits you like a passing train—
your toes feel upraised bumps on the yellow line,
and you instinctively take one, two, three steps back.

Look right, look left: Am I farther back than was Sunando Sen?[1]

In these moments, I am claimed by an entity larger than myself,
one that is prodded at in Uber rides and Starbucks lines.
I am your uncle's favorite FOX News topic.

But I have memorized every verse before and after the ones they like to quote.

1. Sunando Sen, a Hindu man, was killed in 2012 when he was pushed in front of an oncoming train in New York City by a woman who later explained that she pushed him because she thought he was a Muslim.

Now, I am a *rūḥ*[2] with faith tattooed on my soul,
the same *rūḥ* of which Rumi[3] speaks,
the same Rumi that soccer moms keep next to their *50 Shades of Grey*.

In this moment, I'm nothing, nothing but a *rūḥ* tied to You.

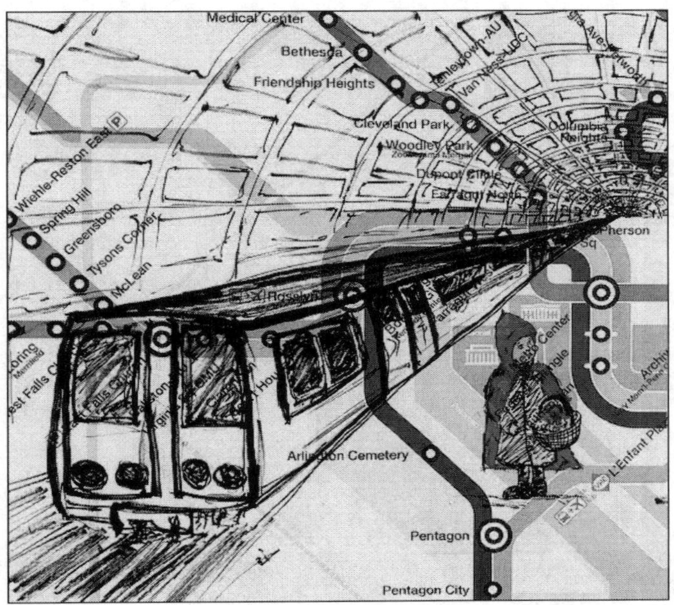

Detail from *Red Riding Hood on the Metro*, by Ahmad Abumraighi[4]

2. *Rūḥ* is the Arabic word for soul or spirit and is a cognate of the Hebrew word for the same entity.

3. Jalāl al-Dīn Muḥammad Rūmī (d. 1273) is one of the most well-known Muslim intellectuals. His poetry is translated into multiple languages and is loved across the world.

4. This detail from a sharpie sketch on a facsimile of a metro map, entitled *Red Riding Hood on the Metro* (24" x 36") was created by Ahmad Abumraighi as part of a live art demonstration held in Dupont Circle in Washington, DC that drew attention to issues of harassment on the metro.

PART II

CROSSING THRESHOLDS

***Solidarity*, photograph by the Greater Boston Interfaith Organization**[1]

OUR FRAUGHT HISTORIES, the many devastating conflicts in our contemporary world, and the pockets of hate in the United States are all evidence that a peaceful and secure society cannot be taken for granted. Religious

1. Boston Mayor Marty Walsh, Massachusetts Senator Elizabeth Warren, and members of the media look on as religious leaders of different traditions greet one another in solidarity following a fraught election cycle (December 2016). Pictured center is Yasir Fahmy, senior imam of the Islamic Society of Boston Cultural Center (ISBCC). Photograph by the Greater Boston Interfaith Organization (GBIO).

bigotry is a direct threat to the stability and sense of security of any polity. But how can we hold onto our own sacred identities, our own sources of joy and spiritual grounding, while being radically open to the identities, joys, and sources of spiritual grounding of other human beings? The art of—let us call it "holding sacred space"—is one that chaplains and religious professionals hone, but the question is one that all of us who live in religiously and philosophically diverse societies can consider in our interactions with our neighbors, friends, and colleagues.[2]

This practice of holding sacred space can ideally also inform relationships in our politics. For instance, in his address to a gathering of several thousand people, as convened by the Greater Boston Interfaith Organization (GBIO) in the wake of the rancorous 2016 presidential election, Boston mayor Marty Walsh, standing at the front of the Islamic Society of Boston Cultural Center, issued a simple but profound challenge to all elected officials: visit with a mosque before the next election.[3] The evening brought together clergy from different persuasions, individuals from across the political spectrum, elected officials, and many from among the city's civil servants and non-profit leaders. It was the first time that many attendees had ever been inside of a mosque, and the atmosphere was abuzz with excitement and conviviality.

Seeking out a positive relationship across lines of difference sometimes requires going out of our way to physically traverse a threshold that we might not otherwise have occasion to cross. Such a simple gesture of crossing an unlikely threshold even holds potential to catalyze a bond of mutual trust. Particularly in the face of geopolitical crises that tear at the social fabric of neighborhoods, countries, and entire regions, it is essential—urgent—that we take deliberate steps—metaphorical and *physical* steps—to know one another, at the very least, so that we can articulate and reaffirm our shared values.

Chaplain Lynn Cooper introduces the theme of sacred liminal moments in her rich descriptions of a Muslim prayer circle as "the meeting of breath and prayer." Then, Unitarian Universalist minister Wil Darcangelo reflects on his memories of being in New York City on September 12, 2001.

2. For a helpful interreligious etiquette guide, see Matlins and Magida, *How to Be a Perfect Stranger*.

3. Out of this effort, the "Out of Many, One: An Interfaith Call for Dignity and Diligence" petition called for a renewal of core civic values, "so that a spirit of dignity and compassion infuses both local and national governmental affairs." See "Out of Many" for the full text of the statement and signatories.

Wil models an ability to sit with the ambiguities, embodied sensations, and insights that may arise when encountering people and ideas across differences. He explores the "felt sense" that arises from learning new spiritual practices. This "felt sense," that is, a preverbal, non-judgmental, and semi-conscious awareness, which arises from gentle, focused attention can provide vital information about our well-being on many levels.[4] Deeply informed and inspired by his universalist inclinations, Wil seeks to experience, firsthand, the spiritual practices of different traditions. I remember vividly my amazement when Wil told me that he was going to fast the entire month of Ramadan in solidarity with Muslims and to *experience* our practice.[5] He did, in fact, fast the month, and over our family's traditional meal of roasted duck, we shared an *ifṭār*.[6]

We may not all have interreligious-ally stamina of Wil's sort, but even smaller-scale acts, done in a spirit of informed exploration and with an earnest desire for solidarity, can help us understand and better appreciate the significances of our different spiritual practices.[7] Textbook learning about different cultures and customs has its place, but textbook learning is most transformative when combined with embodied experience. Throughout his reflection, Wil highlights the value of embodied encounters that give rise to existential questions, including: "Given who I am, how do I relate to those who are markedly different from me?" This is precisely the question that Imam Taymullah Abdur-Rahman is forced to reprise through his early experiences as a prison chaplain on an interfaith chaplaincy team. As Imam Taymullah shows, our answers to existential questions may change as we go through life, but the questioning itself allows for self-awareness and growth.

4. There are many excellent guides to developing this intuition; I personally recommend Rome, *Your Body Knows*.

5. Ramadan is the ninth month of the Islamic lunar calendar and entails refraining from all food and beverage, including water, from the predawn hours until after sunset for those who are not otherwise exempted. Sexual intercourse during the daylight hours is also prohibited. For a great explanation of why Ramadan is not actually a miserable occasion to completely dread every year, see the short clip "Fasting for the First Time."

6. The break-fast meal eaten after sundown on days of fasting.

7. Another such embodied practice for solidarity and embodied learning, albeit a somewhat controversial one for some, is to experience firsthand being visibly Muslim in public by wearing clothing associated with Muslims (a scarf, a kufi head cap, or perhaps the longer fitting abaya-like garment). For a debate on this form of embodied solidarity, see various position pieces in "Do Non-Muslims Help."

In thinking about the potentials and complications of crossing thresholds, physical and metaphorical, Miriam Israel reflects on her time as an American-Jewish teenager living with a Muslim host family in Oman. Finally, Rabbi Nancy Fuchs Kreimer reflects on how communal loyalties and geopolitical realities make crossing the threshold all the more complicated—and simultaneously all the more urgent.

Each of the contributors in this section demonstrates how the willingness to engage—most especially when it requires intellectual or emotional work, vulnerability, and generosity of spirit—can have payoffs in the form of enhanced connections with other human beings and with our own selves. How do we cross thresholds not merely with our bodies, but with our spirits, with the fullness of our identities, and with all of our capacity for compassion and love? How can these encounters with difference deepen and expand our personal identity and spirituality? How can such encounters enrich our sense of community? Such questions are at the heart of this section. To close, Ariella Ruth provides a chillingly beautiful meditation on forging connections across the boundaries of self.

REFERENCES

"Do Non-Muslims Help or Hurt Women by Wearing Hijabs?" *The New York Times*. January 6, 2016. https://www.nytimes.com/roomfordebate/2016/01/06/do-non-muslims-help-or-hurt-women-by-wearing-hijabs.

"Fasting for the First Time for Ramadan: The Other Side of Ramadan." *Real Life* with host Yara Elmjouie. Produced by AJ+/Al Jazeera Media Network. Posted June 10, 2018. https://www.youtube.com/watch?v=h1779_E1A20.

Matlins, Stuart M., and Arthus J. Magida. *How to Be a Perfect Stranger: The Essential Religious Etiquette Handbook*. Woodstock, VT: SkyLight Paths, 2006.

"'Out of Many, One': An Interfaith Call for Dignity and Diligence." Greater Boston Interfaith Organization. https://docs.google.com/forms/d/e/1FAIpQLSeLoywAILdbrE_-oTZwGJ9CA4mrqPIfXoReVoLG5luBWypNhQ/viewform?c=0&w=1.

Rome, David I. *Your Body Knows the Answer: Using Your Felt Sense to Solve Problems, Effect Change, and Liberate Creativity*. Boston: Shambhala, 2014.

Sacred Moments of Liminality

LYNN COOPER

I AM AWASH WITH a case of the *November Strange* as the totality of the evening's darkness settles upon Cambridge streets. The feeling of in-betweenness, the thin place in time, the blurring of perceptions and comforts catches me off guard every year. I have to live the *November Strange* each year—the curious synchrony of turning back the clocks as the northern hemisphere heads toward its shortest day—to truly re-member the experience. Then I say—or rather, my body says—"Oh, yes, this feeling . . . I am home."

The brick sidewalks are slippery with fallen leaves, and I split my attention between the path beneath me and the low-hanging bare branches interrupting the alleyways. As I walk past a steamy café window, I catch a glimpse of my reflection. I am reminded of the tear in my corduroy vest. I have been following this busted shoulder seam since last winter, and I hope, once again, that it doesn't grow too vast before I finally sit down to mend it with imperfect, handsewn stitches. I take a second to nag myself: Why has it taken me so long to tend to this small matter? Am I really that busy?

I press the buzzer, and Naila welcomes me into her home. She and I were classmates in divinity school and have been colleagues in college chaplaincy for a few years. She is someone whose presence immediately puts me at ease—she bears a spirit of hospitality that is new to me. There are three other women in the kitchen, all sitting around the table drinking tea. They pour me a cup. Two more women join us within a short while and we relocate to the living room. We stand facing one another and a woman named Zahra leads us in the *dhikr*.[1] This is my first dhikr circle, and I am

1. *Dhikr* comes from the Arabic root *dh-k-r*, meaning "to mention" or "to remember," and refers to reflecting on God's names and attributes. One can also do *dhikr* by

the only non-Muslim present, but I feel at home. Naila's invitation to this evening prayer continues to unfold before me and within me. The gathering itself is a dynamic invitation—an invitation to commune with these faithful human beings, with God, and with my soul, in all its weariness. These women have invited me into their tradition, into the healing space of this circle, and into a deeper encounter of peace and spiritual consciousness.

As a Roman Catholic, I use the word "mercy" all the time. We speak of the corporal acts of mercy in our work with vulnerable populations. We call out to God for mercy throughout the mass—upward of eight times, depending on some liturgical choices. But it is only in Naila's apartment on this windy November evening that I begin to feel the word "merciful." The reality and profundity bleeds into my bones and I am full of gratitude for the gift of this moment and for clarity, albeit fleeting. I am taken by God's infinite mercy but also our own capacity for mercy and compassion. Reciting and singing attributes of God, I am moved to tears. With each word, I feel something within me expand and an entry point widen. I have long been a believer in the meeting of breath and prayer. It is uncanny, the physiological transformation that takes place when we breathe, sing, chant in repetition. Our bodies are different. We are different. The oxygen and rhythm break us open, making it possible to see with new eyes. I can intellectualize this experience all I want, but the embodied knowing—the practice itself—is what stirs me to a novel state in which peace and wakefulness coexist, nourishing one another.

Two years later, I am meeting with a student at the university's interfaith center. He's a young man from a devout American Catholic family. It's late morning on a Friday and we are just getting to know each other. He tells me about his family and a recent trip to Rome. He dishes on works of art that spoke to him and betrays his zeal for the high churchaesthetics of the Roman Catholic tradition. When we near the noon hour, I mention to him that the center will soon be bustling with our Muslim community gathering for Friday prayer. He nods, says "okay," and our conversation continues. Then we hear it. Traveling down the staircase to my office door, through the hardwood floor and ceiling, out the windows and right back

repenting to God with such repetitive prayers. Many verses in the Qur'an speak about dhikr: "Those who remember (*yadhkurūn*) God standing and sitting and lying on their sides and reflect on the creation of the heavens and the earth: Our Lord! Thou hast not created this in vain! Glory be to Thee; save us then from the chastisement of the fire." Qur'an 3:191. Some Muslims engage in group dhikr, saying God's name aloud in rhythmic chanting.

in—Naila's husband reciting the call to prayer. The young man across from me freezes mid-sentence. His eyes widen and then they close. I watch his body soften in the chair and together we sit in silent reverence, disruptive beauty and divine longing filling the ether between us. He is peaceful. He is full of awe. He is answering the call to prayer.

Though several years have passed since both of these encounters took place, I find myself revisiting these stories over and over again. They are personal landmarks for me—holy moments of transformation and gifts beyond measure—but they have come to inform my whole understanding of interfaith work. It's all about invitation and being awake enough to respond with an open heart. That invitation may come in an email from a trusted colleague or in an unscripted moment of connection—perhaps even at an inconvenient time—but the experience itself is just the beginning. These invitations encourage us to go deeper into our own traditions, enriching the religious imagination and recalibrating our sense of possibility.[2]

A gentleman in my one of my divinity school classes once told me that the greatest gift adult children can give their parents is to be involved in one another's lives as much as possible. I do not always think of God as a parent, but when I do, this is one way I envision our work as people of different faiths. Critical and meaningful interfaith collaboration is deeply concerned with nourishing and nurturing the relationships of brothers, sisters, siblings. We may not have been raised in the same household or indeed in the same religious tradition, but our Merciful Creator and Sustainer is calling us to cultivate a spirit of hospitality in our hearts and in our homes. This is the enduring invitation to create space for a deepening of connection. And likewise, if our hearts, minds, and ears are open to hear the invitations in our midst—the God Already Here—we will no doubt grow in our own love and compassion for God's diverse creation.

REFERENCES

Peace, Jennifer Howe, Or Rose, and Gregory Mobley, eds. *My Neighbor's Faith: Stories of Interreligious Encounter, Growth, and Transformation*. Maryknoll, NY: Orbis, 2012.

2. For more such stories of surprise encounter, see Peace et al., *My Neighbor's Faith*.

The Provenance of Wisdom

Wil Darcangelo

In 1993, I was having lunch in New York City when a few blocks away an explosion went off in the North Tower of the World Trade Center. Then, in 2001, I was planning a trip back to Manhattan and had dinner reservations at the Windows on the World restaurant on top of the North Tower booked for September 12th. I was packing for my trip into the city when I saw in the news the second plane hit the South Tower the morning of the 11th. The restaurant was gone; I could not immediately bring myself to think about all else that was lost. Early the next morning, New York City mayor Rudy Giuliani urged us in his press conference to continue living, and I got on the first train to Manhattan as I had originally planned. I did not know precisely why I was going anymore, but I knew very well why I was not staying home.

Once in the city I smelled the very particular smoke of Ground Zero as it wafted up Sixth Avenue. At that moment, the loss truly hit me. I went to St. Patrick's Cathedral to pray and weep with the faithful and frightened. I did not go near Ground Zero that day. In fact, I avoided anything south of the Village for fifteen years. I returned for the first time only recently. That day, I rode the elevator of the new Freedom Tower to the observation levels nearly a quarter of a mile above the city and looked out at the old view through new windows. The experience prompted me to ask myself: "Who am I today, compared to that young person so many years ago?" No elevator goes all the way to the Answer Department, but I have some new vantage points.

Early on, I had made the choice to separate the actions and ideologies expressed by violent extremists from the faith and teachings of the Prophet

Muhammad, peace be upon him.[1] There are always those of every faith who use God as the unassailable argument to justify terrible deeds; yet, murder is never a religious act by any spiritual metric. I was convinced that in the face of temptation to hate, we must turn our cheek toward love. A sense of empathy and inherent curiosity led me to want to explore what Muslims actually did believe. What was their view on Ultimate Reality? Alongside my lifelong exploration of Christianity, I had explored Judaism, Paganism, Buddhism, and Hinduism. But, in my late forties, I turned my heart toward Mecca to see what I might learn.[2]

I already knew some of the basics of Islam, for instance that Muhammad was regarded as a prophet, and that Muslims interrupt their work or sleep five times a day for a ritual of washing and prayer.[3] To convert to Islam, one pronounces an oath called the *shahāda* with intent: "I testify that there is no god but God and that Muhammad is a messenger of God." I knew these basics; yet, I wondered also about the deeper dimensions of the faith. How do the rituals function as conduits to deeper conviction and spirituality? I could imagine one might faithlessly go through the physical motions of the prayer without a deeper connection, as is true for most faiths. Alternately, can one believe and *not* perform the rituals, as many Christians and Jews do? Islam is a demanding religion, not dissimilar from Judaism with its hundreds of mitzvot, or commandments. How can one possibly fulfill it all? Are there lapsed Muslims? And my curiosities continued . . .

In my proclivity for learning by immersion, I decided to commit to fasting, praying, and studying the Qur'an in observance of the holy month of Ramadan, but to do so as a Christian. It was a very difficult, but fulfilling, contemplative experience, one that a spiritual explorer such as myself could readily access. The ritual prayers and supplications are comforting and physically empowering. The regularity and procedures encourage cleanliness of body and heart, gratitude, mindfulness, and connection with God. Muslims try not only to be connected to God, but also to live in a state of connectivity with their prophet and with one another.

1. By including the phrase "may peace be upon him," Wil is following the Islamic etiquette of saying a short blessing after mentioning the name of a holy figure.

2. In using the imagery of turning toward Mecca, Wil is evoking the Muslim practice of orienting toward Mecca for the daily ritual prayers, known as *ṣalāt*.

3. While the ritual prayer has specific outer forms, the outer form ideally serves as a conduit for cultivating inner states. Hence, the physical purification that Muslims do before ritual prayers bears a connection with the purification of the metaphorical "heart" from ailments such as avarice, pride, and hate.

Muslims believe Muhammad received the Qur'anic revelations from God through the intermediary of the angel Gabriel and that Muhammad was the final prophet of God, bringing a revelation to affirm revelations that had been previously given in various ways to tens of thousands of prophets in the past—Adam, Noah, Abraham, and Jesus among them. In addition to the name "Allah," God also has many other names such as *al-Qarīb*, "the Near One." God is also *al-Qahhār*, "the Compeller," compelling us to orient ourselves so as to arrive at gnosis. God's mercy for creation is another core attribute, and the divine names *al-Raḥmān*, "the All-Merciful," and *al-Raḥīm*, "the Ever-Merciful" are among the most repeated names of God in the Qur'an. But the Arabic words *al-Raḥmān* and *al-Raḥīm* do not have ready translations; in fact, all translations from the Arabic into other languages are interpretations of the original.

Perhaps God is most discernable in the struggle to discern. Perhaps God compels us to sit with one another, and this engagement is part of the wisdom of religious difference. When examining the theology of Islam, my beliefs differ as much from the Qur'an as they do from the Hebrew Bible and the Christian Testament. Each scripture challenges me. Each hints at a deeper life practice. Each also offers grace and opportunity to exhibit compassion toward one another.

I see equal wisdom from each of the three religions that have sprung from the lineage of Abraham, as well as others. Why am I Christian? Is it simply because Christianity is my first spiritual language? How does Christianity intersect with other religions as I study them? Where do these different yet sometimes not-so-different traditions overlap? The intersections *themselves*, I believe, is where the face of God is visible—in a multidimensional view, spoken through the mouths of many different prophets, the Prophet Muhammad included. The Qur'an is an enormous accomplishment regardless of its source. I personally have no difficulty believing that a divine being gave sacred information to a special person who was destined to share it with humanity; I see no reason to disbelieve that Muhammad was a prophet tasked with bringing a scripture to humankind.

The Qur'an is understood by Muslims to be the final and encapsulating word of God. The Qur'an, by its own account, comes to clarify previous revelations, to provide a clearer transmission in a preserved language. Critical biblical scholarship has largely concluded that much of the Gospels are translations of earlier documents now lost. The Hebrew Bible has a varied authorship, mainly attributed to traditional historical figures not literally assumed to have actually written them. But, according to Islamic tradition, the Qur'an was dictated during Muhammad's lifetime, by his own mouth, via transmission from the archangel Gabriel (Jibrīl). In addition to the Qur'an, Muhammad's teachings, passed down in the form of *ḥadīth*, are corroborated by chains of narration and are rigorously graded by early generations of Muslim scholars according to their reliability. None of this careful provenance automatically confers proof of a divine source—that is for the faithful to conclude for themselves.

I am fascinated by Islam partly because it deepens my relationship with the teachings and stories of Christianity and Judaism. The Qur'an is full of many of the same stories and the cast of characters that Christians and Jews well know. Like the satisfying final installment of an epic trilogy, it has a validating, grounding, and reinforcing effect. Reading the narratives of Job, and of Jesus and his mother, among others, told through a different tradition, made them feel even more real. There is more to be learned from the parallel exploration of the three sibling faiths of Abraham. Perhaps God is just waiting patiently for us to not only tolerate but to *accept* one another, waiting for us to become curious about one another, and waiting eventually for us to feel safe enough to reveal our hearts, at which point we might both teach as well as learn.

I am moved by Islam, and while not an adherent, I am appreciative. I will align my heart with the Ka'ba often, and from time to time I may even recite the opening chapter of the Qur'an, *al-Fātiḥa,* just to feel closer to God through the melody of it. In the process of finding where our faiths differ and where we agree, we are given a sacred opportunity to garner a more multifaceted understanding of God. This can happen *only* if we are comfortable enough with our neighbor to share what we believe while remaining humble enough to hear clearly the beliefs of another. Once we are comfortable enough to share, we learn that we have each been given a sacred piece of a puzzle.

Muslims orient themselves toward the Ka'ba when praying, and Jews orient themselves toward Jerusalem. In Judaism a minyan, or quorum of ten or more, is required for public prayer, for Muslims there are special merits to praying in congregation. There is a tenet in Christianity that says when two or more gather in God's name, God is there, and one verse of the Qur'an stresses that in any conversation of three, God is the fourth, and in any conversation among five, God is the sixth.[4] To me, these ideas are each about *sacred orientation* and *relationship*.[5] When we focus our collective energies as a group upon a particular idea at the same time, together, in and toward the same places, the sacred occurs. This collaborative aspect is part of the beauty of organized religion and also part of the essence of prophesy. Jesus and Muhammad (peace be upon them both), as well as the ancient Jewish prophets, are all trying to get us to just *be* with one another and *together* focus on what truly matters.

I believe Jesus was a prophet, a mystic, and a healer. He was a change-maker who knew exactly what humanity must endure in order to survive the age, and he was someone with a direct connection to God. He was someone who was trying to wake us up to the reality that we too are capable of such a connection. Muhammad, like Jesus (peace be upon them both),[6] were and are deserving of respect, emulation, and spiritual orientation. Through multiple prophets over the ages, God has taught us how to improve ourselves, relate with one another, and find the sacred even amid despair. In my experience, God demands the increasingly sophisticated ear and heart of humanity—an ear and heart that hear the plurality of God's voice without conflict, without sorrow, without shame, proving that only Love exists and always has.[7]

REFERENCES

Bouguenaya, Yamina. *Living with Genuine Tawhid: Witnessing the Signs of God through Qur'anic Guidance*. Qur'anic Wisdom Series. Columbia, SC: Receiving Nur, 2016.

4. See Qur'an 58:7: "Hast thou not considered that God knows whatever is in the heavens and whatsoever is on the earth? There is no secret converse among three, but that *He* is their fourth, nor among five, but that *He* is their sixth, nor less than that, nor more, but that *He* is with them Wheresoever they are."

5. For a contemporary Muslim reflection on these themes, see the work of theoretical physicist and Islamic scholar Yamina Bouguenaya, *Living with Genuine Tawhid*.

6. The Qur'an instructs Muslims not to differentiate between prophets as they all brought a message of God's unity and justice: "Say, We believe in God and what has been sent down upon us, and in what was sent down upon Abraham, Ishmael, Isaac, Jacob, and the Tribes, and in what Moses, Jesus, and the prophets were given from their Lord. We make no distinction among any of them, and unto *Him* we submit." Qur'an 3:84.

7. "The loving" (*al-Wadūd*) is one of the many names for God in Islamic theology. For a poetic meditation on different divine names, see the contribution titled "Upon You Peace," by Madonna Arsenault.

***The Sacred Mosque in Mecca, 2018*. Photograph by Hajjah Kamara.**

A Seed of Humility

Taymullah Abdur-Rahman

After the tragedy of September 11, 2001, many American Muslims, myself included, became defensive and hurt after having been wrongfully accused, surveilled, investigated, and suspected of plotting against the country to which we were loyal.[1] So, when I entered Concord prison as Muslim chaplain, I was prepared to be a "defender of the faith," embodying a kind of mythical archetype of the Muslim knight shunning evil, refuting falsehood, and defending the integrity of my religion and values. I had no expectations about how prison chaplaincy would in fact change *me*. Many small life-giving moments occurred during my formative years within prison chaplaincy, but two individuals in particular made an utterly unexpected impact on the way I understood my religion and values.

I shared a large chapel with the Protestant pastor, the Catholic priest, and an occasional visiting rabbi. We each had worship spaces dedicated to our specific tradition. One day, Father George, who was at the time working on his second master's degree, asked if I would give feedback on his thesis comparing *tawhīd* (Islamic monotheism) and the Trinity. Before I could decide how to respond, Father George went into his office, retrieved a copy of his essay and placed it in my hands for review and critique. How could I refuse?

What I read dumbfounded me. The levels of gradation and complexity in his comparison were stunning. Although Islam and Christianity's approach to how we embrace monotheism was different, the fundamental premise of an all-knowing, omniscient creator was at the core of both. Up

1. The backlash of September 11, 2001, did not only impact Muslims in America, but it profoundly impacted other communities of color who also faced heightened xenophobia. For an anthropological account, see Ayer, *We Too Sing America*.

to that moment, I thought of Christian doctrine and practice in little more than caricatures. When I thought of Christianity, I admittedly thought of money-hungry evangelism or a pedophile priesthood full of pomp and indulgence. That day I was humbled by the Lord.

Father George's essay asked questions about God's transcendence, the use of force to protect the faith and faithful, and how to bring to fruition the preferential option for the poor described in the Gospels and echoed in the Qur'an. He concluded by exploring the ways in which synergy could be created around both faiths and their objectives to make a more morally just and compassionate world. Through this and other such encounters, I began to rethink what it meant for me to be Muslim and to have been placed by Allah in some semblance of a leadership position. What was I charged with? How was I to behave among other faith leaders? In a multifaith context, how should I model decency and civility for my Muslim students?

I began to think of these questions and look for answers in the classical books and biographies of Islam. I found stories like Abdur-Ghaffar Khan, a Muslim contemporary and close friend of Gandhi who was a sworn pacifist and leader in the movement that liberated India. I found Abdul-Sattar Edhi, a Pakistani philanthropist who was called the Muslim Mother Theresa for his work on behalf of orphans and the needy. There were many examples of Muslims who were simply good citizens and not heroes in the most superficial sense of the word. My thought was evolving, and I was developing a new kind of temperance.

Then entered an Episcopalian deacon named Bruce Nickerson. Deacon Bruce was a retired seventy-something, blue-collar guy who had pulled himself up from alcoholism and depravity to a life of faith, service, and education. He would come into the prison two times a week to facilitate the Catholic Twelve-Step program. Deacon Bruce would always shake my hand and crack a joke. He was very much aware of and educated in interfaith relations from a historical perspective. He and I began to eat lunch together regularly. I found myself seeking his advice about personal matters; he was an unassuming, wise, and experienced man who had taken the time to get to know a young, black Muslim kid without the assumptions and predispositions that I was accustomed to people having about me.

During our bonding, there was a controversial pastor named Terry Jones who decided that he would burn thousands of Qur'ans in Florida as a protest of Islam and in memoriam to victims of September 11. One day while Deacon Bruce and I were eating lunch together in the prison mosque,

Deacon Bruce expressed his frustration with the lack of solidarity that Christians had shown Muslims during this difficult time. He said, "Lent season is coming. I want you to come to my church and give a three-part lecture about Islam, the Qur'an, and the life of Muhammad. My community needs to hear the truth from you."

Again, I was shocked. *The truth from me?* How could a Christian admit that I had any kind of truth? Why would he allow someone like me in such a sacred place as his church? Was it even permissible for me to enter a church? All of these questions swirled through my mind over the next several days until I decided that this was a moment from the moments of Allah, and that I had to accept.

Deacon Bruce and the congregants of St. Elizabeth's Episcopalian church showed up for all three of my sessions. They were very gracious. The encounters changed the way that I thought of Christians. It wasn't in my heart to think in pejorative caricatures anymore. Deacon Bruce had taught me in several weeks, through his courage and compassion, that practical faith is about encouragement to *all* doers of good; an invitation to expand our understanding of one another and a duty to be protectors of justice and its people.

My visit to St. Elizabeth's changed the trajectory of my life and planted an unexpected seed of humility. I knew then that I would have to work harder at being a true faith leader, not a follower of parochial, isolationist paradigms.

REFERENCES

Ayer, Deepa. *We Too Sing America: South Asian, Arab, Muslim, and Sikh Immigrants Shape Our Multicultural Future*. New York: The New Press, 2015.

A Place to Call Home

Miriam Israel

Moving into a stranger's house, knowing that you'll be staying for nine months, is a bizarre experience, and so, when I met my host family in Muscat, Oman for the first time, I was understandably nervous. I was eighteen and participating in a gap year for intensive language study. From the moment I landed, I was desperately looking for a way to understand my new surroundings and for a place to call home; however, using the word "family" to talk about my hosts seemed to imply a premature degree of intimacy.

This was especially true with my host mother, Samira. Her English was strained, and I arrived with no Arabic, making communication a considerable challenge. Plus, she already had five "real" children so I could hardly expect to be a priority. I had anticipated bonding quickly with my new "mother" and my inability to connect felt like a personal failure. Samira was also the most devout member of my family, which I perceived as an additional barrier. My host family was Muslim, and while they knew that I was Jewish, I was unsure of how to express my religious identity and hesitant to talk about it openly for fear that it would only distance us further.

One day, I found my three-year-old host brother, Tariq, absorbed in a book, and glancing over his shoulder, I discovered familiar characters—Jonah and the whale! I went to tell someone about this development and found the house empty except for Samira; excitedly I tried to explain that I also knew the story of Jonah, hopeful that this might help us relate. To my surprise, she disappeared into her room and returned holding a towering stack of books, each one with a different prophet on the cover. We sat on the floor together and became increasingly animated as we discovered that we shared not just Jonah, but Jacob, Noah, Moses, and more. Suddenly these stories weren't just part of an identity that I kept to myself, but they became the bridge for a gap I hadn't known how to cross. The books were basic enough for me to understand, and for hours we sat together, Samira helping me with pronunciation as I told her the prophets' Hebrew names.

I'd assumed that religion had no place in our relationship, but our shared faith gave us a way to communicate. From then on, religion was our common denominator. We celebrated Hanukkah, complete with my embarrassing attempt at latkes, and she taught me how to put on a hijab. We continued to marvel at each new similarity, from eating restrictions to prayer, and as my language skills improved we were able to move more into the abstract, discussing God and life and death. We were able to forge a deeper, more genuine, connection. Although I never could expect to become Samira's top priority, sharing an important piece of my identity, while learning about hers, helped to eventually make my strange new house feel like a home.

It has been several years since that experience, but I still carry with me the memory of those children's books. I carry something else too: the understanding of the vulnerability that is required to generate spaces that can feel like home. Most importantly, the process of creating a home requires humility—a risky attribute that can sometimes make us feel as if we are compromising our character or values. My initial inability to connect with my host mother was driven partially by arrogance; I assumed how she would react to parts of my identity, and so I purposefully didn't engage as my whole self. As a result, I was initially unable to conceive of her house as a home. Once I was finally able to see past my own misgivings, a door was opened for the both of us.

I didn't know how my host mother would respond to my familiarity with the story of Jonah and the whale, but there was undoubtedly holiness in the connection that followed as we both pushed through the barriers holding us back. Ultimately, it is the act of pushing through insecurity and welcoming other people—into our houses, our places of worship, or our shoes—that allows us to transform our preconceptions of others and of ourselves. This type of engagement requires risk and a degree of vulnerability that can be uncomfortable: it is an act of faith. Although the idealist in me wishes otherwise, humble intentions are useless if not paired with a willingness to meet others where they are to create cross-religious and cross-cultural environments that feel welcoming.

Abraham, one of the most esteemed prophets shared by Jews and Muslims, is lauded for his unfailing generosity and willingness to show hospitality to the stranger. He teaches us how a home can be defined by the people welcomed into it and the openness of its doors. Similarly, in a relationship across difference, we are both the stranger and the host; by being aware of both positions simultaneously, we can increase our capacity for empathy and even construct meaningful places to call home.

My host mother and I didn't speak the same language, and we had very few common cultural reference points; yet, by beginning with a simple point of connection—our shared sacred history—we were able to build a foundation of trust.

A Sign of Connection

Nancy Fuchs Kreimer

For almost fifteen years now, I have had the opportunity of working with Jewish communities to address their interest in and ignorance about their Muslim neighbors. I have taught synagogue members, communal leaders, and rabbinical students across the denominational spectrum. I have seen fear, curiosity, prejudice, and openheartedness—sometimes all in the same community, or even the same individual. In order to prepare myself for this work, I have had the privilege of learning from and with many Muslim Americans.

Over the years, I have watched both our communities struggle to understand each other. I have always led with the claim that we have many issues in common as religious minorities in a Christian majority society. It has become increasingly clear that much is at stake in our country and that we have many reasons to collaborate to uphold our shared values. Given this need to cooperate, it seems wise to avoid an issue that has proved to be divisive, namely the struggle in Israel/Palestine. Pragmatic counsel suggests I duck, as we often do in Muslim-Jewish spaces.

Here, I propose, rather, to dive in. I do so with a great deal of caution, as I am aware of the danger of writing about a topic that is fraught with emotion, and likely to cause tempers to flare in predictable and even unpredictable ways. It is also a topic in flux. On this issue, there are not two sides, but rather many. And, even more importantly, things have changed, are changing, and will change. Indeed, these observations anticipate my thesis. I proceed with humility and faith in the goodwill of my readers.

One of my favorite teaching modalities is working through case studies, chunks of real life, told in narrative form. I have used one particular case study—from the Harvard Pluralism Project—multiple times with

Jewish groups.[1] The case took place in 2007. By tracking the fate of this case as I have taught it over the years, I will reflect upon the dynamics at play in the engagement between Jews and Muslims in America.

The highlights of the case are as follows:

> After months of preparations, Janet Penn and a group of teenagers from Interfaith Action, a youth interfaith group, were busy cooking, making signs, moving tables, and readying Temple Israel for a special event. . . . The teens from Sharon, Massachusetts envisioned an interfaith event they called "Sharing Sacred Seasons." Some four hundred people were expected to attend, and the temple was buzzing with excitement. . . . As guests entered the synagogue they would be greeted by a large sign which read: "We Support Israel." . . . Over the years of her own interfaith involvements, Penn had become aware of another, competing narrative: for many Muslims, Israel was seen as a symbol of oppression. She feared that the sign would be viewed as "an unbelievable insult."

Penn asks the Muslim students if their parents would have a problem with the sign. Their answer: Yes. Part A of the case ends with these words:

> How could she [Penn] ask him [the rabbi of the synagogue] to remove the sign, given the community's dedication to Israel? Yet, how could she invite people to observe their holiday at another house of worship and greet them with a sign they might read as hostile? Penn saw Rabbi Starr approaching down the hallway, and, with some hesitation, asked if she could have a few words with him.

As in any good case study, the learning comes from the group's grappling with the issue: what would you do if you were Rabbi Starr? Will his congregants, noting the sign has been removed, conclude that interfaith means compromising who they are? What if the situation were reversed and you were an imam being asked to take down a sign saying "Free Palestine" when Jewish guests were expected? How are the two situations similar or different? How do we cultivate the virtue of hospitality? How do we plan interfaith encounter with an understanding of the developmental steps involved in engaging with the "other?" The actual outcome in this situation—that Rabbi Starr took down the sign—is much less important than what the group explores about their own feelings, thoughts, and conclusions.

1. "A Sign of Division."

When I first began to teach this case to Jewish groups, it was assumed that the sign belonged in the synagogue, the congregants would want it there, and the question was about removing it for the evening. Similarly, a corresponding sign might well be found in a mosque and Jewish visitors would surely be offended. The majority tended to agree with Rabbi Starr's practical plan. Over the years, more participants began to note the relevance of the power differential between the Jewish community and the Muslim one in the context of Sharon, Massachusetts. A minority of those who studied this case with me would still keep the sign, noting that dialogue can only be real if we insist from the start on our core beliefs.

Today, the very premise of this case is not as secure. Among the Jews whom I teach, it is not obvious that the sign would be missed by all congregants. It is increasingly acknowledged that there is not a neat divide on the issue of Israel/Palestine with a line running between Jews on one side and Muslims on the other. A diversity of views on the issue exist within and among Jewish communities. Similarly, there is no monolithic position on Israel/Palestine among American Muslims. Both of our communities handle these divisions in ways that are painful for those on the margins.

Perhaps in this moment in America, the issue of Israel/Palestine can become an occasion for connection rather than division. In addition to holy days and dietary laws that are out of sync with the majority, in addition to our devotion to a foreign language and an ancient text, in addition to all of the theological frameworks that we Jews and Muslims share, we also find this issue difficult to handle within both of our communities. Both of our traditions teach practices to cultivate compassion, humility, and open-heartedness, and we can learn from each other's struggles, learn to listen to one another better. The jokes about "the elephant in the room" are getting old; we are instead acknowledging that there is an entire zoo in that room.

Rather than lining up on sides around our "dual narratives," we must strive to heal our divides together by adopting much more profoundly intracommunal perspectives. And in this process, we may just help each other to discover, if we are lucky, a way forward.

REFERENCES

"A Sign of Division." The Pluralism Project. Harvard University. 2008. http://pluralism.org/wp-content/uploads/2015/10/Sign-of-Division-A.pdf.

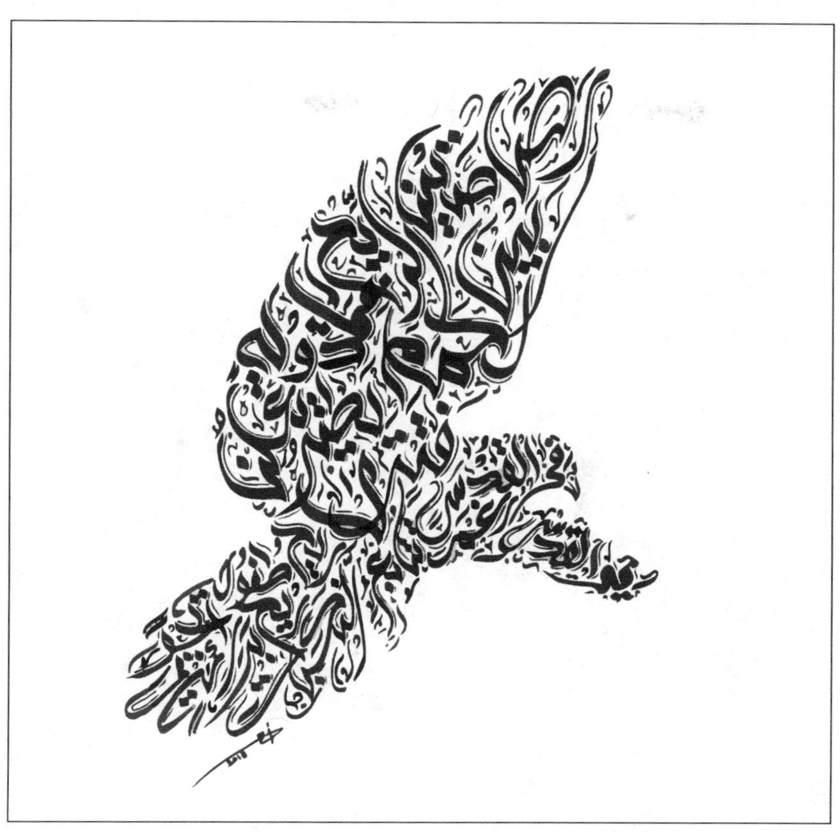

***Hope,* by Ahmad Abumraighi**[2]

2. This image in Arabic calligraphy (18" x 24") is a stanza of the poem "In Jerusalem," by the Palestinian-Egyptian poet Tamim Al-Barghouti. The poem reads, "In Jerusalem, despite successive calamities, a breeze of innocence and childhood fills the air, and you can see doves fly high announcing, between two shots, the birth of a state." In a conversation, Ahmad Abumraighi explains the title of the work: "To me, hope is sacred. Despite all of the tragedies of this world, hope keeps me alive, keeps me longing to a bright future where justice, mercy, and love are not just words but a lived reality."

Sweeping Light Born of Familiar Pathways

ARIELLA RUTH

vulnerability and attentiveness of shared
space, held in our laps between
curved palms

walls resonate
our silence gathered
to let a question linger, echo—

let a thought transpose, renew—

let a note reverberate, rest—we move

alongside each other, corridors of sincere
sweeping light born of familiar
pathways

before and behind us illuminate
through glass
always, glass

Part III

HEALING DIVIDES

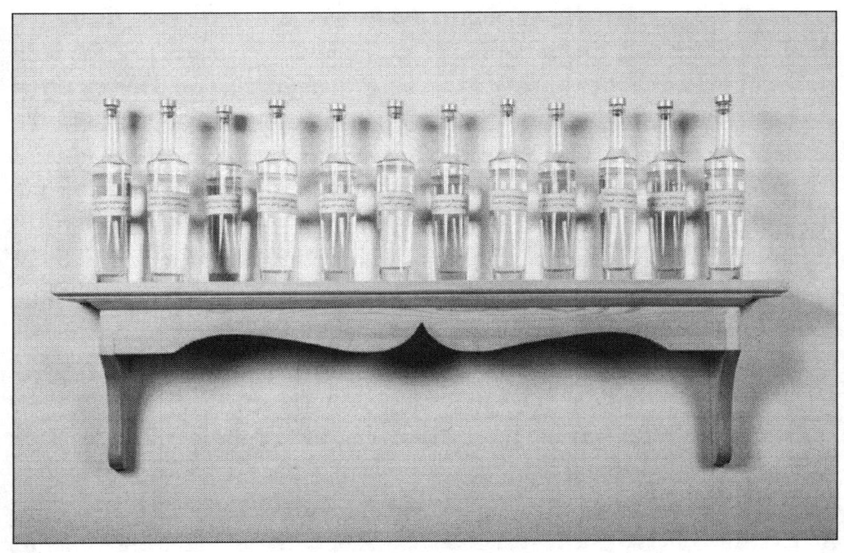

***Castor Oil Detox Formula*, by Huda Lutfi**[1]

1. This three-dimensional wall installation, titled *Castor Oil Detox Formula*, is from the Cut and Paste series, exhibited at the Townhouse Gallery, Cairo, Egypt (2013). Artist and cultural historian Huda Lutfi uses castor oil, a traditional cleansing remedy, as a metaphor for purification of the intellect. "Maybe we also need an internal cleansing, a brain cleansing," she explains in a conversation with AhramOnline, "we need to start with ourselves, question where we're coming from, question our ideologies, our prejudices, and now is the right time for that." Elkamel, "Cut and Paste."

Part III—Healing Divides

In his reflection in the *Harvard Divinity Bulletin* on the demands of contemporary homiletics, Reverend Dr. Matthew Potts observes:

> We need a public speech which honestly addresses the violence and injustice of the world, even if only to condemn it; a form of discourse which admits its own shortcomings, even if only to invite a relationship of response, a homiletics of judgement and humility, of imagination and mystery, of pastoral wisdom and prophetic protest. If the American preacher would find a way to speak of and to our distressing political moment, then let her rise unto the pulpit with some poetry.[2]

The individuals featured in this section are using their pulpits to do just this by helping provoke their constituents, and in turn all of us, into taking action that is informed by wisdom, grace, humility, generosity, and love.

The Reverend Otto O'Connor, the Reverend Soren Hessler, and the Reverend John Soderblom remind us of the ultimate virtues and the high stakes of the current political and social climate in the United States. The Reverend Sam Teitel offers a vision of radical hospitality drawn from the story of Abraham and Sarah in the Bible and the Qur'an. The Reverend Dr. Stephanie Rutt offers pearls of wisdom drawn from the words of the Reverend Dr. Martin Luther King Jr. and intertwined with the words of another Boston sojourner, Sheikh Yasir Fahmy, the current senior imam of the Islamic Society of Boston Cultural Center and the leader of one of the country's most robust institutions for Islamic learning, worship, and community activism. Then, Pastor Jerrell Riggins lifts up the prophetic voice of Micah next to resounding Qur'anic moral imperatives.

How can we dismantle the walls of ignorance and the fears that have cut our communities off from one another? This is the question that animates the following conversations from the pulpit. To close the section, Ariella Ruth offers a poetic reflection on the boundaries of self and other in an experience of sacred space and time.

REFERENCES

Elkamel, Sara. "'Cut and Paste': Artist Huda Lutfi Reflects on Revolutionary Struggle." AhramOnline. December 8, 2013. http://english.ahram.org.eg/NewsContent/5/25

2. Potts, "The Politics of Preaching," 28. For another new interreligious volume that is centered around this need to inspire, provoke, heal, and guide, see Rose et al., *Words to Live By*.

/88561/Arts—Culture/Visual-Art/Cut-and-Paste-Artist-Huda-Lutfi-reflects-on-revolu.aspx.

Potts, Matthew L. "The Politics of Preaching." *Harvard Divinity Bulletin* (Autumn/Winter 2017) 20–28.

Rose, Or, Homayra Zaid, and Soren Hessler, eds. *Words to Live By: Sacred Sources for Interreligious Engagement*. Maryknoll, NY: Orbis, 2018.

Who Do You Think You Are, the Queen of Sheba?

Otto O'Connor

How many times have you been at church and heard the Qur'an as one of the readings? Anyone?[1] (Silence.) I guess I should not be surprised: we are Unitarian Universalists, and we barely read from the Bible; why would we read from the Qur'an? I can hear the barrage of questions: "Is it even relevant? Would it be cultural appropriation? We do not even have any Muslims here." (Not so fast—we are Unitarian Universalists—some of us may also be Muslim!) I personally do not identify as Muslim, but when I took time to study the Qur'an, I became intrigued by its stories, including one in particular.

Did you know that the Qur'an narrates the encounter between the Queen of Sheba and King Solomon? In the Qur'anic version, which differs in notable ways from the biblical account, King Solomon is informed by a hoopoe of a queen who has vast riches and a powerful throne. King Solomon sends her a letter demanding submission and threatening war. She tries to subdue him by sending an envoy with gifts, but he refuses her gifts saying that the provisions that God has given him are better than the queen's wealth. Eventually, the queen personally comes to visit King Solomon and declares her submission to God.

I found myself wondering about how a story from such a different context has relevance today: there was no Queen of Sheba selfie showing her in front of her gorgeous throne and no Twitter post giving updates of

1. In his service design, the Reverend included a reading relating the encounter of the prophet Solomon with the Queen of Sheba as related in the Qur'an (27:29–44). The Reverend then uses the story to develop a commentary on the value of humility and the importance of seeking out relationships across social divides.

her conversion with King Solomon. But the Qur'anic story does have many things to say that resonate at present—about the value of women's leadership, about diplomatic leadership on the part of heads of state, and about the value of humility in particular.

Through this story of the Queen of Sheba and King Solomon, we can begin to dismantle stereotypes about Muslims that we might ourselves hold. Here we have a Qur'anic story of a strong and powerful woman leader who makes the decision not to go to war, despite what her council tells her; she is a leader who thwarts war through diplomacy.[2] Many critics claim that Islam is oriented toward war, is inherently violent, and discourages women from taking active roles in society; yet this Qur'anic story celebrates a woman's acumen and virtues and her diplomatic insight.

The figure of the queen also provides us with a lesson about humility. I am not a Muslim. I do not ultimately know that much about Islam; and if we are honest, many of us do not know much about other cultures and beliefs, even if we study them sometimes. We get into problems when we make judgments about other religions or cultures without having a truly informed perspective. In our world today, information is often instantaneous. We can Google "Muslim," "The Queen of Sheba," or even "Unitarian Universalist," and get an article or two. Then we think that we understand or maybe even that we have mastered the subject. This is a very shallow way of knowing. It is a beginning, but it is not the end. We must strive for a more humanizing way of learning about and engaging with our Muslim neighbors.

The idiom, "Who does she think she is, the Queen of Sheba?" is well known and describes a person who thinks a lot of herself or himself. Part of the wisdom of this story shows that one can have everything—be the Queen of Sheba—and yet still need to change one's mind. We can still be humbled by new knowledge. In particular, as Unitarian Universalists, we must do our best to try to understand the experience of Muslims in the United States. We must think about how we can build bridges of understanding. We have to realize the ways in which we participate in Islamophobia, by condemning a whole religion for being sexist or violent without taking the time to truly examine its tenets or get to know its adherents. We have to be able to admit when we may have been wrong in our beliefs or implicit stereotypes.

2. For further reflections on this point, see the contribution to this volume by Donna Dolham.

At a time when Islamophobia infuses our public discourse, this country can be a difficult place for Muslims to live and practice their faith. And in a country where Christianity is often perceived as normative, Muslim are often stigmatized. "But," I hear you say, "what about us? We are not Christians either!" As Unitarians, *some* of us *are* in fact Christians. But what is more, we are easily *perceived* as Christians, which gives us protection from bigotry directed at religious minorities and those perceived to be foreigners. We have to be allies in the struggle.

In a country where the man who is now president thought it would be a good idea to police "Muslim neighborhoods," I am reminded of the powerful words of Martin Niemöller, a German Lutheran minister, an outspoken critic of Nazism, white supremacist ideologies, and a pacifist: "First they came for the Socialists, and I did not speak out—because I was not a Socialist. Then they came for the Trade Unionists, and I did not speak out—because I was not a Trade Unionist. Then they came for the Jews, and I did not speak out—because I was not a Jew. Then they came for me—and there was no one left to speak for me."[3] I am not saying this to scare you. I am saying this because, in the end, if we are going to protect our own freedom of religion, we have to show leadership in protecting the rights of others. Our right to practice our faith, our non-creedal faith that does not rely on divine revelation, our faith that is most decidedly *not* in line with mainstream Christianity, depends on the freedom that our Muslim siblings have to practice their faith. This is the self-interest based approach, but we cannot afford to sit by while Islamophobia threatens communities of faith and those people who are a part of them.

This is a time for leadership, for diplomacy, and for the humility to recognize that we may learn from and be inspired by Islam and Muslims. The quest for new knowledge can be a part of our commitment to Unitarian Universalism.

REFERENCES

"Martin Niemöller." In *Holocaust Encyclopedia*. United States Holocaust Memorial Museum. Washington, DC. https://encyclopedia.ushmm.org/content/en/article/martin-niemoeller-first-they-came-for-the-socialists.

3. See "Martin Niemöller."

Praying for—and with—the Other

Soren M. Hessler[1]

Jesus said, "Truly I tell you, there is no one who has left house or brothers or sisters or mother or father or children or fields, for my sake and for the sake of the good news, who will not receive a hundredfold now in this age—houses, brothers and sisters, mothers and children, and fields with persecutions—and in the age to come eternal life."[2]

The church understands itself to be a family, and in baptism we are reminded that we are incorporated into a Christian family that transcends space and time. Yet, the family we find in following the will of God through Jesus is not limited to followers of Jesus: "for God all things are possible."[3]

1. This contribution is excerpted and adapted from a sermon delivered at Boston University's Marsh Chapel and broadcast on National Public Radio 90.9 WBUR during the 11 a.m. interdenominational Protestant worship service on Sunday, October 10, 2015. In the course of a Sunday worship service he led at Boston University's Marsh Chapel, the Reverend Soren Hessler, an ordained United Methodist elder, invited a Jewish and a Muslim colleague to share readings from the Hebrew Bible in Hebrew and from the Qur'an in Arabic, likely the first time in the chapel's history that such a Sunday service included a reading from the Qur'an. In this way, Reverend Soren was not simply preaching about the value of interreligious encounter, but he went the next step to introduce non-Christian religious voices into a Christian worship service, and he did so in a time of heightened Islamophobia in the United States. Using a prominent platform, he modeled how forms of thoughtful engagement across religious differences can enrich our own particular encounters with divine mystery. The message of interfaith collaboration, broadcast on public radio, reached audiences across the nation.

2. Mark 10:29–30 NRSV.

3. Mark 10:27, Matt 19:26 NRSV.

When we do the work of God, when we love God and neighbor, we encounter new sisters and brothers, mothers and children who are also on that same journey of doing the work of God. In following Jesus, our new family may come to include those whom we may least expect. Were it not for my relationships across religious divides, I would have trouble knowing or sharing this good news as I now hear it in the Gospel of Mark:

> A crowd was sitting around him; and they said to him, "Your mother and your brothers and sisters are outside asking for you." And he replied, "Who are my mother and my brothers?" And looking at those who sat around him, he said, "Here are my mother and my brothers! Whoever does the will of God is my brother and sister and mother."[4]

As in the opening message of Mark 10:29–30, we are again reminded that we find family not just in the future eschatological promise of resurrection, not just within the four walls of a chapel nave, but in "whoever does the will of God."

A Muslim chaplain colleague noted this week with enthusiasm that her job is to get people of different faiths "to bump into each other." We cannot find new sisters and brothers, parents and children if we don't really, truly engage them. Our reasons for seeking one another out as friends and "new family" in God are different and complex, but a similar call resonates throughout our different faith traditions. Both my personal experience and the exemplary precedent set by Howard Thurman, Marsh Chapel's first dean, tell me that we cannot pray for, and we especially cannot pray *with*, the "other" if we don't know the other.[5] In coming to know the other, we may find that they are not really the "other" at all; they are in fact our sister or our brother, or a mother or a son, on the journey of faith.

Over the course of our many years working together, I've "bumped into" my Muslim colleague a lot. We have shared office space, and I've learned she prays, a lot. In fact, she probably prays more each day than I do in a week. I didn't really know about personal piety until I got to know a Muslim who took her faith seriously.

4. Mark 3:32–35 NRSV.

5. The full sermon references Reverend Howard Thurman's blessing of Rabbi Zalman Schachter-Shalomi's son at the time of the boy's bar mitzvah. Reb Zelman was a student of Thurman's at Boston University in the mid-twentieth century. This blessing, and the special relationship between the two men, is related by Reb Zalman in his memoir, *My Life in Jewish Renewal*, 89–92.

Bob Hill, the dean of Marsh Chapel, and I were recently sitting on a park bench chatting about the consequences of taking seriously three significant creeds spoken at the chapel regularly: (1) We believe that the Sunday morning liturgy is the heartbeat of a Christian religious community; (2) We believe that we communicate the core values of our faith through liturgy; (3) We believe that we are called by the Gospel to be in authentic community with the religious other. In this spirit, think about inviting the neighbor who observes dietary restrictions that you do not to dinner sometime soon. Learn why their food practices are important and meaningful to them. Have a real conversation about how to provide genuine hospitality. Come to know one another by learning of each other's deep love of God, and in that encounter, find the family you are promised in the Gospel lesson today.

May we experience the beauty of each other's traditions, and may we know one another as sisters and brothers, sibling believers who seek to do the will of God.

As the psalmist writes:

> Let the favor of the Lord our God be upon us,
> and prosper for us the work of our hands—
> O prosper the work of our hands![6]

REFERENCES

Shachter-Shalomi, Zalman with Edward Hoffman. *My Life in Jewish Renewal: A Memoir.* Landham, MD: Rowman & Littlefield, 2012.

6. Ps 90:17 NRSV.

They Will Know Us by Our Love

John Soderblom

To Jesus, there were no "others." Jesus reached out to the Roman soldiers around Him and to the tax collectors, people who were loathed because of their connection to an oppressive regime. Much in this way, we too can show God's love through action by having compassion for the many migrants and refugees of all backgrounds and nationalities attempting to find sanctuary in our country. In the same manner that Christ overturned views about the "others" and "outcasts" in His time, we too must care for those who seek our protection and aid.

Even if we may have some fears, we cannot turn our backs on those who ask for our compassion. They are people who come with hope for a better future for their children, as have so many immigrants before them—possibly even including some of our own families. When we see the humanity of refugees seeking asylum, we do Christ's work. We give a new power to our Christian faith by giving others hope, not only by what we give materially, but by what we give from our hearts.

We can look toward the American Muslim communities around us, communities who face undeserved blame and suspicion, with the same compassion. Terrorists may claim to be Muslims, but they are not representative of Islamic values. They have skewed the teachings of the Qur'an and the Prophet Muhammad. Values of compassion and love must remind us that we cannot afford to "other" our fellow American citizens and residents, nor blame them for what fanatics do; fanaticism of any stripe is not representative of a faith community at large.

When we show compassion for refugees and migrants trying to find safety in our country, and when we show compassion to the Muslim community in our midst, we follow the example of Jesus Christ. We walk in the path that Jesus, the prophets of the Hebrew Bible, and Muhammad charted. Our different faiths share so much, including the striving for righteous deeds, the centrality of mercy, the importance of charity. We have far more that unites us than that separates us. It is time to cease to see "others" and start seeing fellow brothers and sisters.

For truly, they will know we are Christian by our love.

***The Fear*, by Sobia Ahmad**[1]

1. Sobia Ahmad, *The Fear*, ceramic tiles, ink, approximately 15" x 15," 2016, Sadat Art for Peace Permanent Collection. Upon closer look, these tiny mosques are made of famous Western towers. The piece is the artist's response to the US government's policy of drastically limiting the number of Syrian refugees offered asylum, and it laments the rampant Islamophobia and collective incapacity to show empathy toward human beings fleeing the horrors of war.

Blessed Are the Strangers

Sam Teitel

If Abraham and Sarah were going to conceive biological children, it would have happened by this point: Abraham is one hundred years old and Sarah is ninety-nine. But when Abraham and Sarah welcome a group of strangers into their home, these strangers bring news that the couple will have a child, despite their old age. The book of Genesis even compares the stars in the sky to their descendants: "Look toward heaven and count the stars, if you are able to count them . . . so shall your descendants be."[1] In the biblical account, Abraham welcomes these strangers who bring him amazing news, Sarah laughs to herself, and all is well. But what can we learn if we look at this story in the Qur'an?

As Unitarian Universalists, we have a special relationship with Islam: quite possibly none of us would be here if it was not for the exchanges between Unitarians and Muslims in Transylvania in the 1500s and the influences of Muslim ideas on Unitarian thought.[2] We must remember this part of who we are at a time when Islamophobia is epidemic in the country where many of us reside. When politicians are shutting our country's doors to refugees and immigrants, we are obligated as people of faith to resist. And as we engage with this struggle, we would do well to remember that for us, this is personal: the people who are being discriminated against are connected to us by history and faith.

One of the ways we honor this connection is by engaging with the Qur'an, particularly when we have a story that is found across scriptures, such as the story of the angels visiting Abraham and Sarah. In one instance, the story is related as follows in the Qur'an:

1. Gen 15:5 NRSV.
2. For a compelling look at this history, see Ritchie, *Children of the Same God*.

> Hast thou heard tell of Abraham's honored guests, / when they entered upon him and said, "Peace!" he said, "Peace—and unfamiliar folk." / Then he went quietly to his family and came with a fattened calf. / He placed it close to them, saying, "Will you not eat?" / Then he conceived a fear of them. They said, "Fear not!" and gave him glad tidings of a knowing son. / Then his wife came forward with a loud cry; she struck her face and said, "A barren old woman!" / They said, "Thus has thy Lord decreed. Truly *He* is the Wise, the Knowing."[3]

Here, too, in the Qur'an, Abraham welcomes the strangers into his home. But then, he immediately becomes afraid of the people that he has just let in and starts waffling, possibly regretting his decision. After this, the strangers give Abraham the news that he is going to be given biological children at his advanced age. And Sarah, his wife, is shocked by this good news.

It is easy to relate to everybody in this story. We can relate to Abraham, as all of us have, at some point, been afraid of what we do not know or understand. We can also relate to Sarah's experience of disbelief in the face of life-changing news. And we can even relate to the strangers, as all of us have tried to tell somebody something they really need to know but will be shocked to hear.

Abraham and Sarah, in both the Bible and the Qur'an, welcome strangers whobring the good news that will ultimately be the beginning of our tradition and others. But the story takes on new meaning for us as scared, confused people, living in a scary, confusing time, watching other people make all of the terrible decisions that scared and confused people make. We are in a position that is not so different from the position Abraham was in when he became afraid of strangers, not knowing that they brought him blessed news.

And we, like all scared and confused people, have choices that we need to make. When our president and our leaders respond to this situation by proclaiming hate, how do we respond? We could go along and jump on the fear wagon. We could do nothing, which is something I wish we were less practiced at doing. Or, we can embrace a spirit of radical welcome, just like Abraham welcomed the strangers to his home with the encouragement of his wife. We can advocate for that kind of welcoming to our political and spiritual leaders who may not be so keen on the idea of hospitality.

3. Qur'an 51:24–30. See also Qur'an 11:69–73 and 15:51–56.

Our sacred texts do not tell us to cut these people a break because of how awesome we are; this is not about us getting a pat on the back for being good. Our sacred texts tell us that we can look at strangers and travelers, visitors and refugees, people of all kinds, from all backgrounds, and know that among them we see messengers from God. We see sacred teachers. We see brilliance, beauty, poetry.

As we move forward, may we greet with enthusiasm the lessons that we have yet to learn, from the sacred people whom we have yet to encounter.

REFERENCES

Ritchie, Susan. *Children of the Same God: The Historical Relationship between Unitarianism, Judaism, and Islam*. Boston: Skinner House, 2014.

The Sheikh and the Preacher

STEPHANIE RUTT

WELL OVER ONE THOUSAND individuals attend Friday prayer at the Islamic Society of Boston Cultural Center each week, and one Friday, I attended as a guest. I listened intently to the senior imam, Sheikh Yasir Fahmy, gave a Friday sermon, a *khuṭba*.[1] As I listened, the words of the Reverend Dr. Martin Luther King Jr. kept coming to mind. As I continued listening, I noticed that if I substituted the Arabic word "Allah" for "God," and the Qur'anic verses for similar biblical ones, I could hear a common message calling us to honor our humanity and celebrate unity over uniformity. I heard an invitation for us to follow the prophetic calling toward a new day when all peoples may look at "others" and see only themselves. The prophetic words of Reverend King and Sheikh Fahmy became intertwined in my mind and heart, laying out a vision of redemption and grace.

ON OUR PERVERSE DESIRE TO EXALT THE SELF

The sheikh describes how we seek recognition at the expense of others: "We want to be uplifted. We want recognition. We want stability. We want to be known and recognized. We want to be justified. Because of our distance from Allah, we think that the only way I am to make myself big is by belittling others . . . The self becomes self-aggrandizing and self-absorbed

1. A *khuṭba* is the Arabic word roughly equivalent to "sermon" or "homily," and is a part of the Friday congregational gathering. The khuṭba is followed by the *ṣalāt*, the Islamic ritual prayer. The time for the prayer is based on the position of the sun at its zenith, and so the precise time for prayer varies slightly from one place to the next and throughout the year.

[thinking about another person]: 'You are a danger to my existence, to my power. You threaten me so I want to destroy you.' [These are] diseases of the heart that exist at the root of this toxic otherizing."[2] The preacher describes our tendency to seek self-gratification, which can become harmful if not checked: "We all have the drum major instinct. We all want to be important, to surpass others, to achieve distinction, to lead the parade. . . . It is a good instinct if you don't distort it and pervert it."[3]

ON THE HUMBLE EXAMINATION OF THE SELF

The sheikh says that we begin with introspection: "We begin by looking in the mirror and thinking, 'Am I a person who otherizes? Am I someone who puts others into other ugly categories and belittles them because of who they are?' I have to ask myself, 'To what extent do some of these diseases exist within me?'" The preacher also reminds us that we begin by analyzing the self: "In order to love your enemies, you must begin by analyzing self. And I'm sure that seems strange to you, that I start out telling you this morning that you love your enemies by beginning with a look at self. . . . There might be something within you that arouses the tragic hate response in the other individual. And this is one of the tragedies of human nature. So, we begin to love our enemies and love those persons that hate us, whether in collective life or individual life, by looking at ourselves."[4]

ON HONORING THE SANCTITY OF THE SOUL

The sheikh urges us to see the dignity of all human beings: "When the Prophet Muhammad stood [in respect] before a Jewish funeral procession and was asked why he stood, he replied, 'Is he not a soul that deserves honor, dignity, and respect?' That is the prophetic ideal. . . . Ask yourself. Am I someone who has genuine honor for others, genuine love? Can I see the sanctity in human beings no matter who they are?" The preacher also

2. Sheikh Yasir Fahmy's quotes have been slightly modified to facilitate ease of reading from the transcript of his remarks at the Islamic Society of Boston Cultural Center (ISBCC) on Friday January 9, 2015. For more on Sheikh Yasir Fahmy's vision to "make America great," see Bell, "This Imam."

3. King, "The Drum Major Instinct." Sermon adapted from the 1952 homily "Drum-Major Instincts" by J. Wallace Hamilton.

4. King, "Loving Your Enemies."

reminds us that when we recognize the common destiny and hopes of all peoples, we are set free: "We will be able to speed up that day when *all* God's children, black men and white men, Jews and Gentiles, Protestants and Catholics, will be able to join hands and sing in the words of the old Negro spiritual, 'free at last!'"[5]

ON CARING FOR ONE ANOTHER

The sheikh urges us to be a mercy to humankind: "To dignify others is to make sure that everyone comes before me. I want people to be lifted high, and if it requires that I bow down, I will do it. That is the prophetic spirit. That is what it means to honor others, to care for others, regardless of religion or ethnicity or race or economic status." The preacher also reminds us to serve with a heart full of grace: "The ultimate measure of a man is not where he stands in moments of comfort and convenience, but where he stands at times of challenge and controversy. The true neighbor will risk his position, his prestige, and even his life for the welfare of others."[6] He reminds us that "everybody can be great because anybody can serve. You don't have to have a college degree to serve. You don't have to make your subject and verb agree to serve. You only need a heart full of grace; a soul generated by love."[7]

ON SEEKING TO KNOW ONE ANOTHER

The sheikh commands us to engage with people as a part of faithfulness *to God:* "The purpose of all creation is 'so you may know one another,' to have an intimate engagement with people. God says, 'I made you into these different tribes that you might know one another.'[8] So, it is through humility—that is the way we begin to heal the pains of our society." The preacher reminds us of our need to communicate better with each other: "People fail to get along because they fear each other; they fear each other because they

5. King, "I Have a Dream."
6. King, *Strength to Love*, 26–27.
7. King, "The Drum Major Instinct."
8. Qur'an 49:13.

don't know each other; they don't know each other because they have not communicated with each other."[9]

ON FORGIVING WRONGS

The sheikh says to treat even your worst enemy with dignity: "Only Allah can measure the God-consciousness of others. It is not your responsibility to identify others as being this or that. . . . We have a distinct desire to see that human life is treated as sacred regardless of the differences that may exist, even in the 'enemy.' No matter your worst enemy, whoever they may be, they deserve dignity as prescribed by Allah." The preacher reminds us to seek love and forgive, even in hard times: "We've been in the mountain of war. We've been in the mountain of violence. We've been in the mountain of hatred long enough. It is necessary to move on now, but only by moving out of this mountain can we move to the promised land of justice and brotherhood and the Kingdom of God."[10] He reminds us that "in spite of the darkness of this hour, we must not despair. We must not become bitter nor must we harbor the desire to retaliate with violence."[11]

ON CULTIVATING A CONSCIOUSNESS OF LOVE

The sheikh urges us to cultivate God-consciousness and seek to rectify hearts: "The most dignified and the most honorable amongst creation is the one who has the most God consciousness. May God make us vehicles for good on this earth. May God make us prophetic vehicles of change toward goodness on this earth. May we be sources of mercy for others on this earth. . . . May Allah rectify the conditions of our humanity on this earth and allow it to begin with us. May Allah guide us, guide through us. May Allah rectify our hearts of the diseases that have caused the problems that we see so that we can see instead a prospering society." The preacher says to never give up the dream: "[Hu]man[kind] must evolve for all human conflict a method which rejects revenge, aggression, and retaliation . . . I

9. King, Advice for Living, 112.
10. King, "Sermon at Temple Israel."
11. King, "Eulogy."

believe that unarmed truth and unconditional love will have the final word in reality."[12]

May it be so, and may we heed these wise words of the preacher and the sheikh.

REFERENCES

Bell, Matthew. "This Imam Wants to Make America Great, Too." *The World*. Public Radio International. March 7, 2017. https://www.wgbh.org/news/2017/03/07/imam-wants-make-america-great-too.

King, Martin Luther Jr. Advice for Living. *Ebony*. May 1958. https://kinginstitute.stanford.edu/encyclopedia/advice-living.

———. "The Drum Major Instinct." Delivered at Ebenezer Baptist Church. February 4, 1968. King Papers. Stanford University Martin Luther King, Jr. Research and Education Institute. https://kinginstitute.stanford.edu/king-papers/documents/drum-major-instinct-sermon-delivered-ebenezer-baptist-church.

———. "Eulogy for the Young Victims of the 16th Street Baptist Church Bombing." Delivered September 18, 1963. MIT Visiting Professors and Scholars Program. http://mlkscholars.mit.edu/king-eulogy-1963/.

———. "I Have a Dream." Delivered at the March on Washington for Jobs and Freedom. August 28, 1963. King Papers. Stanford University Martin Luther King, Jr. Research and Education Institute. https://kinginstitute.stanford.edu/king-papers/documents/i-have-dream-address-delivered-march-washington-jobs-and-freedom.

———. "Loving Your Enemies." Delivered November 17, 1957. King Papers. Stanford University Martin Luther King, Jr. Research and Education Institute. https://kinginstitute.stanford.edu/king-papers/documents/loving-your-enemies-sermon-delivered-dexter-avenue-baptist-church.

———. "Nobel Peace Prize Acceptance Speech." Delivered December 10, 1964. Nobelprize.org. https://www.nobelprize.org/prizes/peace/1964/king/26142-martin-luther-king-jr-acceptance-speech-1964/.

———. "Sermon at Temple Israel." Delivered February 26, 1965. American Rhetoric.com. https://www.americanrhetoric.com/speeches/mlktempleisraelhollywood.htm.

———. *Strength to Love*. 1963. Reprint, Minneapolis: Fortress 2010.

12. King, "Nobel Peace Prize."

Bridge of Peace: Islam, **by Wil Darcangelo**[13]

13. June 2016/Ramadan 1437. Fused glass and metal, from the Windows of Abraham Series. Photograph by Jermaine Stephinger. The Arabic words in the stained glass capture a well-known saying of the Prophet Muhammad: "Not a one of you believes until he loves for his brother what he loves for himself." (*Ṣaḥīḥ al-Bukhārī* 13, Book 2, no. 6. trans. Muhammad Muhsin Khan) Hadith are sayings, teachings, and reports of the actions of the Prophet Muhammad passed down as oral traditions and later also transmitted in compendia. There are hundreds of thousands of hadith, and hadith studies is its own branch of classical Islamic sciences. Several early collections of hadith have had a formative influence, among them, the collection known as *Ṣaḥīḥ al-Bukhārī*.

Stand Up!

JERRELL RIGGINS

"With what shall I come before the Lord, and bow myself before God on high?"[1]

MICAH WAS A COUNTRY prophet who condemned Judah's corrupt rulers, false prophets, ungodly priests, dishonest merchants, and bribed judges. He preached against the sins of injustice, oppression, and immorality, and he warned of severe consequences if the people and their leaders persisted in their wrongdoing. Micah wrote to warn his nation of the certainty of divine judgment and to summarize God's demands for social justice. He addressed injustice with a passion and eloquence that is epitomized in one rhetorical question: "And what does the Lord require of you / but to do justice / and to love kindness, / and to walk humbly with your God?"[2]

The Qur'an frequently expresses these same sentiments. For instance, many passages command care for the poor and socially vulnerable: "And what will apprise thee of the steep pass? [It is] the freeing of a slave, or giving food at a time of famine to an orphan near of kin, or an indigent in the dust, while being one of those who believe, and exhorting one another to patience, and exhorting one another to compassion."[3] Another verse emphasizes protection of the socially vulnerable: "Do not approach the orphan's property, except in the best manner, until *he* comes of age. And observe fully the measure and the balance with justice."[4] There are

1. Mic 6:6 NRSV.
2. Mic 6:8 NRSV.
3. Qur'an 90:12–17.
4. Qur'an 6:152.

many other such verses that bid believers to do justice, love mercy, and walk humbly.

In my studies, I have found the Qur'an to be a guiding light—clear in its social justice priorities and exhibiting a concern particularly for the most disadvantaged in society. The Qur'an also calls me to walk with integrity, for my conscience to be upright, and for me to have balance in my life, including in the physical, mental, spiritual, and leisure dimensions.

For Muslims, the relationship of humanity to God is predicated on the conviction that God has given life, and that humans show gratitude to their Creator through their acts of worship and their treatment of one another. As Lord, God alone "suffices as a Guide and a Helper,"[5] and human beings must strive to be among the guided: "We [God] will indeed test you with something of fear and hunger, and loss of wealth, souls, and fruits; and give glad tidings to the patient—/ those who, when affliction befalls them, say, 'Truly we are God's, and unto Him we return.' / They are those upon whom come the blessings from their Lord, and compassion, and they are those who are rightly guided."[6] To recite the pages of the Qur'an is to become aware of one's own being, the forces of one's own soul, and the journey of life at the end of which stand death and divine judgment.

Micah understood his role to be a preacher of truth—to expose injustice and inequity, to offer a word of hope and salvation, and to make known a vision of a new and transformed way of life for his community and his world. Micah 6:1–8, for instance describes God confronting the people for a breach of covenant: God asks, "O my people / What have I done to you? / In what have I wearied you?"[7] Had God neglected the people or failed to love them sufficiently? The answer is obvious. The people had no excuse or justification for their wrongdoing.

Micah gives a simple definition of what our commitment to God, involves: we must act justly, with fairnesss and honesty. Similarly, in the Qur'an, the notion of witnessing and calling to account is clear: "O You who believe! Establish justice, being witnesses for God, even if the evidence goes against yourselves or against your parents or kinsmen; and irrespective of whether the witness is rich or poor."[8] This duty to uphold justice means that each believer has an obligation before God to be upright, pursue justice,

5. Qur'an 25:31.

6. Qur'an 2:155–57.

7. Mic 6:3 NRSV.

8. Qur'an 4:135.

and give truthful testimony. The Qur'an explicitly states that all believing men and women are the "protecting friends" of one another.[9] This concern is also echoed in many places in the Christian Testament,[10] but how many of us, out of our own selfish desires and our ingratitude, turn our backs on our fellow human beings?

We must be encouraging and protective of each other and uphold our responsibility to God and to each other with integrity and sincerity. We must walk humbly with our God—that is, we must humble ourselves daily, as our purpose is found in the larger purposes of God. Beloveds, what does the Lord require? Do justice, love mercy, and walk humbly with our God. Let us put those words into our heart and mind and carry them within so that we may say: "'Praise be to God, Who was faithful to us in *His* Promise, and has caused us to inherit the land, that we may settle in the Garden wheresoever we will.' How excellent is the reward of the workers!"[11]

Both the Qur'an and Micah's words remind us that life can be rewarding if we choose to love God and love one another. Beloved, plead our case to city hall and Capitol Hill. Do justice for the people who are marginalized: the widows, the fatherless, the orphans, the poor, the hungry, the homeless, the weak, and the oppressed. Tear down the systems of oppression.[12] Stand up! Plead the case for quality healthcare; speak out against transportation racism; fight for affordable housing, for equal pay, and for equity in the distribution of basic resources: "Hear what the Lord says . . . and let the hills hear your voice."[13]

REFERENCES

Esack, Farid. *Qur'ān, Liberation, and Pluralism: An Islamic Perspective on Interreligious Solidarity against Oppression*. Oxford: Oneworld, 1997.

9. Qur'an 9:71.
10. For example, 1 Thess 5:11.
11. Qur'an 39:74.
12. See Esack, *Qur'ān, Liberation, and Pluralism*.
13. Mic 6:1 NRSV.

Detail from *Disruption*, by Nancy Marks[14]

14. This (mixed media and acrylic on canvas, 24 x 24) is from a body of Nancy Marks's work called *Flux* and is based on responding to gentrification in the artist's Boston community. The work explores the city, steeped in its aesthetic and social paradoxes, asking: How does constructed space separate or bring people together? What makes a community and what tears it apart? The image depicts the power and importance of coalition building on issues of socioeconomic equity.

Please Rise

Ariella Ruth

together now
in this expansive air
among sunlit color
we are all quiet
instruments waiting
to sound

we choir
in unison upon
the words "please rise"
and keep standing
we remain
through all those
"you may be seated"
told
rather than a soft
gesture

we light candles
and sit circular
where we face
one another to find
a stranger's gaze
and breathe deeply
as to not
break
the current

Part IV

SEEKING LIBERTY

***Flag Viewing*, photograph by Rahma Ibrahim**[1]

1. A woman contemplates *Flag* (1954) by Jasper Johns. As described by curators, "Johns chose encaustic, a mixture of pigment and molten wax that has left a surface of lumps and smears; so that even though one recognizes the image in a second, close

Over the din of materialism, the clang of elitism, and the dangers of sheer apathy, the contributors in this section lift up the voices of sages, ancient and contemporary, to inspire, to provoke, and to guide.

Matthew Blair Hoyt, the Reverend Kevin Bryant, and Gabriela De Golia explore different aspects of the value of submission in spiritual formation. The Reverend David Kohlmeier, a Unitarian Universalist minister, looks for spiritual provocation in the Qur'an in conversation with insights from Henry David Thoreau. The Reverend Dr. Linda Hartley contemplates renewal and resurrection in the Qur'an and in Ezekiel. Then, the Reverend Pamela Wannie invites us to contemplate an encyclical of Pope Francis, alongside Qur'anic verses and a famous Christian hymn.

To close the section, Madonna Arsenault offers a poetic reflection drawing upon her Native American spirituality, the traditional Muslim greeting of peace, and Arabic names for God.

REFERENCES

Museum of Modern Art. *MoMA Highlights*. 1999. Reprint, New York: The Museum of Modern Art, 2004. Accessible online at: https://www.moma.org/collection/works/78805.

up it becomes textured and elaborate. It is at once impersonal, or public, and personal; abstract and representational; easily grasped and demanding of close attention." Museum of Modern Art, *MoMA Highlights*, 232.

Freedom to Submit

David M. Kohlmeier

In America, we value our freedom. Anytime we imagine there is a threat to our freedom, especially our individual freedom, we react viscerally, and sometimes aggressively. It seemingly goes against the American ethos to submit to any kind of authority. I wonder if this dynamic feeds into so much of the bigotry and fear many Americans have toward the religion of Islam? After all, the word "Islam" means "submission."[1] The holy book of Islam, the Qur'an, says clearly, "Whosoever seeks a religion other than submission, it shall not be accepted of them."[2]

Many of us are fighting all kinds of obstacles in order to be free. Why on earth would we ever submit to anything? And yet, in my own journey of faith, I have come to learn that submission can be a spiritual virtue, even a necessary one. To illustrate this, I look at a piece of writing that is very close to my heart, one of the great American literary celebrations of freedom, *Walden* by Henry David Thoreau. Then, I go back to the Qur'an and see how these two very different texts are saying very similar things about what it means to truly be free.

1. Most Arabic words have a trilateral root. In the Arabic language, the root of "Muslim" and "Islam" are the consonants *s-l-m*. This root also forms words that mean wholeness, completeness, peace, safety, and security. The meaning of the root has many significances. For instance, the metaphorical heart of a Muslim experiences a sense of spiritual peace and security from its connection to God, and a Muslim should, by their actions, bring about peace and security for others. The Prophet Muhammad is reported to have said: "A Muslim is one from whose tongue and hand Muslims are safe." See the hadith collection of *Ṣaḥīḥ al-Bukhārī*, no. 211. The Prophet Muhammad said three times, "By God, he does not believe!" His companions asked him, "Who does not believe, O Messenger of God?" He replied, "the one whose neighbor does not believe he is safe from his harm." See the hadith collection of *Ṣaḥīḥ al-Bukhārī*, no. 5670.

2. Qur'an 3:85.

I first discovered *Walden*[3] as a teenager and was immediately captivated. *Walden* is taken from Thoreau's journal, written while he lived for two years in a cabin in the woods that he built with his own hands near Walden Pond, right outside Concord, Massachusetts. The year he began his experiment in simple living was 1845, when he was twenty-eight years old. Thoreau's record of his time at Walden has become one of the great classics of American literature, a moving commentary on what it is to find meaning and purpose in life.

Thoreau looked around at the frantic life of his neighbors, and it seemed a horrible waste of time. "Why should we live in such a hurry and waste of life?" he writes. "We are determined to be starved before we are hungry."[4] He wondered: Why do people spend all day in jobs they hate, go into debt to buy things they do not need, such as houses too big for them, just because they feel they have to? Why do people fill their few precious moments of freedom with shallow drivel, with gossip, or with trivia? How could this possibly be what life is supposed to be? He wrote, "I wish to live deliberately, to front only the essential facts of life. I wish to learn what life has to teach, and not, when I come to die, discover that I have not lived . . . I wish to live deep and suck out all the marrow of life, I want to cut a broad swath, to drive life into a corner, and reduce it to its lowest terms."[5]

One of the reasons his text has endured the test of time is that it still resonates with so much of what we experience in our culture, this constant pressure to conform to some other notion of who we should be, when who we long to be is ourselves. And if Thoreau was worried that newspapers and telegraphs filled too much free time with meaningless news, what would he think about cable TV and Facebook? He would likely call them what he called most technology of his time: "improved means to an unimproved end."[6] What good is more information if we stay small, ignorant, and distracted? Why, Thoreau wondered, do we care more about wearing the latest fashions than improving who we are inside? What is the point to having better "stuff" if we have not grown or evolved in our character?

Thoreau was baptized in the Unitarian faith and was a believer in the Unitarian doctrine of "self-culture." Just like agriculture is the careful cultivation of the soil, so "self-culture" is the cultivation of the soul, the true

3. Thoreau, *Walden*.

4. Ibid., 59.

5. Ibid.

6. Ibid., 33.

self. This is what Unitarians, drawing from the Bible, called the inner image of God, which contains, like little seeds, the potential for compassion, justice, courage, and all the other things we admire in great human beings. Many Unitarians believed, and Thoreau believed, that "salvation" is not a one-time conversion experience, but the lifetime work of cultivating these seeds in our soul, weeding out harmful influences and ideas and nurturing our best potential. The reason Thoreau wanted to throw off conformity and start living his own life was not merely to be a wild, carefree, selfish individual; instead, he felt that only by getting back to nature, only by stripping off all this unnecessary clutter, could he hear the call of his true self. The work of freedom was, for him, spiritual work. *Walden* is not just a work of freedom, it is a work of faith.

It may surprise you to learn that the Qur'an is saying something very similar. Muhammad was a merchant in seventh-century Arabia; the book we now call the Qur'an was delivered gradually over a period of twenty-three years. This wasn't a book he wrote, Muhammad was illiterate; these were, instead, long and elaborate verses that he recited. He recited these words to a culture that he felt put clan loyalty and wealth over the needs of the poor and over personal accountability, and he heard, like Thoreau, something calling to his soul, something he then proclaimed aloud: a call for his people to turn their hearts toward nature and hear what it has to say. And the lesson nature teaches? Muhammad taught the words of the Qur'an: "Do they seek other than God's religion, while whosoever is in the heavens and on the earth submits to *Him*, willingly or unwillingly, and unto *Him* they will be returned?"[7]

What does "everything submits to God, willingly or unwillingly" mean? This reminds us that everything in nature is true to its own purpose automatically: birds do not obsess over how to be better birds, trees do not fret because they are ashamed of not being better trees. All things in nature simply are what they are, and so, by being true to their nature and purpose, they are in submission to the will of the Creator.[8] Muhammad's call for his people to submit was a call for them to join their place in the family of things, to find true purpose in forsaking greed and exploitation of the poor and instead yielding to the call of their deepest selves.

7. Qur'an 3:83.

8. The Qur'an also asks its listeners: "Hast thou not considered that unto God prostrates whosoever is in the heavens and whosoever is on the earth, the sun, the moon, the stars, the mountains, the trees, and the beasts, and many among humankind?" Qur'an 22:18.

Thoreau went into the woods to cultivate his soul, and he knew that in being present to the natural world he would discover what he called "higher laws" waiting within himself. The Qur'an says something very similar. It says that to Adam, the first human, "God taught all the names," meaning, according to one interpretation, God's names,[9] names such as "the Compassionate," "the Just," "the Shaper of Beauty," "the Forgiver," and that these names were put inside Adam, and, thus, as Adam's children, they are inside each of us. The Qur'anic admonition to remember the names of God is a call to remember ourselves, the potential for us ourselves to be compassionate, just, shapers of beauty, forgiving, and so much more.

So, like Unitarianism in Thoreau's day, the Qur'an teaches that the answers we long for are lying buried within us, just waiting for us to wake up and remember them. But whereas Unitarians, like most Americans, have tended to see this inner voice as calling us primarily to freedom, the Qur'an instead sees it as a call to serve God and each other, to create a just society in harmony with nature, and to do what the Qur'an refers to as carrying "the Trust."[10] So the Qur'an agrees with Thoreau that the best use of freedom is to voluntarily submit to the best potential within ourselves.

One of the seven Unitarian Universalist principles is that we "affirm and promote a free and responsible search for truth and meaning." The "free" part is easy. We love our free search for truth, but how do I keep this freedom from just turning into spiritual shallowness? The key is the second part: "responsible." Thoreau may have run off into the woods for two years, but look closer and see that while he was there he went to jail for refusing to financially support a war, and his cabin at Walden was a stop on the Underground Railroad. Thoreau's spiritual journey was free, but it was also responsible.

The Qur'an and Thoreau also call us to balance our freedom with humility. While the American in me recoils at the Qur'an's use of "slave" as the primary metaphor for how humans relate to the Holy, if I am honest, the metaphor is apt, because like a slave in Muhammad's time, I am totally dependent for my survival on that which owns me. We are all owned by the universe. Even if I could survive all alone in the woods, I would die quickly if the soil stopped producing food, or if all of the oxygen left the air. I am

9. Qur'an 2:31.

10. One such verse describes the "Trust" as follows: "Truly We [God] offered the Trust unto the heavens and the earth and the mountains, but they refused to bear it, and were wary of it—yet the human being bore it; truly *he* [who has broken the Trust] has proved *himself* an ignorant wrongdoer." Qur'an 33:72.

radically dependent, every moment, on everything else that exists, and so are all of us. Once we throw off the shackles of conformity to the world, once we reject being a servant of dominant culture, we discover that we are bound by shackles we can never be rid of; we are bound to a wider universe. Just like Thoreau relied on food from the Emersons in order not to starve in the forest, and just like he relied on his mom to do his laundry, so, if we are honest with ourselves, we cannot do it alone. Thoreau's pursuit of freedom taught him he could not be free alone. Will we submit to this truth?

I have worked so hard in my life to be free, and I still find myself wrestling with external and internal forces trying to twist me into someone other than who I long to be. In these moments, I find Thoreau an ally, a friend, reminding me to turn off the news, stop worrying about how others judge me, and just listen. Listen to the birds, the air, the waves, my own beating heart, my own wildness. He still calls to me like he did when I was in high school. But I am now learning that he is not calling me *only* to be a rebellious non-conforming hippie. The Qur'an too wants us to listen to nature, to observe its "signs" calling us to our better selves. Like Thoreau, the Qur'an is unflinching in its condemnation of cowardly conformity to unjust social norms. And like Thoreau, the Qur'an is a call to submit; to yield, willingly, to the quiet call of the true self that is deep within.

Thoreau by the waters of Walden, and Muhammad reciting the Qur'an to the greedy merchants of Mecca—they both call to freedom, the freedom to finally submit of our own free will to what really matters. And the promise is that in this submission we will not lose our freedom. Perhaps paradoxically, in submitting to the call of our best selves we will in fact find the reason we have freedom in the first place. And so, may we live deliberately, surrendering at last to the best within us, accepting our place in the family of things.

REFERENCES

Thoreau, Henry David. *Walden; or Life in the Woods.* 1854. Reprint, New York: Dover, 1995.

Let Truth Come

Matthew Blair Hoyt

My first encounter with the Qur'an was at a horse farm in the bucolic hills along the central coast of California. I was in the beginning of my teen years and traveling with my parents on a tour of local farms. I was standing in the tack room surrounded by saddles, brushes, and dust, searching through a glossy magazine with pictures of various horses for sale. At the bottom of one page was a passage of scripture that I did not recognize. They were words that snuck themselves into the deep storage of my mind, into a place that I would not revisit until many years later when deciding to take a course on Islam. More than a quarter century later, I read this verse of the Qur'an, and it brings me back to that barn:

> In the creation of the heavens and the earth, and the alternation of night and day, and the ships that run in the sea with that which profits men, and the water that God sends down from the sky, then gives life therewith to the earth after its death and spreads in it all kinds of animals, and the changing of the winds and the clouds made subservient between heaven and earth, there are surely signs for a people who understand.[1]

Reliving that experience, I can see in my mind's eye those ships on the sea, crossing the globe. I see the rain falling from the sky and giving life to everything. I see the world of animals, and winds, and everything as a whole as a sign that there was a God in the heavens. That day in the barn, I felt an awe at the majesty of the world as the confirmation of a Divine Creator. It wasn't the first time that I had had that impression.

It is a feeling that I experienced when I read one of the holy books of my childhood—the Book of Mormon. In a story from that book, the

1. Qur'an 2:164.

prophet Alma is speaking to Korihor—a man who denies the existence of the Divine and is asking for the prophet to show him a sign from Heaven. The prophet Alma points to the world around them as evidence:

> The scriptures are laid before thee, yea, and all things denote there is a God; yea, even the earth, and all things that are upon the face of it, yea, and its motion, yea, and also all the planets which move in their regular form do witness that there is a Supreme Creator.[2]

Alma seems to have experienced something similar to what I had; Alma observed that the world around him did more than imply the existence of God. It implied the importance of submission to divine power. In another passage, the prophet Alma preaches to people who were believers but who had briefly strayed from the path. Unlike Korihor, they were not deniers of the Divine. After preaching to them of the need for salvation, Alma concludes with this statement:

> And now I would that ye should be humble, and be submissive and gentle; easy to be entreated; full of patience and long-suffering; being temperate in all things; being diligent in keeping the commandments of God at all times; asking for whatsoever things ye stand in need, both spiritual and temporal; always returning thanks unto God for whatsoever things ye do receive.[3]

Forgiveness, mighty rewards, and light on the pathway home are blessings we can receive by submitting ourselves to the Almighty. In the Qur'an, there is a verse that echoes the prophet Alma's teaching. It speaks to me, like Alma's teaching, of the virtue of submitting to God:

> For submitting men and submitting women, believing men and believing women, devout men and devout women, truthful men and truthful women, patient men and patient women, humble men and humble women, charitable men and charitable women, men who fast and women who fast, men who guard their private parts and women who guard [their private parts], men who remember God often and women who remember [God often], God has prepared forgiveness and a great reward.[4]

There are many things I appreciate, but forgiveness and mighty rewards are near the top of the list. And in this list of attributes men and women must

2. Alma 30:44, Book of Mormon.
3. Alma 7:23, Book of Mormon.
4. Qur'an 33:35.

possess to receive the forgiveness and rewards, the first, and I believe the gateway attribute, is submission.

The idea of submission, particularly to something that we cannot see or touch, may seem strange, even dangerous. For me, and I suspect for many others, this is largely the result of history. Submission, as a political idea, has had poor representatives arguing in its favor throughout time—every example from the neighborhood bully to the global tyrant argue against it. The list of men who have used the cudgel of obedience in tandem with the demand for submission could be endless. Thus, in our contemporary environment, submission is viewed negatively, as an indication of weakness, and sometimes as a cowardly succumbing to evil. But the idea of submission as a theological principle is different. As I have come to learn from my Muslim sisters and brothers, submission is the idea of acquiescing to the One God, the idea that men and women who seek the wisdom and blessings of an all-powerful God must first submit themselves to God and God's commands.

I had no idea when I was a young boy that I was reading from the Qur'an, but I recognized truth when I saw it. This is largely because in my childhood home, my parents lived the ideas taught by the prophet Joseph Smith: "One of the grand fundamental principles of 'Mormonism' is to receive truth, let it come from whence it may."[5] Members of the Church of Jesus Christ of Latter-day Saints can learn much from our Muslim friends and neighbors. The principle of submission to God, as taught in the Qur'an, confirms the truths in our own scripture. Together, these holy books witness that there is a Divine Power in the universe, and that our willingness to submit to God will yield more than we can see, more than we can imagine.

REFERENCES

Joseph Smith History. July 1, 1843–30 April 30, 1844, p. 1666. The Joseph Smith Papers. http://www.josephsmithpapers.org/paper-summary/history-1838–1856-volume-e-1–1-july-1843–30-april-1844/36.

5. Joseph Smith, History.

Spiritual Humility

Kevin Bryant

The servants of the Most Merciful are those who walk upon the earth in humility, and when the ignorant address them, they say words of peace.[1]

As a seminary student, I took an introductory course on the Qur'an. I studied the scripture, history, role, and theology of the Holy Qur'an in Muslim devotion. My classmates and I shared our opinions openly and caringly with each other. Yet, as we progressed, I soon realized that I was not as open-minded as I initially thought. In one class, we watched a popular American Muslim sheikh who preached a line that kept ringing in my ears about God being our Master and we *His* slaves. Now, as an African American man, slavery is a tough concept to say the least. As I ruminated on this concept, I knew I needed to make a choice: shut down or open my mind.

I opened my mind in the spirit of humility. I learned that slave (*'abd* in Arabic) means the one who submits and humbles himself to God. For instance, the popular Muslim name Abdullah means "slave of God." Biblical verses began to come to mind: "For whoever was called in the Lord as a slave is a freed person belonging to the Lord, just as whoever was free when called is a slave of Christ."[2] And moreover, "you, having been set free from sin, have become slaves of righteousness."[3] And then came this verse from Ephesians:

1. Qur'an 25:63.
2. 1 Cor 7:22 NRSV.
3. Rom 6:18 NRSV.

> Slaves, obey your earthly masters with fear and trembling, in singleness of heart, as you obey Christ; not only while being watched, and in order to please them, but as slaves of Christ, doing the will of God from the heart. Render service with enthusiasm, as to the Lord and not to men and women, knowing that whatever good we do, we will receive the same again from the Lord, whether we are slaves or free. And, masters, do the same to them. Stop threatening them, for you know that both of you have the same Master in heaven, and with him there is no partiality.[4]

Through such verses, I began to profoundly see anew a concept that was in fact embedded in my own religion, and I began to appreciate the value of spiritual humility in both the Bible and the Qur'an.

For instance, the Bible regularly encourages humility: "Do nothing from selfish ambition or conceit, but in humility regard others as better than yourselves. Let each of you look not to your own interests, but to the interests of others."[5] The Qur'an too enjoins humility, forbids boasting, and urges kindness and fairness in many verses. For instance, the Qur'an instructs, "Turn not your cheek at people in scorn, nor walk exultantly upon the earth. Surely God loves not any vainglorious boaster. / And be moderate in thy pace and lower thy voice. Truly the vilest of voices are those of asses."[6] Another verse commands, "Worship God, and ascribe not partners unto *Him*. And be virtuous toward parents and kinsfolk, toward orphans and the indigent, toward the neighbor who is of kin and the neighbor who is not of kin, toward the companion at your side and the traveler, and toward those [servants] whom your right hands possess. Truly God loves not one who is a vainglorious boaster."[7] Clearly, Christianity and Islam are religions of humility.[8]

For Muslims, the devil represents the epitome of arrogance and tempts humans to make the wrong spiritual choices. God gave the devil permission to roam the earth tempting people, but the devil cannot compel people to sin; rather, he can only lure people to make their own choice to sin. He is aided by sinning people who serve him.

4. Eph 6:5–9 NRSV.

5. Phil 2:3–4 NRSV.

6. Qur'an 31:18–19.

7. Qur'an 4:36.

8. For a multilayered reflection on the contemporary relevance of humility among "Abrahamic" faiths, see Heft et al., *Learned Ignorance*.

Like the devil in the Qur'an, when we lack humility, we become arrogant and judgmental, something that the Bible warns against: "Do not judge, so that you may not be judged. For with the judgment you make you will be judged, and the measure you give will be the measure you get."[9] How can it be so easy for us to judge a person or group of people because they do not worship the way we do, or because they do not look like us or dress like us? Why is it so easy for us to think that we are better than other people? This is the exact sin that the devil commits in the Qur'an when he proclaims himself as better than Adam.

But how do we stop falling into patterns that cause resentment, bitterness, hatred, self-righteousness, and discrimination? We must build relationships with people from other cultures and faith backgrounds. We must make a conscious decision to establish friendships with people from other cultures and religions. We must put ourselves in situations where we meet people who are different from us in cultural or religious background. We must listen to people tell their stories; we must be bold enough to ask questions when we do not understand and be courageous enough to risk making mistakes in order to learn. By doing these things, we can come to a more robust appreciation of all of our brothers and sisters. As the late Kofi Annan reminds, "We may have different religions, different languages, different colored skin, but we all belong to one human race."[10]

REFERENCES

Heft, James, Reuven Firestone, and Omid Safi. *Learned Ignorance: Intellectual Humility among Jews, Christians, and Muslims*. New York: Oxford University Press, 2011.

Pashollari, Ediola. "The Role of Youth in Promoting Cultural Diversity." In *Agree to Differ*, edited by Jacqui Griffiths, compiled by Sean Nicklin and Ben Cornwell, 54–56. Paris: UNESCO, 2015.

9. Matt 7:1–2 NRSV.

10. Pashollari, "The Role of Youth," 56.

Liberation through Submission

GABRIELA DE GOLIA

As servants of God, live as free people, yet do not use your freedom as a pretext for evil.[1]

WHAT DO WE ACTUALLY mean when we say, "I am free," or "the land of the free"? Answers to these questions might seem obvious, but in our times of political and social unrest it is vital to reflect deeply on the meaning of freedom for us as individuals and as communities. If you are anything like me when you are struggling to define a concept, you first go to Google. According to my search, freedom is: "the power or right to act, speak, or think as one wants without hindrance or restraint."[2] This is roughly the definition many of us have of freedom, a value we idealize so fervently in the United States.

On some level, we all yearn for freedom, no matter how exactly we define the term. Yet, at an early age, I started doubting the idea that action without restraint was healthy or that it equates to true liberation for individuals and communities. I am, of course, grateful for having certain civil liberties as a result of my American citizenship; however, I have reservations about the notion of freedom being equated to doing what one wants without restraint and I have long questioned many of our so-called "liberties," including but not limited to our country's "freedom to bear arms."

Part of my skepticism toward a conception of freedom as "the power or right to act, speak, or think as one wants without hindrance or restraint"

1. 1 Pet 2:16.
2. Gammon, "What Is Freedom?"

is that it negates some basic facts of life. For instance, *none* of us, even if social circumstances permit it, can ever do whatever we want when we want; *none* of us is in full control of our circumstances; and some options are simply *not available* to us, no matter how much we try to make them possible. Every single human being has restraints on their circumstances that are beyond their control. How can true freedom, then, be possible?

From a theologically grounded perspective, God makes freedom possible precisely *through* restraint. Let me give an example: as you may know, the first, critical steps toward freedom from addiction in Twelve-Step programs is the acceptance of one's own powerlessness over the addiction, followed by a surrender to the will of God, as follows:

1. We admitted we were powerless over our addictions, that our lives had become unmanageable.
2. Came to believe that a power greater than ourselves could restore us to sanity.
3. Made a decision to turn our will and our lives over to the care of God as we understood him.[3]

Willpower does not free an addict from addiction; abandoning one's self-will does. It is precisely at this nexus of powerlessness and surrender to God that the door to recovery and freedom from addiction is opened.

There is something very powerful in Twelve-Step programs that everyone—not just recovering addicts and their loved ones—can benefit from. The freedom offered through recovery programs is not centered on the ability to do whatever one wants without restraint. Rather, freedom from addiction arises from abandoning one's own desires and impulses and following God's plan through discernment and action. This may sound contradictory, but the path of liberation proposed by Twelve-Step programs is actually reflected in many faith and wisdom traditions, including Christianity.

In many Bible passages, the Word has an amazing tendency to turn our certainties on their heads. It claims that the first shall be last and the last first; that the grief-stricken and downtrodden will be given the greatest gifts; and that crucifixion leads to eternal and abundant life. As destabilizing as this biblical tendency of upending our intellectual security is, it is perhaps God's way of enabling us to discover even more solid ground than

3. "The Twelve Steps."

our current thinking provides. Consider, for instance, a beautifully poetic and seemingly contradictory statement in 1 Peter: "As servants of God, live as free people, yet do not use your freedom as a pretext for evil."[4] Notice how being free here is *not* the opposite of being a servant; nor does it equate to having free rein to do whatever one wants. Rather, we are told that in order to live as free people we must be *servants* of God, a God who is love.

Do you see how the Bible is once again turning everything on its head? To be free, I must enslave myself. I can choose not to enslave myself to God, but then I would not gain liberation. It is beautifully paradoxical. There is a deeper truth hiding here that Jesus's teaching is encouraging us to see and embrace—one that does not pit freedom against servitude but rather brings the two together, therein ushering us into a realm that transcends the boundaries we currently place on ourselves.

Living in submission to a higher reality—the God of love—is our doorway to a deeper freedom than we could possibly achieve through our own self-will. Such profound teachings on freedom are present in spiritual texts beyond the Bible, including in the Qur'an. Like Christianity, Islam is described by many as a path of liberation through communion with God. As the Qur'an asserts: "Truly the religion in the sight of God is submission."[5]

Here too, we see the binary between freedom and submission being broken apart in Islamic teachings. We are ultimately at the mercy of whatever fate God has planned for us. To accept this position of our relative powerlessness in the face of God's will is not a sign of weakness, but rather a holy understanding that is in perfect resonance with God's design of the human being. Islam makes explicit that to be submissive to this divinely ordained reality is a way of being that yields true freedom through God's guidance and loving care.[6] Submission is the state that all of the rest of creation is in by default, and we, as human beings, are called to be in this state willingly, as the only creature with a rational intellect who can choose to be in submission.

In Christianity, Islam, Twelve-Step programs, and many other spiritual paths, we are told again and again that to find true freedom, we must *consensually submit* to the will of God—who is love—to the best of our abilities. Freedom for ourselves and our communities is therefore not about

4. 1 Pet 2:16 NRSV.

5. Qur'an 3:19.

6. See Qur'an 2:257, "God is the Protector of those who believe. *He* brings them out of the darkness into the light."

doing whatever we desire; freedom is the task of diligently staying a course whose North Star is love. It is not so much our ability to choose that grants us freedom, but our decision to choose, over and over, to follow God's will for us that allows us to achieve liberation. For God's plan is far greater and more benevolent than any plan we could ever create for ourselves. May each of us, and our whole community, find radical freedom through the grace of God, our only true source of liberation.

REFERENCES

Gammon, Katharine. "What Is Freedom?" LiveScience.com. June 27, 2012. https://www.livescience.com/21212-what-is-freedom.html.

"The Twelve Steps." All Addicts Anonymous. https://alladdictsanonymous.org/the-aaa-program/.

The Promise of New Life

LINDA HARTLEY

Then He said to me, "Mortal, these bones are the whole house of Israel. They say, 'Our bones are dried up, and our hope is lost; we are cut off completely.' Therefore, prophesy, and say to them, 'Thus says the Lord God: I am going to open your graves and bring you up from your graves, O My people; and I will bring you back to the land of Israel. You shall know that I am the Lord, when I open your graves, and bring you up from your graves, O My people.'"[1]

EZEKIEL SPEAKS TO A people whose "bones are dried up." Life and hope have gone. With their temple destroyed, the people of Israel perceive that God has abandoned them, but God shows Ezekiel that what appears impossible to human understanding *is* possible for God. In God's omnipotence, nothing is impossible, and God shows Ezekiel, and ultimately the people of Israel, that God can bring life from death.

This passage from Ezekiel has a special place in my heart. During a time of tremendous transition in my life—getting divorced, selling my home, and beginning seminary—I held steadfastly to God's promise of resurrection in this passage, to God's ability to bring new life to my tired bones. Reading the Qur'an for the first time in seminary, I was struck by the similarity in beliefs about God's ability to renew our lives through an omnipotent creative power that can create something out of nothing.

Standing now on the other side of so many transitions and uncertainties, I am in awe of God's resurrecting power. The Qur'an preaches a

1. Ezek 37:11–13 NRSV.

message similar to the Gospels about God's ability to "give life to the dead."[2] The Qur'an describes the various ways that human beings see life emerging out of death in the world—plants come back to life in the spring after a form of "death" during the winter, and each morning the return of sunlight brings the earth back to life after the darkness of night.[3] In one section of the Qur'an, God advises the people not to allow themselves to be led astray into disbelief by those who question God's ability to resurrect the dead. In response to the question, "Who revives these bones, decayed as they are?" the Qur'an asserts of God: "*He* will revive them Who brought them forth the first time, and *He* knows every creation."[4]

The Qur'an refers specifically to God's ability to bring about the physical resurrection of the dead on the Day of Judgment. The concept of a Day of Judgment is also evident in Christianity, even though many mainline Protestant churches do not talk about it very much. The concept of physical resurrection is also a position held by many Christians, although not all, who look to the resurrection of Jesus as evidence not only of eternal life, but also of the physical resurrection from death that awaits his followers. Individual views about life after death vary greatly among Christian denominations and even among members of the same congregation. But most who share a belief in eternal life probably identify it with a sense of peace—a place or time when the trials, pains, and oppression of this world will cease to exist; a place or time in which we will live fully in the presence of God.

One of the names for God in the Qur'an is the Returner, evoking a sense of our returning to God as a final destination. But the name the Returner can also mean the God who, out of infinite mercy, forgives transgressions and causes a person to return to guidance. In this way, the Day of Judgment depicted in the Qur'an is not merely about a point in time in the future. It is about what we do *now*. Even so, Qur'anic depictions of the Paradise awaiting those who have lived faithful lives also portray this as a garden in which there are "trees, rivers, and delicious fruits," and as a place where we will be reunited with those we love.[5] The sense of plenty and goodness is magnified by being close to the presence of the Omnipotent.[6]

2. See, for instance, Qur'an 36:12.
3. Qur'an 36:33 and 37.
4. Qur'an 36:78–79.
5. Abdel Haleem, "Paradise in the Qur'an," 93.
6. Sells, "The *Sura* of the Compassionate," 151.

In fact, the Qur'an makes far more references to the spiritual and moral rewards in Paradise than to material rewards.[7]

Because our experience in the hereafter is determined by our actions in this life, the message of the Qur'an is a call to us to awaken to our true nature, to live lives faithful to our purpose as God has intended. We are called upon to recognize God's omnipotence now—to faithfully carry out what God requires of us. And we can do this as we become aware of the sense of right and wrong that God has placed in each human heart at the moment of creation. In a sense, the Qur'anic message is that God calls us to new life each day, to examine our actions and thoughts that we may find our home with God, both here and in the hereafter.

No matter how we parse the language of the passages in Ezekiel or in the Qur'an, we should not overlook the most important part of the message in both, and that is recognizing the omnipotence of God. It is God alone who joins the bones as Ezekiel prophesies over them. Ezekiel does not resurrect the bodies, God does. Ezekiel prophesies as God commands, and he bears witness to God's omnipotence. God, who formed the world in the beginning and created humankind upon it, brings life out of death. This theme is also evident in the Qur'an with verses repeatedly noting that God, who created life in the first instance, can surely resurrect the dead.[8] God's creative power is so great that God need only say, "'Be!' and it is."[9] This is not unlike the language of creation in the first chapter of Genesis, where God's omnipotence is succinctly stated: "Then God said, 'Let there be light'; and there was light."[10]

Ezekiel's words call us to recognize God's omnipotence here and now, to trust that God can do that which, in our limited understanding, we cannot imagine. His words call us to trust that God can renew our lives. His words call us to turn to the omnipotent God by whose power and guidance we may find the way to renewal. Ultimately, the Word, spoken by the prophets Ezekiel and Muhammad, call us to faithfully acknowledge God's omnipotence, to trust in God's mercy and goodness, and to come home to the One Creator, so that we may experience the newness of life promised in the resurrection, and so that we may feel our spirits renewed through times of trial in this life.

7. Abdel Haleem, "Paradise in the Qur'an," 102.

8. See, for instance, Qur'an 36:81.

9. Qur'an 36:82.

10. Gen 1:3 NRSV.

REFERENCES

Abdel Haleem, Muhammad. "Paradise in the Qur'an." In *Understanding the Qur'an: Themes and Styles*, 96–109. London: I. B. Tauris, 2001.

Sells, Michael. "The *Sura* of the Compassionate." In *Approaching the Qur'an: The Early Revelations*, 143–58. 2nd ed. Ashland, OR: White Cloud Press, 1999.

Our Common Home

Pamela Wannie

In the United Church of Christ (UCC) tradition, we hold that "God Is Still Speaking"[1] and that the Bible is a living Bible offering relevance in every stage of our personal and corporal development. There are many other sources in which we find God's wisdom, including poetry, music, and visual arts, as well as spiritual texts from a variety of sources. Drawing together elements from Pope Francis's encyclical on climate change, wisdom from the Bible and the Qur'an, and inspiration from a hymn, I offer a meditation on our interdependence, as human beings, with all of creation.

> ***For the beauty of the earth, for the glory of the skies,***
> ***for the love which from our birth, over and around us lies.***[2]

In the Qur'an, "God is the one who created the heavens and the earth, and makes water descend from the sky, so bringing forth fruit to nourish you . . . and has made rivers to be of service to you; and puts the sun and the moon, constant in their courses, at your service, and has made serve you also night and day."[3] Another Qur'anic verse states: "It is *He* who has made you successors on the earth and raised some of you in rank above others so that *He* may test you in respect to what *He* has given you."[4] In the first book of Genesis, God created the heavens and the earth, waters,

1. The notion that "God Is Still Speaking" (tagline "stillspeaking"), was developed in 2004 as a new identity and marketing campaign of the United Church of Christ in order to underscore the "welcoming, justice-minded Christian community" that the denomination strives to be. See "God Is Still Speaking."

2. All offset verses are from Pierpoint, "For the Beauty of the Earth."

3. Qur'an 14:32–33.

4. Qur'an 6:165.

vegetation, living creatures, and finally male and female humans to which God gave dominion over all of creation.[5] The Qur'an in many verses also calls humans to recognize that God created animals, plants, and minerals for humans to use, and that God filled the earth with such blessings for humans to find shelter, sustenance, and livelihood.[6] At the same time, the Qur'an is also clear that humans have the responsibility to care for creation and to not exploit it.

According to Pope Francis, rather than exercising absolute dominion over creation, we must till and keep, cultivate and care, plough and protect it in "a relationship of mutual responsibility between human beings and nature."[7] In Qur'anic logic, we care for the earth because God knows our actions and knows what is in our hearts, and it is our duty to care for what God has created out of respect. Does that mandate not also hold true for Christians? As expressed in the psalms: "O God, you know my folly; the wrongs I have done are not hidden from You."[8] God knows what we do, God knows our intentions, and with the free will that God has given us, we readily receive the fruits of creation with responsibility, respect, and mindfulness.

Lord of all to thee we raise, this our hymn of grateful praise.

In the Qur'an too, we are reminded that all good comes from God, "Indeed We [God] have given you abundance."[9] "All praise belongs to God."[10] God is the creator of all and sustains us through this creation. If we are open to it, we will be gifted with the knowledge of both how God intends for us to deal with the harm to the earth that has been caused, and how to care for the earth in times to come. For all that God has created, we must be grateful. We have so much for which to raise a hymn of gratitude.

5. See Gen 1:26–29 NRSV.

6. One of the core tenets of the Qur'an is that God's provisions should lead human beings to feel an immense amount of gratitude. In fact, this theme is at the core of *Surāt al-Raḥmān*, the fifty-fifth of the Qur'an, a particularly beloved segment of the Qur'an for many Muslims and one that takes its name from the appellation of God, "the All-Merciful."

7. Francis, *Laudato si'*, 20.

8. Ps 69:5 NRSV.

9. Qur'an 108:1.

10. Qur'an 27:59.

For the wonder of each hour of the day and of the night,
hill and vale and tree and flower, sun and moon and stars of night.

The Qur'an asks:

> Have they not then observed the sky above them, how We have built and adorned it, and how there are no cracks in it? And We spread out the earth, and cast in it firm mountains, and caused every delightful kind to grow in it. [In this there is] an insight and admonition for every penitent servant. And We send down from the sky salubrious water, with which We grow gardens and the grain which is harvested, and tall date palms with regularly set spathes as a provision for servants; and with it We revive a dead country.[11]

While we can be in awe of the beauty that surrounds us, and while we are nourished by all that the earth provides, and while we can ponder the stars and the vast heavens and oceans, we need to continually be aware that we are negatively impacting our glorious home. This beautiful earth that God has provided for all of creation is in peril. As another Qur'anic verse sums up: "they denied the truth when it came to them so they are now in a perplexed state of affairs."[12]

In his encyclical on climate change, Pope Francis reminds us that creation is "groaning"[13] from exploitation of the earth for the benefit of industry, groaning from use of technology for economic growth, and groaning from the consumeristic mentality that uses up rather than respects the earth's bounty.[14] We are mandated by our faith to act as an instrument of God in the care of God's creation.[15] Being faithful comes in the form of worship, praise, and action. This action could simply be mindfulness, for the Kingdom of God is like a mustard seed; that one little seed grew into a tree that became a shelter for the birds of the air.[16] One small change could help lead to cleaner water, a reduction in our carbon footprint, and more sustainable uses of our food sources.

11. Qur'an 50:6–11.

12. Qur'an 50:5.

13. "We know that the whole earth has been groaning in labor pains until now," reads Rom 8:22 NRSV.

14. Francis, *Laudato si'*, 1.

15. Ibid., 5.

16. See Luke 13:18–20 NRSV.

For the joy of human love, brother sister parent child,
friends on earth and friends above, for all gentle thoughts and mild.

Through the miracle of technology, we are able to be in contact with our brothers and sisters all over the globe. As a global community, we must work to be in concert, celebrating our culturally unique gifts and graces. The apostle Paul in the Book of Romans reminds us that God gave each of us our own distinctive gifts: "For as in one body we have many members, and not all the members have the same function."[17]

God has provided all that we need, and we are beholden to then share with all other members of the body. The Qur'an acknowledges our differences, saying that God could have made "one community" but instead created our differences in order to "test us in respect to what *He* has given us."[18] Each person and each community has a unique purpose that will allow us, in faith, to work toward healing. Qur'anic scholar Daniel Madigan calls attention to this relationship, asking us to see that "we are bound to God in a relationship of gratitude realizing that much of creation is shaped around our human needs."[19]

Yet, there is a symbiosis between humans and nature that has broken down because of the self-absorption that can come with the idea that creation is shaped around our needs, and thus, is meant solely for us.[20] Human beings are prone to egocentricity, and we fail to consider how our actions affect all of creation. We must develop the moral character to recognize the interconnectivity between all of God's creatures.[21] The Qur'an speaks regularly to our interconnections, and the apostle Paul says, "there may be no dissension within the body, but the members may have the same care for one another."[22]

For yourself, best gift divine, to the world so freely given,
agents of God's grand design, peace on earth and joy in heaven.

The psalmist asks for all of creation to praise God: "Praise him, sun and moon; praise him, all you shining stars! Praise him, you highest heavens, and you waters above the heavens! Let them praise the name of the Lord,

17. Romans 12:4 NRSV.
18. Qur'an 5:48.
19. Madigan, "Themes and Topics," 82.
20. Francis, *Laudato si'*, 20.
21. Ibid., 2.
22. 1 Cor 12:25 NRSV.

for he commanded and they were created."[23] The Bible offers guidance about how to not overwork the soil, how to leave the gleanings for the poor, and how to deal fairly with our neighbors. These teachings lead to a synergy of peace and prosperity in the highest form.

God provides too through the teachings of the holy texts that allow us to learn, to develop, and to grow into compassionate caring hearers of the Word. The Qur'an speaks of Heaven as gardens with streams or rivers, milk and honey and fruits for nourishment, and trees that provide shade. These beautiful visions of the heavenly realm give us a glimpse of what we could have, what is possible right here on earth.

God is speaking and working in and among us. The Spirit of God has filled the universe with possibilities. As God says in Isaiah, "I am about to do a new thing; now it springs forth, do you not perceive it? I will make way in the wilderness and rivers in the desert."[24] In the words of the Qur'an: "Glorify the Name of your Lord, the Most High, Who created, then fashioned, Who measured out, then guided."[25] In the words of the psalm, "Let everything that breathes praise the Lord. Praise the Lord!"[26] In the words of our Christian Bible, "And let the peace of Christ rule in your hearts, to which indeed you were called in the one body. And be thankful."[27]

Lord of all to thee we raise, this our hymn of grateful praise.

REFERENCES

Francis. Encyclical letter *Laudato si': On Care for Our Common Home*, May 24, 2015.

"God Is Still Speaking." United Church of Christ. http://www.ucc.org/god-is-still-speaking.

Madigan, Daniel. "Themes and Topics." In *The Cambridge Companion to the Qur'an*, edited by Jane Dammen McAuliffe, 79–96. Cambridge Companion to Religion. Cambridge: Cambridge University Press, 2006.

Pierpoint, Folliot Sandford. "For the Beauty of the Earth." In *Singing the Living Tradition*, edited by the Unitarian Universalist Association, no. 21. Boston: Beacon, 1993.

23. Ps 148:3–5 NRSV.
24. Isa 43:19 NRSV.
25. Qur'an 87:1–3.
26. Ps 150:6 NRSV.
27. Col 3:15 NRSV.

Upon You Peace

Madonna J. C. Arsenault

My heart cried
in a sudden awareness.
I did not know!
Humility kissed the soul.
"as-salām 'alaykum"
Peace be unto you,
"wa-'alaykum as-salām"
and upon you the Peace.[1]

I have been cast into being,
from a single soul.[2]
All of creation is
United in the Breath of the Compassionate,
Outside of the Name we do not exist,
Yā Wāḥid, yā Qayyūm.[3]

1. This is the greeting that Muslims exchange upon meeting and upon parting ways. Like many aspects of the religion, exchanging this particular greeting is a practice that can be traced to a teaching of the Prophet Muhammad, who instructed his followers to spread greetings of peace. The Qur'an too reinforces the importance of greeting with courtesy: "And when you are offered a greeting, respond with a greeting that is better, or return it; surely God takes account of all things." Qur'an 4:86.

2. See Qur'an 4:1, "O humankind! Reverence your Lord, Who created you from a single soul and from *her* created *her* mate, and from the two has spread abroad a multitude of men and women." Multiple other Qur'anic verses make reference to this concept of one original soul. The Arabic word for soul here (*nafs*) is gendered feminine; as with the pronouns used for God, this is a grammatical feature that does not necessarily correspond to ontological gender.

3. These names, *Wāḥid* and *Qayyūm,* evoke God's unity and sustaining power respectively.

The orphan and the widow
come from the single soul,
created by You,
Knower of the Unseen.
I enter the Gardens with rivers from where we began;
veil me in Your purity,
Yā Ghafūr, yā Ḥakīm.[4]

I come from the people of the dawn, from Your breath.
Before the rising sun, I praise You
with love,
the first drop of ink
flowing into my soul,
returning
as Pure Honey,
Yā Quddūs, yā Razzāq.[5]

Born to pray
at the edge of my soul,
my limbs pray,
establishing the direction of generations.
You hold the well of hope,
Yā Māniʿ, yā Karīm.[6]

Waters of Life,
Breath of Compassion,
feeding the generations,
accept my supplication.
I submit my love to you.
Find me in the forgiveness.
Yā Wadūd, yā Salām.[7]

4. O Ever-Forgiving, O Wise One.

5. O Holy One, O Nourisher.

6. O Bestower, O Generous/Noble One. Generous and noble are the same word in Arabic, underscoring the centrality of generosity in the conception of virtue.

7. O Lover, O Giver of Peace.

Part V

CELEBRATING FEMININE WISDOM

***Covered*, by Yusef Abdul Jaleel**[1]

1. This graphic illustration by Yusef Abdul Jaleel is from the 2018 exhibition *Covered: Celebrating Muslim Women*, which consists of an abundant series of brightly colored graphic designs depicting the variety and beauty of Muslim styles of head covering.

As an American woman who is presumably liberated by her Americanness, and as a Muslim woman who is supposedly oppressed by her Muslimness—or so the storylines often go—I have often been asked about "the status of women in Islam." This is an impossible query to answer satisfactorily without overgeneralizing to the point of abstraction or appearing suspiciously apologetic. We have well over a millennium of Muslim women's history and over half a billion female Muslims currently on the planet; we are poets and homemakers, diplomats and taxi drivers, software engineers, radio hosts, lawyers, religious leaders, and much more. We look to our histories, cultures, and religion to make sense of our present, and we make history, too.

"Where will life and passion take my daughter?" I often wonder about the child who was born on "Pyramid Road" in a hospital overlooking the tombs of a civilization whose relics are now strewn about the globe in collections and hidden in yet undiscovered tombs. Cleopatra and Nefertiti may now be household names in America, but less well known are the later queens of Egypt, including the likes of Shajar al-Durr, a former slave who ruled Egypt for a stint in the thirteenth century[2] until she was put to death, it seems, at the bidding of a rival empress.

Women, ancient and contemporary alike—whether entitled heiresses or political upstarts—are heralded as repositories of virtue and sometimes feared as threats to the political order. Queen and slave, women's stories have been preserved in our traditions, but at times we, as women, must also reread our presence in texts and in history. From the ancient world to the contemporary one, we struggle, at times, for safety, security, voice, credibility, and dignity. Even as we celebrate the liberating aspects of faith, we must contend with disquieting forms of cultural and institutional misogynism.

In light of these struggles, this section lifts up just a few of the legendary women that the Qur'an shares with its sister traditions. In a sermon, Jewish interfaith activist Allyson Zacharoff reflects on the cohort of female figures who save the infant Moses. Then, Unitarian Universalist minister Donna Dolham draws lessons from the diplomacy of a clever queen. John Torrey discovers Qur'anic matriarchs, and the Reverend Lauren Seganos Cohen explores Qur'anic depictions of the mother of Jesus, asking: "What happens when individuals' ideologies and beliefs directly oppose our own?" The section concludes with Madonna Arsenault's striking reflection on the mysteries of the womb.

2. This corresponds to the seventh century on the Islamic calendar, a calendar that begins in the Common Era year of 622, when the Prophet Muhammad migrated from the city of Mecca to the city of Medina.

Love, **by Yusef Abdul Jaleel.**

Finding the Missing Pieces

Allyson Zacharoff

What is missing from the Torah? It may be a strange question, but every time we engage in Torah study we essentially ask ourselves: what is behind this particular story; what is not written in the text? We ponder what lies behind the basic meaning of the text—the *peshat*—to try to uncover an even deeper meaning. Often, this means attempting to fill in the narrative by imagining what characters said behind the scenes, or what they were feeling but did not articulate. We ask, to put it simply—*what is missing*? What did Eve say to Adam after they were expelled from the Garden of Eden? How did Isaac feel as his father bound him in preparation for sacrifice? How did Naomi feel when her husband and sons died? We have, of course, a myriad of options for interpretation, as we sit alone or in *havruta*[1] and consider what else might have happened. How else could we have sustained all these centuries of discussions on the Torah?

We have always needed to fill in the missing pieces. And perhaps surprisingly, we need look no further than the religion of Islam for some inspiration. Many of the same characters in our biblical stories appear in the Qur'an; at times, the stories follow a similar narrative arc, while in other instances, the stories differ significantly or include additional information. While the Qur'an is, of course, not part of our sacred scripture, it provides interpretive possibilities that we can consider in filling in the blanks in our own understanding of the stories. As someone who specializes in building bridges between our Jewish community and other faith communities, I can

1. Havruta is an ancient and still popular form of Jewish study wherein partners develop a relationship with one another and with texts through ongoing, reflective conversations.

find in the Qur'an provocative suggestions for how figures from our stories of sacred history may have lived their lives beyond the text of the Torah.

One major issue we need to address as Jews, and one for which we can perhaps look toward the Qur'an, is a devastating lack of female voices in the Torah. We certainly have some matriarchs to whom we can turn—Sarah, Leah, Rachel, and others. But their stories are limited and short compared to their male counterparts. You would be hard-pressed to find a Jew who could not relate at least some portion of Moses's story; I imagine you would find far less acquaintance with the story of Ruth. So, in our age that values equality, when so many of us crave more female leaders to whom we can turn for inspiration, what can we do but try to fill in the blanks—perhaps with a little help from the tradition of our Muslim sisters and brothers.

Now, some people may be under the impression that the Islamic religion oppresses women, or that women are regarded as less than men. Much could be said about gender roles in Islamic thought and Muslim cultures, but from a basic Muslim perspective, I want to emphasize that men and women have equal worth before G-d,[2] a notion reiterated emphatically in the Qur'an.[3] The Qur'an also contains stories of several female exemplars of piety, and as an example, I would like us to look at the women from the Exodus story—that is, the women around Moses.

Take, for example, Yocheved, the mother of Moses. In the Torah, we have a brief mention of how she saw Moses's beauty and hid him for three months from the murderous henchmen of Pharaoh, before putting him in a wicker basket and sending him down the Nile. She was even able to nurse her baby and raise him, something to which Pharaoh's daughter agreed, presumably without knowing that Yocheved was the baby's birth mother. Several rabbinic sources discuss Yocheved in more detail, but her description in the Torah is limited.

The Qur'an, however, offers us a passage with some possible further insight into this biblical figure. We hear about her intense pain at having

2. Judaism prohibits the erasure or defacement of the name of G-d. To protect against this happening due to ignorance or accident, many Jews write G-d.

3. For one such instance, see Qur'an 33:35: "For submitting men and submitting women, believing men and believing women, devout men and devout women, truthful men and truthful women, patient men and patient women, humble men and humble women, charitable men and charitable women, men who fast and women who fast, men who guard their private parts and women who guard [their private parts], men who remember God often and women who remember [God often], God has prepared forgiveness and a great reward."

had to cast out her infant. She is overcome with grief, wondering what happened to her baby when she placed him in the river. The Qur'an poetically describes her raw emotions: "The heart of Moses's mother became empty, and she would have disclosed it [meaning told the Egyptians what she had done to save her child], had We [G-d] not fortified her heart, that she might be among the believers."[4] Yocheved in the Qur'anic telling was so overcome with emotion that only G-d could help her keep her secret. The fact that the Qur'an offers up this information about her emotional state is inspiring. All too often, we as women are taught that we must suppress our emotions: Had a bad breakup? Get over it. Upset over losing out on an academic fellowship? Keep it together. But how moving is it that the Qur'an in this moment allows us to truly *feel* with Yocheved, to ache with her paining heart, and this is not the only time the Qur'an allows us a deeper glimpse into the emotional and spiritual lives of the women in Moses's life.

Another woman of import in this story is Miriam, Moses's older sister. She bravely chases after her brother in the basket, seeking to follow him and discover where he has gone. She even—in both the Torah and the Qur'anic versions—has the chutzpah to go up to Pharaoh's household and offer them a Hebrew woman (really hers and Moses's own mother) as a nurse for the infant, inquiring: "Shall I direct you to the people of a house who will take care of him for you and treat him with good will?"[5] But what the Qur'an adds that we do not see in our own text is that Miriam does this as a direct result of her mother's deep need. Yocheved instructs Miriam to go and follow her baby brother, and it is then that Miriam follows him and speaks to the women of Pharaoh's court in order to have her mother suckle the baby. This focus on female connection in the Qur'anic version of the story is one we should celebrate. Miriam's courage was spurred on by her mother's aching heart, and Yocheved trusted her daughter with a most weighty charge.

Even the Egyptian women, those around Pharaoh, deserve more recognition for their key roles in this story, and yet we rarely, if ever, raise them for discussion in our circles. Why did Pharaoh's daughter decide to take a baby she knew was a Hebrew into her heart?[6] Today, adoption or fostering

4. Qur'an 28:10.

5. Qur'an 28:12. See also Ex 2:7 and Qur'an 20:40.

6. In the Qur'anic story, the "family of Pharaoh" picks Moses from the river, and the woman who advocates for Moses's adoption specifically is the wife of Pharaoh: "Then the house of Pharaoh picked him up, such that he would become unto them an enemy and a sorrow. Truly Pharaoh and Hāmān and their hosts were sinners. / And the wife of Pharaoh said, 'A comfort for me and for you! Slay him not; it may be that he will bring

of this kind can come from many motivations—fertility issues, single wanting to raise children, an impulse of care toward a fellow human being. It was apparently this woman who even gave Moses his name, a name meaning, "I drew him out of the water."[7] Why did she take this baby into her life? If she truly took Moses into her heart as a son, knowing he was a Hebrew, then what was her relationship with the way her blood relatives treated the family of her adopted son? Did she recognize the evils of her society? Was adopting Moses one way to rebel against such terrible acts?

This woman, who took baby Moses out of the water and saved him, changed the world as we know it. She was no small character in the history of our people, as she saved the very life of one of our great leaders when she saved the baby Moses, and the Qur'an can offer a glimpse of what might have motivated her actions that fateful day. Inspired by G-d, this Egyptian woman saw the evils committed by her people and asked for guidance, praying, "My Lord, build for me a house near Thee in the Garden, deliver me from Pharaoh and his deeds, and deliver me from the wrongdoing people."[8] In this Qur'anic version, we might read her act not only as one of love, but one of rebellion against an unjust society around her. What a passionate way to view a woman who barely receives mention in our own text.

Unfortunately for us, our tradition and so many other religious traditions minimize the role of our matriarchs. But imagine if we could know, truly know, the full stories and spiritual lives of these and other women from our tradition. What if we could know more about the relationship between Miriam and Yocheved or the experiences of Leah and Rachel? We have a moral obligation as people committed to gender equality as a core tenet of our faith to search for those missing pieces. I am not proposing anything different than what we have done for millennia as Jews: ask the hard questions about what is missing from the text and try to figure out possible answers. Yes, it may be unorthodox, but we should consider looking to the Qur'an to fill in those blanks, as it offers us new possibilities and perspectives for what might have happened behind the scenes.

Maybe what we discover there will prove to be the exact scripture we need.

---

us some benefit, or that we may take him as a son.' Yet they were unaware." See Qur'an 28:8–9.

7. Ex 2:10 JPS.

8. Qur'an 66:11.

A Queen of Peacemaking

Donna Dolham

Unitarian Universalist principles call us to respect the inherent dignity of every person and to recognize our interdependence with all of creation.[1] As the hymn says, "If we agree in love, there is no disagreement that can do us any injury, but if we do not, no other agreement can do us any good. Let us endeavor to keep the unity of the spirit in the bonds of peace."[2] In light of these lofty aspirations, let us consider a rather enchanting Qur'anic story that provides insight into our living these core Unitarian Universalist principles.

As the story begins, King Solomon is marching with his troops of humans, birds, and jinn.[3] King Solomon is aware of the speech of a tiny ant, and he is aware of which animals are present and which are not: "he surveyed the birds and said, 'How is it that I do not see the hoopoe? Or is he among those who are absent?'"[4] Upon returning, the hoopoe tells the king about a foreign land where a great queen leads her people: "Verily, I found a woman ruling over them, and she has been given of all things, and hers is a mighty throne!"[5] King Solomon writes a letter to the Queen of Sheba, beckoning that she come to him: "In the Name of God, the Compassionate, the Merciful," he writes, "Do not exalt yourselves against me, but come unto me in submission."[6]

1. Preface to *Singing the Living Tradition.*

2. Ballou, "If We Agree in Love."

3. The jinn (from which the idea of genie derives) are beings with free will that are part of the "unseen" world described by the Qur'an.

4. Qur'an 27:20.

5. Qur'an 27:23.

6. Qur'an 27:30–31.

Unitarian Universalists embrace a wide range of theological expressions or none at all; we might not see the sun worship by the queen and her subjects in this Qur'anic story as theologically problematic, as King Solomon did. I invite you to think, however, about how this story can be seen as one of bridging communities, building trust, listening, and truly hearing as well as engaging the mystery involved in connection and self-discovery. The story of King Solomon's encounter with the Queen of Sheba is about a political mastermind, a powerful woman who avoids war through diplomatic communication. In responding to the king's letter, she had options. She had access to strong military troops and the resources to support them; she could choose military action or peaceful engagement.[7] The queen's council remind the queen of their strength and might, encouraging her to go to war: "They said, 'We are possessed of strength and possessed of great might. But the command is thine; so consider what thou wouldst command.'"[8] Her council recognizes and respects her authority; they listen to her guidance and wisdom even when it contradicts their own impulses.

Falling into acts of violence is a risk, whether we are living in tenth-century Jerusalem or Sheba or in the United States today.[9] The Queen of Sheba recognizes the travesty to her people if she goes to war. We too have a role in choosing a path of peace instead of the politics of violence. We are called to live into greater connection with our neighbors and to engage in relationships built on communication, honesty, and even wonder. As the Scottish Qur'anic scholar Sohaib Saeed points out in a commentary on this story, "none of us are free from environmental and cultural contexts and a brave soul is one who thinks beyond these."[10] Despite being advised to go to war, the queen instead decides that it is best to send a tribute. And even after King Solomon refuses her gifts, she continues to engage in a peaceful and principled approach based on communication and alliance-building between the two kingdoms. Ultimately the queen is transformed by encountering the unexpected with humility and openness.

The queen had the kind of experience that breaks through certain belief systems and sometimes changes who we are. Now, I am not preaching religious conversion, but I am encouraging you to be open to transformation in life, to be open to engaging something new, to have the kind of

7. Lamrabet, *Woman in the Qur'an*, 25–27.

8. Qur'an 27:33.

9. Nahida, "In Islam and the Qur'an."

10. Hindawi and Saeed, *Solomon and the Queen*.

humility that leaves room to explore the unknown. Imagine a new story of transformation where we commit to building relationships with peaceful communication and with wonder instead of with warfare. Will you join me in the work to change the politics of violence, separation, and division toward peace and connection? Take courage friends, step into relationships, take time to wonder, pause, and connect to all of creation, and let us build together a world where all human beings can experience peace.

REFERENCES

Ballou, Hosea. "If We Agree In Love." In *Singing the Living Tradition*, edited by the Unitarian Universalist Association, no. 705. Boston: Beacon, 1993.

Hindawi, Hajjaj al-, and Sohaib Saeed. *Solomon and the Queen (Qur'anic Story Telling)*. YouTube.com. September 13, 2015. https://www.youtube.com/watch?v=3wj2mN4G3Zo.

Lamrabet, Asma. *Woman in the Qur'an: An Emancipatory Reading*. Translated by Myriam François-Cerrah. New York: Kube Publishing, 2016.

Nahida. "In Islam and the Qur'an, The Queen of Sheba." *The Fatal Feminist* (blog). August 2, 2017. https://thefatalfeminist.com/2011/08/02/in-islam-and-the-Qur'an-the-queen-of-sheba/.

Unitarian Universalist Association. *Singing the Living Tradition*. Boston: Beacon, 1993.

Heroine Matriarchs

John Torrey

I am the kind of person who likes to know what is coming down the road, to have things planned out, and to always have a sense of control in life so as not to ruminate about distant and daunting possibilities. Yet, as I read about the heroines of Islam, I encounter figures who are the epitome of how to navigate with faith in the face of uncertainty. In fact, this very steadfastness in tempestuous times is what makes them heroic. Three women in particular from the Islamic tradition, three matriarchs, provide inspiration to me with their stories of extraordinary courage in uncertain times.

In Muslim sacred history, Hagar's son, the prophet Ishmael, together with his father, the prophet Abraham, built the *Ka'ba*, the central marker of Islamic ritual devotion and the direction for Islamic ritual prayer for Muslims throughout the globe and throughout history.[1] As in the biblical narrative, Hagar and young Ishmael are close to perishing of thirst in the desert, but according to Islamic sacred history, their story unfolds in the valley of Mecca. Hagar runs between two hills in search of help,[2] and at long last, the angel Gabriel created a spring out of which water gushed, a spring

1. The word *ka'ba* literally means "cube" in Arabic. According to accounts in Muslim sacred history, the prophet Adam, the prototypical human being, initially built this sanctuary but it was later destroyed and forgotten. The prophet Abraham was instructed by God to rebuild the Ka'ba along with one of his sons, Ishmael or Isma'īl in Arabic. Of this reconstruction the Qur'an says: "And [remember] when Abraham and Ishmael were raising the foundations of the House [saying], 'Our Lord, accept [it] from us. Truly Thou are the Hearing, the Knowing.'" Qur'an 2:127.

2. Emulating Hagar by walking back and forth between the hills of Ṣafā and Marwah is an action that pilgrims to Mecca today still perform, honoring this woman. As the Qur'an describes: "Truly Ṣafā and Marwah are among the rituals of God; so whoever performs the Hajj [the pilgrimage that is a "pillar" of Islam] to the House, or makes the '*umra* [a pilgrimage that resembles the Hajj], there is not blame on *him* in going to

that to this day provides water to the pilgrims of Mecca.[3] Hagar's faith was rewarded, and a habitable oasis created.

Even though biblical and Qur'anic narratives do not agree on the place where the miraculous events transpired, the moral of the story is a shared one: when we are faced with bitter challenges, God never abandons faithful servants. Once we, like Hagar, recognize God's omnipresence and omnipotence, we can have profound assurance. Even when we are stuck in the desert, there are springs to nourish us. Like Hagar, we must still run, striving to obtain what will sustain us, but even as we strive, we can know that God has each of us on a journey and is the ultimate Provider.

The mother of the prophet Moses is another example of how deep faith guides a woman to help fulfill the destiny of an entire people. When Pharaoh was slaughtering the infants of the Hebrews, God told Moses's mother to nurse him and place him in a basket in the river: "Do not fear or grieve, for We will restore him to you and make him one of the apostles."[4] Moses's mother had faith and did what God commanded. It must have been terrifying for her to abandon her son in the river, but God told her to, and so she did. God then fulfilled the promise when another Qur'anic heroine, Pharaoh's wife, decided to adopt the infant Moses after he was found in the river: "And the wife of Pharaoh said, 'A comfort for me and for you! Slay him not; it may be that he will bring us some benefit, or that we may take him as a son.'"[5] In her child's absence, Moses's mother's heart "became desolate, and indeed she was about to divulge it had We [God] not fortified her heart so that she might have faith."[6] God recognizes the needs of a servant and responds; even the most faithful need strengthening support.

God subsequently rewards Moses's mother's faith by having her chosen to suckle the baby Moses while her identity remains secret: "And We forbade him to be suckled by foster mothers before that; so she [Moses's

---

and fro between them. And whoever volunteers good, truly God is Thankful, Knowing." Qur'an 2:158.

3. The Qur'an places the story in Mecca, the birthplace of the Prophet Muhammad. The spring in Hagar's story is the spring of Zamzam, an ancient pre-Islamic spring associated with Hagar and her son that still runs today. Their bodies are thought by many to be buried in an area adjacent to the Ka'ba. Those familiar with the stories of the Bible will note a difference in that Hagar, in the Islamic tradition, was resettled by God's command so as to establish Abraham's descendants in this sacred place.

4. Qur'an 28:7.

5. Qur'an 28:9.

6. Qur'an 28:10.

sister] said, "Shall I direct you to the people of a house who will take care of him for you and treat him with good will? Thus We returned him to his mother, that she might be comforted and not grieve, and that she might know that God's Promise is true. But most of them know not."[7] Like Hagar, Moses's mother almost loses her child, but her faith in God's promise is strong and her son grows to lead the Hebrews out of Egypt.

Maryam, the mother of Jesus, also exemplifies this strength, and her chastity, obedience, and faith are examples for the believers. As a child, God supplied Maryam with provisions in the temple sanctuary. Her guardian, the prophet Zachariah, asked her where they came from and she replied, "It comes from God. God provides to whomever *He* wishes without any reckoning."[8] Maryam had complete faith in God's provisions even as a young child. This faith would serve her well as her life progressed. It would make her into one of the most revered women in human history. Maryam endured what for many would be a highly strange visitation by an angel who told her she was to conceive, though she was a virgin.[9] She believed in God and allowed *His* creative power to work through her. When she was giving birth, she cried out to God in pain that she wished she had died and become a "forgotten thing," and God rewarded her perseverance with pure drinking water, fresh dates, and words of comfort.[10] Maryam is both a witness and a testament of God's power, and she stands at the center of the Islamic faith due to her monumental connection to God. She is "chosen above the women of the worlds."[11]

These heroines of the Qur'an show that God is working in the world, even in what seems like the most desolate of times. For me, it is a reminder that God has a plan for my life and my ministerial witness, too. In particular, I see that the poor are suffering en masse as a result of human-caused climate change. I have faith that God will work through me and other concerned global citizens to bear witness to this horrific fact. It may often seem that we climate activists are fighting an uphill battle, but I know that God will supply the provisions and that our witness will be carried to minds and hearts.

7. Qur'an 28:12–13.
8. Qur'an 3:37.
9. Qur'an 19:19–21.
10. Qur'an 19:23–26.
11. Qur'an 3:24.

Mary, a Different Perspective

Lauren Seganos Cohen

What can the stories about Mary in the Qur'an teach us about the theological similarities between Islam and Christianity? What can the stories teach us about our perceptions, as Christians, of Islam and Muslims?[1] Many women are mentioned in the Qur'an, but Mary is the only woman identified by her first name; her name appears thirty-four times in the Qur'an, which is actually more times than in the entire New Testament. Mary even has an entire sura of the Qur'an named in her honor. Muslims throughout history have admired and celebrated her as an example of faith for all believers.

There are two major storylines about Mary in the Qur'an: the first is about her own birth and childhood, and the second is about the conception and birth of Jesus. Here is what the Qur'an narrates about Mary's birth:

> [Remember] when the wife of 'Imrān said, "My Lord, truly I dedicate to Thee what is in my belly, in consecration. So accept it from me. Truly Thou art the Hearing, the Knowing." / And when she bore her [Mary], she said, "My Lord, I have borne a female,"—and God knows best what she bore—and the male is not like the female, "and I have named her Mary, and I seek refuge for her in

1. Lauren offered this sermon for a worship service of Living Stream Church of the Brethren, an online Church of the Brethren congregation. This worship service included a video and song of Mary's Magnificat, prayer, and scripture readings from Luke 1:26–38 (Gabriel's announcement to Mary) and Luke 2:1–7 (Jesus's birth in Bethlehem). In the preface to her sermon, Lauren clearly outlined her goals and uses a helpful rhetorical posture to "disarm" potential feelings of fear and invite her listeners into a reflective and engaged framework by saying: "Feel free to pose thoughtful questions, engage in creative discussions, and agree or disagree with any of my conclusions." In her original sermon, Lauren also included a few basic words about the Qur'an for those who were learning about it for the first time.

> Thee, and for her progeny, from Satan the outcast." / So her Lord accepted her with a beautiful acceptance, and made her to grow in a beautiful way, and placed her under the care of Zachariah. Whenever Zachariah entered upon her in the sanctuary he found provision with her. He said, "Mary, whence comes this unto thee?" She said, "It is from God. Truly God provides for whomsoever *He* will without reckoning."[2]

In this passage, we read that when Mary's mother, the wife of 'Imrān, found out that she was pregnant, she dedicated the child in her womb to God.

While the story of Mary's birth is not in our Bible, we see this theme of dedicating a child frequently in the Judeo-Christian-Muslim stories; consider, for just one example, Hannah, the mother of the prophet Samuel. In the Hebrew Bible, in the book of 1 Samuel, we read that Hannah dedicated her son to the temple before he was born, and then he grew up under the care of the priest Eli. In the ancient world, dedicating boys to be servants of God was not uncommon, and this seems to be what Mary's mother was doing for her child. The passage goes on to say that God appeared to know all along that the baby would be female and accepted her all the same. So just like young Samuel under the care of Eli, young Mary was raised in the temple under the care of Zachariah, the prophet who acted as her guardian.

In the story of young Mary in the sanctuary, Mary receives provisions from God that surprise even her prophetic caregiver, Zachariah. Zachariah was learning lessons from the young Mary, lessons about how God will always provide. When I first read this story, I was struck by the similarities to the child Jesus in the temple as told in the Gospel of Luke, where Mary and Joseph find Jesus in the temple talking with the elders and priests. They were all amazed at his understanding and his answers. In the same way, Zachariah seems to be amazed at Mary's understanding about God.

As we hear the second major passage about Mary in the Qur'an, Mary goes on to become an extraordinary mother:

> And remember Mary in the Book, when she withdrew from her family to an eastern place. / And she veiled herself from them. Then We sent unto her Our Spirit, and it assumed for her the likeness of a perfect man. / She said, "I seek refuge from thee in the Compassionate, if you are reverent!" / He said, "I am but a messenger of thy Lord, to bestow unto thee a pure boy." / She said, "How shall I have a boy when no man has touched me, nor have I been unchaste?" / He said, "Thus shall it be. Thy Lord says, 'It is easy for Me.'" And

2. Qur'an 3:35–37.

> [it is thus] that We might make him a sign unto humankind, and a mercy from Us. And it is a matter decreed. / So she conceived him and withdrew with him to a place far off. / And the pangs of childbirth drove her to the trunk of a date palm. She said, "Would that I had died before this and was a thing forgotten, utterly forgotten!" / So he called out to her from below her, "Grieve not! Thy Lord has placed a rivulet beneath thee. / And shake toward thyself the trunk of the date palm; fresh, ripe dates shall fall upon thee. / So eat and drink and cool thine eye. And if thou seest any human being, say, 'Verily I have vowed a fast unto the Compassionate, so I shall not speak this day to any man.'" / Then she came with him unto her people, carrying him. They said, "O Mary! Thou hast brought an amazing thing! / O sister of Aaron! Thy father was not an evil man, nor was thy mother unchaste." / Then she pointed to him. They said, "How shall we speak to one who is yet a child in the cradle?" / He said, "Truly I am a servant of God. *He* has given me the Book and made me a prophet. / *He* has made me blessed wheresoever I may be, and has enjoined upon me prayer and almsgiving so long as I live, / and [has made me] dutiful toward my mother. And *He* has not made me domineering, wretched. / Peace be upon me the day I was born, the day I die, and the day I am raised alive!" / That is Jesus son of Mary—a statement of the truth, which they doubt. / It is not for God to take a child. Glory be to *Him*! When *He* decrees a thing, *He* only says to it, "Be!" and it is. / "Truly God is my Lord and your Lord; so worship *Him*. This is a straight path."[3]

There are clear similarities between the announcement of the birth of Jesus in the Qur'an and the announcement of the birth of Jesus in the Gospel of Luke. In both stories, the angel Gabriel appears to Mary to give her the news, and in both stories, Mary responds in confusion because she is a virgin. In the ancient world, stories of miraculous births were told to indicate something special about the baby, and clearly in the Qur'an, the baby Jesus is something special, indicated both by Mary's virginity and by Jesus's ability to speak as an infant later on in the story.

But there is also something that differs quite drastically between the New Testament account of Jesus's birth and the Qur'anic account. In the Gospel of Luke, when it comes time for Mary to give birth, she is with her husband Joseph in Bethlehem, and she lays her newborn in a manger. But in the Qur'an, Mary is quite alone; in fact, she withdraws during the birth. In her pain and desperation, she even cries out, wishing she had died

3. Qur'an 19:16–36.

before this trial. The more I read this passage, the more I find it remarkable that this woman, one of the most highly regarded women in Islam, has so much in common with young, unmarried, pregnant women who are often stigmatized and looked down on by our society.

Another facet of the story has implications for Christian and Muslim relations today. Muslims believe that the stories of Mary in the Qur'an were revealed to the Prophet in order to refute any notions that Jesus was divine, which Muslims view as a violation of the oneness of God. Despite Mary's holy childhood, despite Jesus's virgin birth, and despite Jesus's miraculous ability to defend his mother as a baby in a cradle, the stories of Mary in the Qur'an emphasize the humanity of Mary and Jesus.

As a Christian, I find great inspiration in the esteem that both Jesus and Mary are given by Muslims, yet I must always remember that one of the core beliefs of my faith is the divinity of Christ, and this is in contrast to the conception of Jesus in my Muslim neighbors' faith, where Jesus is a prophet—not an incarnation of God. This has interesting implications for interfaith work. What happens when individuals' ideologies and beliefs directly oppose our own?

One of the core tenets of responsible interfaith dialogue is the importance of bringing one's whole self to the table. Dialogue is not genuine if we must leave some of our beliefs and convictions at the door. So, how do we maintain respect for the beliefs and tenets of our neighbors' faith while not apologizing for our own deeply held convictions? One way is to find common ground. Realizing our shared values and beliefs can give us a solid foundation on which we can then safely examine and discuss our many differences.

Appreciating all that we hold in common can be a pathway to building authentic, intentional relationships, even across lines of difference. I am sure everyone can think of an important relationship in their life that thrives despite vast differences in geography, race, political leanings, or even theology. The same is true for relationships across lines of religious difference. As a historic peace church, the Church of the Brethren values creating and sustaining communities where all peoples can live with respect and in service to others. Building relationships despite opposing theology or ideology is an ideal way to contribute to the kingdom of God as peace-seekers and peacemakers.

I hope you have found something inspiring, something challenging, and something to ponder about Mary or about our relationships with our

Muslim neighbors who also admire and celebrate the mother of Jesus. Like Mary, may we come before our God with wonder and amazement, may we trust in what seems miraculous, and may we find hope in new birth and the promises of God to come.

This Is the Straight Path

Madonna J. C. Arsenault

Maryam sings of the fruit of her womb:
"Indeed God is my Lord and your Lord, so worship *Him*."[1]

Maryam calls me to stay and see God
in the hard, dark places of my own life.

"And I cast upon you a love from *Me*."[2]
Be comforted in My Compassion.

You are the fruit in and out of season.[3]
You are closer than my own soul.[4]

Come, open to *al-Raḥīm, al-Wadūd*.[5]
Purify your devotion. Submit to God alone.

Love nourishes, Love creates,
Conceiving revelations in the womb.

1. These are the words of Jesus in the Qur'an, see 19:36.
2. See Qur'an 20:39 and Ps 22:10.
3. See Qur'an 3:37.
4. See Qur'an 50:16.
5. The Compassionate, the Loving.

Part VI

BEYOND COMFORT ZONES

Camera Tutorial, by Saskia Keeley[1]

1. In this photography workshop in the West Bank, facilitated by New York-based photojournalist Saskia Keeley in cooperation with Roots, a grassroots organization promoting nonviolence and encounter across difference for Israelis and Palestinians, Jewish and Muslim women paired up across religious divides and seized an opportunity to take portraits of one another. By the final session of the workshop, the women captured striking details of their subject's physical appearance, like earrings or a hijab, in a process that allowed for rare intimate proximity. Such a safe space for conversation and exploration across difference is crucial given the tangled history of violence, trauma, fear, and bias.

Part VI—Beyond Comfort Zones

MUCH OF THIS VOLUME has been about the benefits and challenges of intentionally stepping beyond our comfort zones to forge new relationships, to experience new ways of being, and to achieve a deeper sense of connection with other human beings. Are we capable of appreciating the spiritual lives of other human beings, even if their creed is different from our own? Can we appreciate the ways in which other individuals relate to the deeper mysteries of life, and in doing so, can we enrich our sense of self? How can we dismantle fear and establish trust so that we can do the work of justice within our wider social worlds? These questions are at the heart of this section.

When attempting to navigate our very real human differences, we could simply make snap judgements. But, interrupting our judgemnets with a spirit of genuine curiosity and presence creates a potential opening. In other words, if you ever feel the urge to say: "*You're* clearly delusional." Instead, try saying, while holding back the sarcastic undertones: "I wonder what in your experience has made you believe that. . . ." (Holiday dinners with extended family make for ideal opportunities to practice this reframing skill. They're *family*! Aren't they *obliged* to find us endearing?)

In this spirit, the contributors in this section challenge us to approach interreligious, intercultural, and intra-human experiences as occasions to shift our perceptions and self-understandings. Gayle Bartley, a self-described "city gal," opens with a poetic inspiration on the time she found herself in a remote Muslim retreat center. By putting aside her acute—and quite well-founded—concerns about the mountain lions, scorpions, and rattlesnakes who also on occasion inhabited the retreat center, Gayle survived to convey the exhilaration of her journey "across time zones, mountains, and language barriers."

Cheryl Stromski continues the theme of learning through embodied relationships as she vividly describes how this same Muslim retreat center reenergized her Christian identity. Lisa Loughlin, meanwhile, doesn't shy away from asking the difficult questions about where Islam and Christianity differ profoundly. She models how to sit with the complexity, rather than with anxiety. Then, Rabbi Lenny Gordon sees some familiar ideas in the most oft-recited verses of the Qur'an, and Kevin Singer explores why, against the tides, some Evangelical Christians are taking note of Muslim prayer practices and feeling what former Harvard Divinity School Dean Krister Stendhal aptly described as "holy envy."[2]

2. Gustafson, *Learning from Other Religious Traditions*, 2–3.

Then, Nora Zaki, a Muslim chaplain, shares stories about the relationships she kindled with intimate strangers within a Florida trauma hospital, and Charity Terry-Lorenzo reflects vividly upon her mesmerizing, but also unsettling, first encounters with the Qur'an. She asks: "By holding tight to safety and comfort, what are you withholding?" To close the section, Ariz Saleem reflects on being Muslim in the workplace and discovering something akin to friendship across divides, and Kythe Heller offers a poetic eulogy for a fellow traveler with a hunger for mystic experience.

REFERENCES

Gustafson, Hans, ed. *Learning from Other Religious Traditions: Leaving Room for Holy Envy*. New York: Palgrave Macmillan, 2018.

***Seeing One Another Anew*, by Saskia Keeley**

Border Crossing

Gayle Bartley

Why *would* I—
Cover my head?
Remove my shoes?
Wake up before dawn,
in the dark and cold—
Answering a call to prayer?

Why *would* I—
City gal, urban to the core,
Born and raised
Surrounded by concrete and glass,
This Womanist,
This product of Rosa Parks and Gloria Steinem, now—
moved to tears, in a far-off wilderness.

Moved to sit with other women
in a place of honor and respect,
crossing time zones, mountains, language barriers,
Trusting in the power of Spirit and community,
Crossing borders—
al-ḥamdu-li-llāh![1]

1. A common Arabic phrase in Muslim devotion meaning "Praise be to God."

Allahu Akbar!

Cheryl Stromski

Are not hearts at peace in the remembrance of God?[1]

"*Allahu akbar!*" God Is Greater![2] Echoing through the hills, these words awoke me every morning during my visit at the Shadhiliyya Sufi Center in Sonoma, California. As I hurriedly dressed, covering ankles, arms, and head, I became aware of the sounds of other women shuffling through the hallway, making their way to the *masjid*.[3] We were being summoned to come alive, to wake up, physically and spiritually.[4] As we entered, lining up, shoulder to shoulder behind the men,[5] all of us still crumpled from sleep, the large-hearted, large-bodied imam started intoning emotive praises. In

1. Qur'an 13:28.

2. How unfortunate it is that this sacred phrase that begins the call to prayer has been so often deployed in contemporary contexts by those committing acts of violent criminality.

3. A *masjid* is a place dedicated for Muslim ritual prayer; the word is derived from the root *s-j-d*, which signifies "prostration."

4. Sells, *Approaching the Qur'án*, 147.

5. Generally, in congregational settings, prayer rows are divided into men's and women's rows. The placement of women's prayer rows behind men's rows is a practical arrangement to ensure that women can bow and prostrate without being observed from behind by men. Some prayer spaces also offer women privacy through adjacent rooms or separate floors. In the contemporary context in particular, the suitability of women's spaces in some mosques has been an issue of communal concern. In this context, Hink Makki has developed a photoblog dedicated to documenting women's spaces in mosques around the world, including, as the site describes, "the beautiful, the adequate, and the pathetic." See Makki, "Side Entrance."

the predawn light, we were doing first what was most important: we were remembering Allah.

Remembering Allah, or *dhikr*, can take the form of prayer, or a mantra, a teaching, a moment of contemplation that reminds the human being of Allah. For the Muslim, it is practiced at least five times a day as followers are called out from their everyday preoccupation, from the heedless arrogance of the human ego that tends to engulf us, from their separation from the divine, called to turn back to Allah, the Merciful and Compassionate. To many Muslims, the remembrances of Allah and matters of ultimate concern are constant throughout the day. Allah is all that there is. Allah is the ultimate reality, present in all things while not being comparable to anything.[6] All will pass away, is passing away, and what is real is Allah and our heart that we will one day present to *Him*. The purification of this heart by letting go of worldly pursuits and ego is why believers walk the path, constantly reorienting themselves toward Allah.

As I spent many days immersed in Islamic culture at the Sufi Center in Sonoma, I realized that the Muslims I was spending time with could see God's creative power in everything. They were seeking to enslave themselves to God, constantly murmuring prayers and praises, viewing each situation as a mirror to reflect God's compassion and mercy as well as *His* guidance and truth. Seeing this total emptying of self in those moments gave me new eyes through which to view the prayers, the spiritual healing traditions, the art, and the history of Muslims. In my encounter with different Muslims, I acquired more than just a literary knowledge about Islam; I acquired an experiential knowledge of Muslim faith and spiritual practice. I grew to appreciate many things that stretched and inspired my own spiritual practice as I saw how Islam is a religion of both heart and head, with an emphasis on both individual development and communal upliftment.

Muhammad was visited by the angel Gabriel who brought him the words of Allah to guide people away from tribalism and into a life of unity and compassion. As with most prophets who teach that personal wealth and fame is meaningless without generosity and humility, Muhammad was chased from his hometown. He fled from Mecca to Medina where his following began to grow exponentially. While initially persecuted by other Arabs from Mecca, his followers eventually drew together the entire Arabian Peninsula under the banner of Islam. The polity continued to grow over time to become a vast empire that promoted great works of art and

6. Cornell, "Fruit of the Tree," 70.

science as well as advancements in math, philosophy, architecture, engineering, urban planning, medicine, public health, and much more.

The idea that Allah's majesty is revealed in *His* creation has enabled Muslims to pursue both scientific knowledge and spiritual experience as they connect head and heart, seeking Allah's pleasure. Likewise, Muslim scholars have emphasized different levels of knowing. The first is an intellectual, conceptual, theoretical knowledge; the second is a knowledge based on seeing something for oneself; and the third is an experiential knowing that brings absolute certainty, a type of knowing that is developed over time through contemplation and spiritual practice.[7] At some point, intellectual faith becomes an even more profound experiential knowing, a progression that I could even begin to see and experience for myself.

On the final day of our trip, we were invited for dinner and prayer at the home of Ahmed and his wife Karima. With passion and strength, I witnessed Ahmed's "knowing" as he led his family and friends in dhikr, or prayerful remembrance of God. We were all fed with food not of this world. I was challenged by the intimacy that the group shared that went beyond intellectual knowledge of Allah to a place of knowing, experiencing, and reveling in the Divine Presence. The group possessed a spiritual intelligence that must have been present in the early days of the Christian Church, a type of knowledge by presence, a state that comes from direct inspiration. The emphasis on complete self-emptying, and the striving toward it in community, reminded me of the spiritual relationship to which Jesus calls us as Christians.

REFERENCES

Cornell, Vincent J. "Fruit of the Tree of Knowledge." In *The Oxford History of Islam*, edited by John Esposito, 63–106. New York: Oxford University Press, 1999.

Makki, Hink. *Side Entrance* (blog). http://sideentrance.tumblr.com/.

Sells, Michael Anthony. *Approaching the Qur'án: The Early Revelations*. Ashland, OR: White Cloud Press, 2007.

7. Ibid, 63–66.

Asking Difficult Questions

LISA LOUGHLIN

Let the words of my mouth and the meditation of my heart
be acceptable to you, O Lord, my rock and my redeemer.[1]

I HAVE BEEN BLESSED to have diverse Muslims in my life, mainly as a result of my work in the restaurant business. Through these relationships, I learned a little about Ramadan, some Islamic rules around alcohol and dating, and some of the core Islamic values. My recent studies of the Qur'an have confirmed much of what I had learned in my twenties, but at the same time, I have also been challenged to deeply question.

I even experienced some sleepless nights after reading Qur'anic verses that emphatically rebuke those who claim that Jesus is God, including verses such as the following:

> And when God said, "O Jesus son of Mary! Didst thou say unto humankind, 'Take me and my mother as gods apart from God?'" He said, "Glory be to Thee! It is not for me to utter that to which I have no right. Had I said it, Thou wouldst surely have known it. Thou knowest what is in my self and I know not what is in Thy Self. Truly it is Thou Who knowest best the things unseen. I said naught to them save that which Thou commanded me: 'Worship God, my Lord and your Lord.' And I was a witness over them, so long as I remained among them. But when Thou didst take me [to Thyself], it was Thou Who wast the Watcher over them. And Thou art Witness over all things. If Thou punisheth them, they are

1. Ps 19:14 NRSV.

> indeed Thy servants, but if Thou forgiveth them, then indeed Thou art the Mighty, the Wise."[2]

I have been haunted by this Qur'anic text in which Jesus seems to be saying, "Hey, I tried. They didn't listen. Do what You must."

Yet, *before* I got to these passages, my dialogue with the Qur'an went something like this:

> Remember My Blessing which I bestowed upon you, and fulfill My covenant, and I shall fulfill your covenant, and be in awe of Me.[3]

Check!

> Nay, whoever submits his face to God, while being virtuous, shall have his reward with his Lord. No fear shall come upon them; nor shall they grieve.[4]

Check!

> Whosoever works righteousness, whether male or female, and is a believer, We shall give them new life, a good life, and We shall surely render unto them their reward in accordance with the best of that which they used to do.[5]

Check!

> Your Lord knows best that which is in your souls. If you are righteous, then verily God is Forgiving toward the penitent.[6]

(And that is the one I am counting on!)

These passages are easy to reconcile with my Christian belief. At the same time, the Qur'an teaches that ascribing partners to God is the worst offense: "Truly God forgives not that any partner be ascribed unto *Him*, but *He* forgives what is less than that for whomsoever *He* will, for whosoever ascribes partners unto God has surely fabricated a tremendous sin."[7]

Cue internal dialogue number two:

"Yikes! Did the Qur'an just say that God forgives anything besides worshipping Jesus? How could that be? Is this the all-merciful,

2. Qur'an 5:116–17.
3. Qur'an 2:40.
4. Qur'an 2:112.
5. Qur'an 16:97.
6. Qur'an 17:25.
7. Qur'an 4:48.

all-compassionate God that I have come to know through the words of the Qur'an? What happened to the promises of admission into the gardens for those who have faith and do righteous deeds?[8] What about rewarding the virtuous with whatever they wish near the Lord?[9] What about all of those other values that please the Lord?"

My faith in the mercy of God is strong, and I comfort myself with the belief that God is all-forgiving. Yet, some Qur'anic verses leave me questioning what the phrase "Holy Trinity" means to me and how this could be reason enough to incur God's displeasure, as described so forcefully in the Qur'an:

> O People of the Book! Do not exaggerate in your religion, nor utter anything concerning God save the truth. Verily the Messiah, Jesus son of Mary, was only a messenger of God, and *His* Word, which *He* committed to Mary, and a Spirit from *Him*. So believe in God and *His* Messengers, and say not "Three." Refrain! It is better for you. God is only one God; Glory be to *Him* that *He* should have a child. Unto *Him* belongs whatsoever is in the heavens and whatsoever is on the earth, and God suffices as a Guardian.[10]

Through prayer and conversations with people I trust, I have realized that what is troubling me is the idea that God may not be pleased with me in the end. This brings about a profound question underlying my anxieties: "How do I know if I am truly in submission to God?"[11]

The Qur'an tells the story of Iblīs (Satan) who opposes God's command and displays arrogance. The jinn, of which Iblīs is one, are among God's creations before humankind. Like humans, the jinn were created to worship God.[12] After breathing life into Adam, God told the angels and the jinn to "fall down in prostration before him." Iblīs refused to bow before a human and God cursed Iblīs and cast him out until the Day of Resurrection.[13] Iblīs asks for and is granted respite until Judgment Day.

8. See, for instance, Qur'an 4:57.

9. See, for instance, Qur'an 39:34.

10. Qur'an 4:171.

11. In her reflection Lisa asks: "Am I in submission to God?" This is a profound question about human moral accountability and divine authority with which believers must constantly wrestle.

12. See, for instance, Qur'an 51:56.

13. See, for instance, Qur'an 15:26–31.

If this is the punishment for failing to humble oneself before humankind, imagine the severity we face if we do not humble ourselves before God. Similar to Iblīs, we humans seem to forget the rewards of living a life of submission to God, or even if we remember, we do not always act on that understanding or recognize the many blessings that God has put in our lives. When we refuse to submit to God we are left to live a life of constant frustration, blame, and questioning. Yet, when we gratefully acknowledge that all blessings come from God, it is impossible to forget that God is in charge. I am not about to try to solve the theological difference at the heart of the world's two largest faith traditions, but when I wake up each morning willing to submit myself to God and live in a spirit of gratitude, it is almost impossible to not feel blessed.

I have been ruminating on a saying, a hadith, attributed to the Prophet Muhammad about the accountability of individuals to spend their blessings in a way that is pleasing to God: "No person will leave the judgment place before being asked about four things: his life span and how he spent it, his knowledge and what he did with it, his body and in which things he wore it out, and his wealth, from where he collected it and how he spent it." Despite our different theological views, may God continue to bless us all with a desire to lead a righteous life, to pursue knowledge, to tire ourselves with the good, and to spend on those in need. May we seek *His* Word, and may God give us a willingness to use our faith and blessings in ways that bring benefit and goodness.

Opening the Qur'an

LEONARD GORDON

MY WORK IN THE interfaith arena has largely focused on Jewish-Christian relationship-building around the hard work of having conversations about Israel/Palestine. I have been privileged to lead groups of rabbis and ministers on learning visits to Israel/Palestine that include encounters with Muslims who live and work there and who share their struggles, challenges, and efforts toward coexistence. The clergy on these trips come with questions, prejudices, and opinions. We are building toward dialogue and more fully inclusionary experiences, and I have become convinced that text study is a fruitful path toward relationship-building because shared learning is surprisingly intimate and heart-opening.

Much of my work begins in my own Jewish community, teaching colleagues and coreligionists some of the fundamentals of Islam, with an emphasis on text study. I have discovered that preparatory study is a discipline that paves the way toward encounter. In my own experience—studying basic Arabic, meeting the Jewish and Muslim leaders of Israeli NGOs, and planning programs for Christian-Jewish leaders that include engagement with Muslims—I have had to accept the limitations of my training and approach these engagements with deep humility, as a learner. This posture of modesty can be the starting place for interfaith engagement.

The question of starting point looms especially large when you are considering interfaith dialogue across a painful divide, such as that which can exist between Muslims and Jews in America. Both groups are diverse, and individuals harbor prejudices, both conscious and unconscious. I have witnessed the effects of cultural stereotypes and the consequences of a history of conflicts, imagined and real, over Middle East politics. For some Jews, a first encounter with a Muslim might be seen as an opportunity to ask questions whose original context was polemical—"Why don't Muslims condemn terror?" Or: "Isn't it true that the Qur'an calls Jews monkeys?" I have discovered that for many people in the Jewish community, the best first step is a textual rather than personal encounter, an encounter with texts that illustrate the complex and fruitful relationship between Islamic and Jewish spirituality.

In that spirit, I offer this Jewish reading of the first sura of the Qur'an. As I show, many of these verses can be easily translated from Arabic into Hebrew cognates. God is named with appellations that are familiar from Jewish prayer, and the Day of Judgment translates into the name for Judaism's most holy and awesome day, Yom Kippur. The balancing act in the sura between God's mercy and judgment also reflects a familiar theme from Jewish mysticism and from the High Holiday liturgy. Exposing Jews to these teachings as an introduction to Islam can restart the dialogue on a warmer basis. We proceed from here to discover how much more we share in our respective religious and spiritual practices, for example, fasting, pilgrimage, and charitable giving. In this way, our focus shifts away from that which divides our communities to that which we share, despite our variegated religious identities.

A JEW READS AL-FĀTIḤA, "THE OPENER"

These seven initial verses known as the "*Fātiḥa*" (Arabic for "opener") open the Qur'an and play a special role in Muslim devotion, including being recited in every unit of daily ritual prayer.[1] As a Jewish reader, when I hear the *Fātiḥa* recited, I hear echoes from the Jewish liturgy and textual tradition. While most of the Qur'an's suras are arranged in approximate size order—as are the books of the first text of Rabbinic Judaism, the Mishnah—this short sura stands out as a prologue. It mirrors the practice in medieval Jewish texts of placing a poetic introduction at the start of works of commentary or law. The title of this sura, or segment, signals its position as the first of the Qur'an. This text offers the possibility of an opening, a new beginning, a vision of Islam in its fullness.

1. The title of this sura, or segment of the Qur'an, signals its position as the opener of the Qur'an, and from an esoteric perspective, as the opener of hearts. The Qur'an itself refers to these verses in a later sura: "And certainly, We have given you seven of the oft-repeated verses" (Qur'an 15:87). It is generally the first part of the Qur'an that small Muslim children and new Muslims learn. For an excellent, concise commentary on the meanings and significances of *al-Fātiḥa*, see *The Study Quran*, 3–11.

IN THE NAME OF GOD, THE COMPASSIONATE, THE MERCIFUL.[2]

The first verse of the *Fātiḥa* translates easily into liturgical Hebrew; both Islam and Judaism begin a new venture or text "in the name of God" as an act of piety and humility. Everything that follows is done on behalf of our desire to do God's will and make God manifest in the world. God is then named as "merciful," the word for which derives from the same root in both Arabic and Hebrew, a root that means "womb." God loves humanity as a mother loves the product of her womb, or with womb-love. Like Jewish thought, Islamic theology depicts God as balancing the traits of mercy and judgment; here God's mercy is solely and dramatically highlighted. A subsequent verse, however, points to God as ruler over the "Day of Judgment," often interpreted to mean the day when debts are settled, evoking the imagery of justice.

PRAISE BE TO GOD, LORD OF THE WORLDS.[3]

The second verse deepens our appreciation for God who is named as Master and Sustainer of the worlds. In Jewish liturgy, we also praise God as Creator and Sustainer, which is the opening theme of Jewish worship morning and evening in the first blessing before the Shema[4] and the following liturgy. What does the text mean by "worlds"? Reflecting on parallel usages in Jewish worship, the plural "worlds" might refer to this world and the world that is coming, or it may reflect on the multiple worlds that coexist simultaneously in the present, perhaps harkening to the concept of the four cosmic realms that is shared by Jewish and Islamic mystics. In Islam: the realms of matter, souls, spirits, and of God. In Judaism: the realms of action, formation, creation, and emanation.

THE COMPASSIONATE, THE MERCIFUL.[5]

Strikingly, this short sura repeats the designations for God provided in the first verse. The repetition underscores the centrality of mercy as a divine

2. Qur'an 1:1.
3. Qur'an 1:2.
4. Deut 6:4.
5. Qur'an 1:3.

attribute and it serves as a loving frame for the verse evoking judgment to follow.

MASTER OF THE DAY OF RECKONING.[6]

This phrase also translates easily into liturgical Hebrew. The reference is to a final day of judgment, a time anticipated during Judaism's High Holidays of Rosh Hashanah (when God is enthroned as Ruler/Master) and Yom Kippur. Having named God as merciful and praised God as our Creator and Sustainer, we now acknowledge a more challenging reality: there is a day when God will sit as our Ruler in judgment. Similarly, in the liturgy for the Jewish High Holidays, Jews repeat God's traits of mercy known as the "thirteen divine attributes" and enthrone God as Ruler and Creator before confessing sins. In both traditions, we approach God as judge only from a place of security in God's mercy and appreciation for God's gift of life.

In the context of this sura we are now at the midpoint, the hinge. We move from God as Creator/Sustainer to God as Judge/Redeemer in the end times. In Jewish worship, the order of prayer is Creator-Revealer-Redeemer, as reflected in the blessings before and after the Shema and in the flow of Shabbat worship from evening to morning to afternoon. God created the world and then gives us law and will, in the end, redeem. In the *Fātiḥa*, the movement is different. Here we acknowledge God as the ultimate judge, and then we ask God for the guidance we need to receive a good outcome on the Day of Reckoning.

THEE WE WORSHIP AND FROM THEE WE SEEK HELP.[7]

A prayer from the *Zohar*, the classic text of medieval Jewish mysticism, reads as follows: "Not on mortals, nor on angels do I rely, but rather on the God of heaven, the God of truth, whose Torah is truth and whose prophets are true, and who abounds in deeds of goodness and truth."[8] In this passage, which is found in the Sabbath morning service, replacing the word "Torah" with "Qur'an," points to the parallels in theological sensibility: God is the object of our worship and the source of our salvation.

6. Qur'an 1:4.
7. Qur'an 1:5.
8. Feld, *Siddur Lev Shalem*, 170.

GUIDE US UPON THE STRAIGHT PATH[9]

This request echoes the familiar words of the twenty-third psalm, "*He* guides me in right paths as befits *His* name."[10] The world offers many paths, and most are crooked and perilous. We seek guidance to select the straight path and to avoid the voice of Shaytān (Satan) who whispers to us to drive us in other directions. In worship this sura is introduced with a line placing our hope in God to protect us from the accursed Shaytān. Judaism names the internal and external forces that tempt humanity the "evil inclination," often understood as the id of modern psychology. We can recall, for instance, the verse in Genesis: "Surely, if you do right, / There is uplift. But if you do not do right, / Sin crouches at the door; / Its urge is toward you, / Yet you can be its master."[11]

THE PATH OF THOSE WHOM THOU HAST BLESSED, NOT OF THOSE WHO INCUR WRATH, NOR OF THOSE WHO ARE ASTRAY.[12]

The poetic closure is strengthened by the length of this final verse in contrast to the earlier, staccato verses. Here, the two paths recall imagery in Deuteronomy: "See, I set before you this day life and prosperity, death and adversity."[13] While many biblical passages, especially in the writings of the prophets, also end exhortations with a note of warning, Jewish liturgy tends to avoid such endings by cutting off the negative or adding a verse that ends on a note of hope. Though the sura ends with a stark warning, we will begin the next sura with the invocation called the bismillah, "In the Name of God, the Compassionate, the Merciful," reminding us of God's unbounded mercy.

In these ways and more, the opening of the Qur'an provides me with an opportunity, an opening, to reread my own tradition, its liturgy and theology, with fresh eyes. Each verse points to a shared heritage of deeds and thoughts, a heritage that offers hope for a shared future. My own explorations of Islam are enriching conversations within my Jewish circles. For

9. Qur'an 1:5.
10. Ps 23:3 JPS.
11. Gen 4:7 JPS.
12. Qur'an 1:7.
13. Deut 30:15 JPS.

instance, I recently had the opportunity to teach four sessions on Islam for Jews to a group on a retreat sponsored by the Federation of Jewish Men's Clubs, an organization of the Conservative denomination of Judaism. Alongside this text we studied the story of Joseph and the story of King Solomon and the Queen of Sheba in Jewish and Muslim sacred texts. In this way, we encountered Islam as an alternative interpretive tradition rather than as a rival. Studying in this way generated mutually respectful encounters in which we were all teachers and learners, gift-givers and receivers, humbled before a cosmic Presence and Wisdom that is greater than we and embracing of all.

REFERENCES

Feld, Edward, ed. *Siddur Lev Shalem*. New York: Rabbinical Assembly, 2016.

Muslims Inspiring Evangelicals

KEVIN SINGER

IN DECEMBER 2015, DR. Larycia Hawkins, a tenured political science professor at Wheaton College and one of the college's few black tenured women professors, posted a picture on Facebook of herself donning a hijab to show solidarity with Muslim women. She accompanied the picture with a statement asserting that Christians and Muslims worship the same God. A public spat ensued between Hawkins and the historically Evangelical, predominantly white institution, eventually leading to her departure a few months later.[1]

In the same month, Liberty University president Jerry Falwell Jr. remarked at an all-university chapel after the 2015 San Bernardino attack that students ought to consider arming themselves in preparation for a Muslim threat. Though there were a few jeers, a majority of the predominantly white student audience erupted in applause.[2] Some may also remember Christine Weick grabbing the microphone from a speaker at the Texas Muslim Capitol Day in 2015 and exclaiming, "Islam will never dominate the United States, and by the grace of God, it will not dominate Texas!" As she walked away, she shouted, "America was built on Christian principles!"[3]

Such events gave the watching world a window into how predominantly white Evangelical communities in America were wrestling with Islam and Muslims in America, and also wrestling with underlying dynamics involving racial difference. The world saw communities that seemed ill-prepared to address systemic xenophobia and who were potentially

1. Smietana, "Wheaton College."

2. Bailey, "Jerry Falwell, Jr."

3. *Christine Weick*. For a more informed perspective on the historical contributions of Muslims to the building of America, see Hussein, *Muslims*.

even fostering Islamophobia. Indeed, recent Pew research found that white Evangelical Christians in particular have greater concerns about Muslim Americans than American adults overall, including those of other religious groups.[4]

The overarching attitudes of Evangelicals, as depicted in Pew polling data and other such sources, are not surprising. White Evangelicals, in particular, have historically harbored some of the most negative attitudes toward Muslims, either on account of their religion or racial identities.[5] What is behind these negative attitudes? What has caused Muslims to become, in the eyes of Evangelicals, a "modern-day equivalent of the Evil Empire"?[6] For some, this "threat" is bound up with a vision of America as a Christian nation. Charles Kimball, a professor of religion at Wake Forest University, noted that Islam is the only religious tradition to ever threaten Christianity on an existential level, causing tensions that are "deeply woven into our subconscious, into Western literature and culture," anxieties that can be readily triggered.[7]

Given the patterns of events and thinking described above, it might be easy to dismiss the idea that American Evangelicals would ever appreciate the religious practice of their Muslim neighbors, and given the overwhelming trends, it might be easy to overlook instances where Evangelical groups and individuals have shown inclinations of appreciation. However, a small but growing segment of white Evangelical voices have indeed expressed appreciation for Muslims' commitment to prayer, in particular. The appreciation is typically framed as a good *reminder* of how Christians have been taught to pray to the triune God in the Bible and in their communities. This appreciation is not an endorsement of Muslim *theology*, but is rather an acknowledgment of the endurance, humility, and the theocentric spirit that informs Muslim religious *practice*.

4. For example, 66 percent of white Evangelicals agreed that "Islam is not part of mainstream American society," compared to 50 percent of all American adults, while 63 percent agreed that Islam "encourages violence more than other faiths," compared to 41 percent of all American adults. Pew Research Center, "U.S. Muslims."

5. Bhatia, "American Evangelicals and Islam," 26–37; Cimino, "No God in Common," 162–74; Larson, "Will Evangelical Attitudes"; Wadsworth, "The Racial Demons."

6. In a 2003 article in the *New York Times*, Rev. Richard Cizik of the National Association of Evangelicals suggested that Muslims become the next Soviet Union. Goodstein, "Seeing Islam as 'Evil' Faith."

7. Ibid.

In his book *World Religions: An Indispensable Introduction* (2011), Evangelical author Gerald McDermott remarks, "We can learn from Muslims the importance of having set times for prayer, instead of relying on our own fickle sense of when we have the time and inclination to pray."[8] In this respect, Muslims' commitment to pray five times daily, even when it is inconvenient, has proven to be inspirational. Bob Roberts Jr., pastor of a Texas-based Southern Baptist church with over 1,500 members, has written about several instances of being inspired by Muslims to take time to pray. In his book *Bold as Love* (2012), he tells the story of his visit to Syria for a peacebuilding conference, where three times a day an imam would gather the Muslims at the conference to pray. After watching them do this a few times, he felt compelled to join them. "I'd like to be over there praying with them," he wrote, "I love to pray."[9] He asked the imam if it was okay to kneel and pray to Christ alongside of them, and the imam agreed warmly.

In his book, *Can Evangelicals Learn from World Religions?* (2000), Evangelical author Gerald McDermott noted that the humble and submissive posture taken by Muslims in prayer can help Evangelicals better appreciate the reverence with which Isaiah, Daniel, and Cornelius approached God, while helping them to break free from self-indulgence and narcissism.[10] Robynn Bliss, an Evangelical blogger who grew up in Pakistan, discussed her appreciation for how Muslims incorporate movement into their prayers. This challenged her to rethink the connection between body, soul, and spirit, writing: "Our bodies are not disconnected from our inner reality. . . . I was challenged to bring my own self into alignment. [Now], my prayers are directed to a living God and often they are moving and motional."[11]

The sense of appreciation for the God-centric emphasis of Muslim prayer on the part of Evangelical leaders has also prompted a focus on common ground. Eric Demeter, a popular Evangelical speaker, recalled a time when he asked to pray alongside a Muslim in Thailand: "He faced west, toward Mecca; I looked upward, facing the ceiling. He kneeled on a rug; I stood on the floor with outstretched arms. Our styles were different, but our intentions were the same—we both wanted to connect with God."[12]

8. McDermott, *World Religions*, 130.

9. Roberts, *Bold as Love*.

10. McDermott, *Can Evangelicals Learn*.

11. Bliss, "6 Things."

12. Demeter, "4 Spiritual Lessons."

Similarly, Muslims reaffirm that God is the ultimate concern by reciting aloud central aspects of Islamic belief at the beginning of each call to prayer, including belief in one God and in Muhammad as the final prophet of God. Evangelical blogger Robynn Bliss wondered how this repetitive act of "deliberately remembering what is true" might strengthen the faith of Christians.[13] Citing the Apostles' and Nicene Creeds, she asked, "What if we recited back to our weary-from-life souls the character of God, his faithfulness, his sacrifice, his provision? Imagine the reassurance that might wash over our reactive emotions, our crises, our desperations, our superficial happiness."[14]

In fielding the question of whether God hears the prayers of Muslims, Evangelical author Susie Hawkins came to realize through reflection on the story of Cornelius, a Jew who is described as "God-fearing" even before following Jesus (Acts 10:2), that "God is not bound by anything except His love, which is limitless, and His Word, which is eternal. If He wishes to hear the prayers of God-fearing Muslims . . . who might seek him with a humble and sincere heart, He can respond to them in ways we may not understand."[15]

The endurance, posture, and spirit of Muslim prayer have prompted Evangelicals to revisit their own practices and have helped them to see the religious other in a favorable light. Yet, it is not just Muslims' consistency but their humility and reverence in approaching God that has made an impression. Developing an appreciation for Muslim prayer could prove to be a promising conduit for correcting some of the misconceptions that Evangelicals have about Muslims. This was true for Pastor Bob Roberts Jr., who acknowledges, in *Lessons from the East* (2016) that he previously thought Muslims prayed rote prayers. He came to learn that they, like him, pray from their hearts about a variety of issues.[16]

Though this cohort of white Evangelical voices is admittedly still small, they could prove to be trailblazers for others to follow their lead. As codirector of Neighborly Faith, an organization helping Evangelicals to be good neighbors to people of other faiths, it is my hope that more Evangelicals and their communities will try to find the good in other expressions of faith, rather than focusing solely on what they see as the shortcomings.

13. Bliss, "6 Things."

14. Ibid.

15. Hawkins, "Does God Hear?"

16. Roberts, *Lessons from the East.*

Though there will always be a theological divide with respect to the nature of God between Muslims and Christians, these voices provide hope that Evangelicals, as a wider demographic, might eventually more enthusiastically celebrate the faith practices of their Muslim neighbors.

REFERENCES

Bailey, Sarah Pulliam. "Jerry Falwell, Jr.: 'If More Good People Had Concealed-Carry Permits, Then We Could End Those Islamist Terrorists.'" *The Washington Post*. December 5, 2015. https://www.washingtonpost.com/news/acts-of-faith/wp/2015/12/05/liberty-university-president-if-more-good-people-had-concealed-guns-we-could-end-those-muslims/?utm_term=.80168cfd661a.

Bhatia, Amit A. "American Evangelicals and Islam: Their Perspectives, Attitudes and Practices towards Muslims in the US." *Transformation: An International Journal of Holistic Mission Studies* 34, no. 1 (February 2016) 26–37.

Bliss, Robyn. "6 Things Christians Can Learn from Muslims about Prayer." Zwemer Center for Muslim Studies. http://www.zwemercenter.com/6-things-christians-can-learn-about-prayer-from-muslims.

Christine Weick Interrupts Texas Muslim Capitol Day Speaker. KTBC Fox 7 Austin. January 29, 2015. Published on YouTube. https://www.youtube.com/watch?v=t4-CoaZ3V1Q.

Cimino, Richard. "'No God in Common': American Evangelical Discourse on Islam after 9/11." *Review of Religious* 47, no. 2 (December 2005) 162–74.

Demeter, Eric. "4 Spiritual Lessons Muslims Can Teach Christians." OnFaith. https://www.onfaith.co/onfaith/2015/06/26/4-spiritual-practices-muslims-can-teach-christians/37205.

Goodstein, Laurie. "Seeing Islam as 'Evil' Faith, Evangelicals Seek Converts." *New York Times*. May 27, 2003. https://www.nytimes.com/2003/05/27/us/seeing-islam-as-evil-faith-evangelicals-seek-converts.html.

Hawkins, Susie. "Does God Hear the Prayer of a Muslim?" *Planter Wives Blog*. July 15, 2015. https://www.namb.net/planter-wives-blog/does-god-hear-the-prayer-of-a-muslim/.

Hussein, Amir. *Muslims and the Making of America*. Waco: Baylor University Press, 2016.

Larson, Warren. "Will Evangelical Attitudes toward Muslims Continue to Harden?" Zwemer Center for Muslim Studies. http://www.zwemercenter.com/will-evangelical-attitudes-toward-muslims-continue-to-harden.

McDermott, Gerald R. *Can Evangelicals Learn from World Religions? Jesus, Revelation, and Religious Traditions*. Downers Grove, IL: InterVarsity Academic, 2010.

———. *World Religions: An Indispensable Introduction*. Wheaton, IL: Thomas Nelson, 2011.

Pew Research Center. "U.S. Muslims Concerned about Their Place in Society, but Continue to Believe in the American Dream." Pew Research Center: Religion and Public Life. July 26, 2017. http://www.pewforum.org/2017/07/26/demographic-portrait-of-muslim-americans/.

Roberts, Bob Jr. *Bold as Love: What Can Happen When We See People the Way God Does*? Wheaton, IL: Thomas Nelson, 2012.

———. *Lessons from the East: Finding the Future of Western Christianity in the Global Church*. Colorado Springs, CO: David C. Cook, 2016.

Smietana, Bob. "Wheaton College Suspends Hijab-Wearing Professor after 'Same God' Comment." *Christianity Today*. December 15, 2015. https://www.christianitytoday.com/news/2015/december/wheaton-college-hijab-professor-same-god-larycia-hawkins.html.

Wadsworth, Nancy D. "The Racial Demons That Help Explain Evangelical Support for Trump." *Vox*. April 30, 2018. https://www.vox.com/the-big-idea/2018/4/30/17301282/race-evangelicals-trump-support-gerson-atlantic-sexism-segregation-south.

Intimate Strangers

NORA ZAKI

AS THE FIRST MUSLIM to complete clinical pastoral education[1] in hospital chaplaincy at a nationally renowned Florida trauma hospital—all eight hundred hours of it—I was conscious of the ways in which I was visible as Muslim. A woman in a headscarf, I offered pastoral care to people of different faith backgrounds as well as patients without a tradition-specific faith background who requested spiritual care.

The stories I heard from patients, the traumas, the tears, the blood, the snot—all of the vulnerabilities—stretched my capacities: I was called upon to offer comfort for immigrant Hispanic children whose mother died from stage-four cancer. I offered comfort to a seventy-year-old Christian man as he cried and cried while relating to me stories about his intubated wife. An eighty-year-old Hindu woman wanted me to listen to Hindi songs on her old laptop since she had no family to visit her. A grieving African American family told me, "you're family now—stay with us," as they watched an uncle in palliative care slowly deteriorate. A ninety-four-year-old Jewish woman, a Holocaust survivor, offered *me* words of encouragement in one of my lower moments.

As the intimate stranger that hospital chaplains are called upon to be, I saw the humanity in all these patients and the love and pain in the eyes of their family members. It is not always easy to be merciful and compassionate to strangers, and the vast majority of the people I visited with were

1. Clinical Pastoral Education (CPE) is a standard component of ministerial training and typically includes lessons on family systems, theological reflection, practice with active listening, discussions about the importance of self-care, study of palliative care, gaining familiarity with grief processes and different kinds of trauma, and studies of behavioral science that impact pastoral caregiving. Increasingly, programs are also providing training in how to provide care in multifaith settings.

from a different faith tradition than mine. I was even rejected by some patients because I was a *Muslim* chaplain, and I can say that the rejection and stereotyping hurt, even as I strove to rise above it. I reminded myself not to take such encounters personally, and that, well, I was not exactly the typecast image of a hospital chaplain, the white Christian man that some people might have expected when they called for a chaplain.

What propelled me to continue was my belief in the unending compassion of God, the Most Merciful One. Visiting with the sick and comforting people in need are core Islamic mandates that the Prophet Muhammad himself taught by word and example. There is a prophetic saying, a hadith, from the Prophet that on the Day of Judgment, God Most High will announce: "'O son of Adam, I was sick, yet you did not visit *Me*.' He will reply, 'O God, how could I have visited *You* since *You* are the Lord of the worlds?' God Most High will say: 'Did you not know that this servant of mine was sick, and yet you did not visit him? Should you have visited him you would have found *Me* by him.'"[2]

The Prophet Muhammad taught mercy, *exuded* mercy, not only for humans, but also animals and all living things. My faith and also my family history call me to this work. My late father was a medical doctor who cared tremendously about justice and exuded compassion. He died when I was just fifteen years old. As an Egyptian immigrant to America, he expressed himself openly and sincerely by trying to explain to other Americans that Arabs and Muslims were not "terrorists," but that they too had compassion and the will to serve. He practiced Islam, my mother converted to Islam, and we continue to maintain good relations with our Christian extended family.

These early influences and experiences with positive interfaith relations carried me through the days when my own capacities were stretched to their limits. Sometimes, the extent of the pain and trauma I witnessed stretched my capacity for compassionate service so much that my head would literally ache, but I extended ministry and care to all people regardless of their faith, cultural background, gender, age, sexual orientation, socioeconomic background, or any other distinguishing characteristic.

2. *Ṣaḥīḥ Muslim* 2569. This prophetic narration is referred to as a "*ḥadīth qudsī*," meaning that the meaning of the revelation is given to the Prophet Muhammad directly from God but the phrasing is from the Prophet Muhammad himself. This differs from the Qur'an itself, which is held to be the Word as given directly by God.

Even when I came face-to-face with anti-Muslim bigotry that was expressed by the patients that I was called upon to serve, I took it as an opportunity to shrink my own ego and grow my own capacity for patience and compassion. This process of struggle against the lower impulses of the ego is called "*mujāhada al-nafs*" (struggle against the soul), and is very much at the center of Islamic character formation. The ultimate goal of such a spiritual struggle is to bring about a clean, pure spiritual heart (*qalb salīm*), a heart that is free from the "diseases" of greed, pride, hatred, and so forth, much like our physical hearts also need to be free of diseases to function properly. The Qur'an instructs human beings to come to God on the Day of Judgment with a sound heart (*qalb salīm*) because on that day, every soul possessing sound faculties will be responsible for the moral weight of his or her actions in the world. I believe it is incumbent upon me as a Muslim to be introspective and to take myself into account, rather than seeking to find faults in others.

As Muslims, we are called to engage in a struggle with our own egos in order to make ourselves more compassionate, better able to persevere in the face of adversity, and ultimately better able to serve humanity. In serving humanity, we serve God.

REFERENCES

Mawlud, Muhammad al-, *Purification of the Heart (Maṭharat al-Qulūb)*: *Signs, Symptoms and Cures of the Spiritual Diseases of the Heart.* Translation and commentary by Hamza Yusuf. Chicago: Starlatch, 2004.

Withholdings and Openings

Charity Terry-Lorenzo

And indeed We have set forth for humankind in this Qur'an every kind of parable, that haply they may remember.[1]

I learned about swaddling when my first child was born. Swaddling provides a sense of comfort to the newly born, a comfort that comes from restricting the baby's freedom of movement. It entails placing a baby on a blanket and then wrapping the blanket around the baby, firmly trapping its arms and legs like a baby burrito. If you are like a midwife I once knew, you hold the baby up with its bum balanced in one palm: *Voilà!*

Since our family's swaddling days, I have noticed the ways in which I swaddle myself. Not literally—that would be complicated—but in the sense that I seek structure for my thoughts and actions. Structures are useful; they help the world feel more predictable, more comfortable, less overwhelming. When I first started engaging with the Qur'an, I went in with an intellectual swaddle that went something like this: "I know this drill: analyze passages, discuss historical context, and use a detached observer approach." That was my intellectual swaddle. It was not intentional. I didn't even know it was there until it stopped working.

I tried hard to stay within a comfortable structure, but the structure seemed to fall apart when I listened to Qur'anic recitation.[2] According to

1. Qur'an 39:37.

2. "Qur'an" means "recitation" in Arabic. In Arabic morphology, most words are derived from trilateral roots, and the root letters for "read" and "recite" are the same, *q-r-'*. The last radical, called *hamza*, is a letter that does not have an English equivalent and that is made by a glottal stop. The first letter, the one transliterated as "q" here, is also a

the Qur'an itself, it is a revelation from God to the Prophet Muhammad via the angel Gabriel. The Qur'an was "sent down" in this manner over the course of twenty-three years, from the time the Prophet Muhammad was forty years of age until his passing at sixty-three years in the year 632 of the Common Era. Qur'anic revelations speak of this orality: "Recite the Qur'an in a measured pace. Truly We [God] shall soon cast upon thee a weighty Word."[3] Muslims aim to recite the Qur'an just as the Prophet Muhammad taught it, and hence his followers preserved detailed instructions for how to recite it. These instructions, known as *tajwīd*,[4] specify things like how long to hold different vowel sounds, or whether to stop short at the end of a line or draw it out. The purpose of this is to provide, as best one can, the experience of reciting the Qur'an as the Prophet Muhammad recited it and as the angel Gabriel recited it to Muhammad. For Muslims, the Qur'an is God's words coming from a human throat, as the Qur'an says: "God has sent down the most beautiful discourse, a Book consimilar, paired, whereat quivers the skin of those who fear their Lord. Then their skin and their hearts soften into the remembrance of God. That is God's Guidance, wherewith *He* guides whomsoever *He* will; and whomsoever God leads astray, no guide has *he*."[5]

Now, I am at best a tentative theist; I am definitely not keen on the notion of a guy-in-the-sky anthropomorphic God (which, by the way, is not at all a part of the Islamic worldview). But that image of quivering skin was powerful to me. Then, when I listened to recordings of the Qur'an being recited by men and women in Arabic, it became clear that the detached intellectual mindset was not going to work for approaching the Qur'an. I

---

letter sound that is foreign to English. It is also made in the back of the throat by quickly constraining the air flow with the back of the tongue.

3. Qur'an 73:4–5.

4. During the foundational period of Islam, the Prophet Muhammad and his followers taught the Qur'an primarily aurally, and it was not compiled into book form for wider distribution until after the Prophet Muhammad's passing. *Tajwīd* describes the practice of reciting with a precise and correct recitation as was originally practiced by the earliest Muslims. See Qur'an 73:4, which specifies that the Qur'an is to be recited in a slow, measured pace. Muslims will commonly learn the rules of tajwīd from a young age, and there are even Qur'an recitation competitions globally, as captured in the feature-length documentary *Koran by Heart*, directed by Greg Barker (2011), available for streaming at https://www.hbo.com/content/hboweb/en/documentaries/koran-by-heart/koran-by-heart.html. For information on tajwīd, see Mattson, "The Voice and the Pen." See also Kristina Nelson, *The Art of Reciting*.

5. Qur'an 39:23.

made a point of listening to the Arabic first without looking at the translation. Even though I did not know what the words meant, it did not matter as the words bypassed my brain and went straight to my heart. I got chills. This was intense. This was direct.[6] This was also scary. I am not accustomed to the intense and direct in my religious experiences, which I usually route through my brain before letting them get anywhere near my heart.

And then when I went and looked at the translation, particular passages kept jumping out at me that had common themes with Buddhism, a worldview that was familiar to me. Take for instance, the segment of the Qur'an called *Sūrat al-Ḥadīd* (Arabic for "iron"), the fifty-seventh sura of the Qur'an, the exact middle of the Qur'an's 114 segments.[7] In this section, the Qur'an speaks of the delusion of this worldly life with an admonition:

> Know that the life of this world is but play, diversion, ornament, mutual boasting among you, and vying for increase in property and children—the likeness of a rain whose vegetation impresses the farmers; then it withers such that you see it turn yellow; then it becomes chaff. And in the Hereafter, there shall be severe punishment, forgiveness from God, and contentment, and the life of this world is naught but the enjoyment of delusion.[8]

With a similar sentiment, the Dalai Lama writes: "Ordinary happiness is like dew on the tip of a blade of grass, disappearing very quickly. That it vanishes reveals that it is impermanent and under the control of other forces, causes, and conditions."[9] Here was this concept of impermanence, with which I was familiar from Buddhist thought, showing up in the Qur'an, but in theistic terms.[10]

Other verses of the Qur'an talk at length about how, at the moment of death, the veil of delusions is removed from our eyes, and we can see things for what they really are:

6. Here Charity captures beautifully the affective experience, the physical sensations and sense of awe, that many Muslims experience when listening to a recitation of the Holy Qur'an.

7. Iron is the core of our planet and the structural center of the Qur'an; this correspondence is one example of how the Qur'anic revelation, for Muslims, points to wonderous phenomenon in the physical universe.

8. Qur'an 57:20.

9. Dalai Lama, *How to See Yourself*, 217.

10. For more on the similarities and differences between Buddhist and Islamic thought, see Kazemi, *Common Ground*. See in particular the provocative essay by Hamza Yusuf entitled "Buddha in the Qur'ān?," 113–36.

> Did We [God] then weary in the first creation? Nay. But they are in doubt regarding a new creation. / We [God] did indeed create the human being, and We know what *his* soul whispers to him; and We are nearer to him than *his* jugular vein. / When the two receivers receive, seated on the right and on the left, no word does *he* utter without a ready watcher beside him. / And the agony of death comes with the truth. That is what you were avoiding. / And the trumpet is blown. That is the Day of the Threat. / Then every soul comes, with it a driver and a witness: / "You were indeed heedless of this. Now We [God] have removed from you your cover; so today your sight is piercing."[11]

This last part of the passage reminds me of the insight we are expected to derive from Buddhist meditation while focusing on the breath or non-judgmental awareness. This cultivation of awareness helps to strip away the distractions, the delusions, the veils, and allows us to see clearly, helps free us from the filter of our egos.

So, rather than a detached intellectual swaddle, I was instead experiencing: "Wow, this is amazing! Count me in!" Yet, for every "Wow!" moment, for every passage that sent chills through my body, there were others that made my Unitarian Universalist antennae quiver. For example, *Sūrat al-Raḥmān*, the "All-Merciful One" (number fifty-five in the Qur'an), contains many vivid descriptions of the hour of judgment when each human being stands before God and deeds are weighed. Those with heavier good deeds go to a very pleasant garden with other worthy people to dwell in peace. Those whose bad deeds are heavier—well, they do not have such a pleasant eternal end.

Much of the Qur'an is about Heaven and Hell, punishment, moral accountability, and reward in the afterlife. The existence of the afterlife is the main message of the Qur'an, after Islam's central creed "there is no god but God." As someone who does not believe in an active deity, nor in Heaven or Hell as actual, physical places, nor really in the survival of the ego after the death of the physical body, this was a tough aspect of the Qur'an. It wouldn't have been as tough had it not stuck with me so persistently. I felt I couldn't simply accept the other powerful experiences I had and reject the parts of the Qur'an that were uncomfortable to me.

11. Qur'an 50:15–22. The "ready watcher" in this verse is generally held to refer to attendant recording angels that capture a person's good and bad deeds as a witness to the individual's moral stature when records are reviewed on the Day of Judgment.

This was not the detached, intellectual experience I had expected, and I did not know what to do with it. I felt frustrated and a bit angry, to be honest. I needed something to help direct me. Then, I read these verses: "And indeed We [God] have made the Qur'an easy to remember."[12] And, "We have only made this easy upon thy tongue, that haply they may remember."[13] In the seventh century, this referred to the fact that the revelation was in Arabic, revealed most immediately for the people of the Arabian Peninsula. But this message applies not only to the people of the Arabian Peninsula. In the spirit of this sentiment, I took a leap and began to think figuratively when approaching the Qur'an so that I might personally better appreciate the fullness of its messages. Then, I looked again at one passage about Hell that had particularly seared itself into my mind: "This is Hell that the guilty deny; / to and fro shall they pass, between it and boiling waters."[14]

As I read the passage, the thought came to me that each human has the ability to judge her own actions in every moment, and it is only the distractions and delusion of this life that make it possible to sidestep that self-judgment. Once God removes the veil of illusion, one can no longer turn away from the truth of one's actions, and yet, by the time this happens, there's no way of going back and changing things. Here, the constant circling between Hell and boiling water reminds me of the tormented ruminations of a person who's aware both of having done wrong and of the inability to right that wrong. Possibly we experience this inner judgment of the self-reproaching soul in the moment between the realization of impending death and the actual death itself. Maybe that moment, disconnected from our earthly experience of time, feels like an eternity. Or maybe it actually is eternity. In either case, by engaging with the Qur'an through figurative language, I had accessed the powerful meaning in an image I might otherwise have just discarded.

I do not speak Arabic; I don't believe in a deity who acts directly in the world; I don't believe in a literal Heaven and Hell. But when I can reach outside of these boundaries, I find that the Qur'an actually does speak my language. By loosening my intellectual swaddle, I let myself be open to the transcending mystery and wonder affirmed in the Qur'an, and I feel a renewal of my spirit, and an openness to the forces that create and uphold life.

12. Qur'an 54:17, 54:22, 54:32, 54:40.

13. Qur'an 44:58.

14. Qur'an 55:43–44.

I love Unitarian Universalism. Yet, most of the time, Unitarian Universalism feels very safe, very comfortable. Safety and comfort are good things, but too often it seems like we Unitarian Universalists are engaged in a process of keeping everyone comfortable at the expense of the intense experience. We are so afraid of causing discomfort that we file off all the sharp edges. At the same time, in Unitarian Universalism, we have seven principles drawn from six sources. The seven principles get a lot of airtime, but we do not talk so much about the six sources. The first source is "direct experience of that transcending mystery and wonder, affirmed in all cultures, which moves us to a renewal of the spirit and an openness to the forces which create and uphold life." This is a spirit of openness that must animate Unitarian Universalist congregations in our efforts to engage with the wisdom traditions of the world.

With this spirit, I invite you to look at your personal swaddles. What boundaries have you set up to keep you feeling safe and comfortable? By holding tight to safety and comfort, what are you withholding? Where might there be possibility for opening?

REFERENCES

Dalai Lama. *How to See Yourself as You Really Are.* Translated and edited by Jeffery Hopkins. New York: Atria Books, 2006.

Kazemi, Reza Shah. *Common Ground between Islam and Buddhism.* Louisville, KY: Fons Vitae, 2010.

Mattson, Ingrid. "The Voice and the Pen." In *The Story of the Qur'an: Its History and Place in Muslim Life*, 76–136. 2nd ed. Malden, MA: Blackwell, 2013.

Nelson, Kristina. *The Art of Reciting the Qur'an.* Austin: University of Texas Press, 1985.

Trust at the Precipice

Ariz Saleem

Ron typically began his morning routine by approaching my desk for a daily personal check-in; the dry corporate environment we both grudgingly tolerated was no place for so lively a soul as Ron's. He had a peculiar habit of wearing a tie to work every day, which wasn't necessarily a reflection of how seriously he took the job. More tellingly, I believe it spoke to his deep-seated inclination to imbibe positivity wherever he found himself.

Ron was hired around the time of our company's annual employee appreciation "Summerfest." I still recall how the golden cross necklace that Ron wore that day was even more apparent against the dark backdrop of his T-shirt. His cross caught my attention; it seemed almost out of place in the workplace. Yet, as someone who deeply appreciates my own faith, I was intrigued.

"Do you wanna do the obstacle course?" Ron asked regarding the inflatable adult toy that stood before us. "Sure," I responded, despite feeling my reserved nature pushing back against his extroverted friendliness. In our first real interaction at Summerfest that day, I didn't see in Ron's eyes the reserved estrangement that hovers in the background of niceties, but rather a refreshing genuineness that became the gateway to our friendly accord.

Ron wasn't shy about becoming a grown-up kid in an obstacle course at Summerfest, and neither was he hesitant in bringing up religion at work. In fact, on several occasions, he questioned me about the faith I belong to and its tenets. Although I truly appreciated the interest he took in trying to understand me, those conversations didn't always end pleasantly.

"Are you getting breakfast?" Ron asked casually one morning. "No, today I'm fasting," I replied, knowing inevitably that I would have to explain further. “Oh, so just water and fruits?” he inquired. “No food or water from sun up ‘til sun down,” I responded, anticipating some form of surprise, and Ron did not disappoint: “That’s stupid. Why would you do that?” I was just as surprised by his tactless remark. “To please God . . . to get close to Him,” I offered with great hesitation, unsure if the conversation was already too far out of line. “Oh, yeah, cause I’m sure God wants you to starve, right?” he blurted out sarcastically. Now it was unmistakable. He *had* crossed a line. I felt his words wrap around my heart wringing it of the trust that had developed between us. A mumbled refutation was all I could muster. As he walked off, I remember sitting with the feeling of betrayal coupled with an intense need to set the record straight.

So, I set out on a Google search to collect all the verses in the Bible that speak of fasting. It wasn’t only Islam, after all, that required a level of sacrifice to achieve something of divinity in return. Perhaps he would consider that carefully before disrespecting another person’s tradition, I thought to myself, as I sent him links meant to school him on his own faith. Much to my chagrin, he didn’t make any meaningful connection between the verses I sent him and his insensitive comment about the futility of fasting. Eventually, I brushed the incident aside, vowing to be more assertive the next time around.

“How was your night?” He initiated one of our morning ritual conversations. In truth, I had passed the previous evening in a state of gloom. I had listened to a lecture by a prominent American Muslim academic reflect on what the most recent Muslim ban being upheld by the Supreme Court of the United States meant for the future of Muslims in this country. Listening to the professor’s analysis, a commingled sense of estrangement, despair, and fear followed me the rest of the day.

Estrangement was not a new feeling; truthfully, I cannot remember a time when I’ve felt a deep sense of belonging to this country. In middle school, I was the foreign boy who had a mustache much too early and who happened to be an easy target for school bullies. In high school, I was the reserved kid who no one really bothered to befriend. College was probably the first time I felt more at home. The Muslim Students’ Association on campus marked a space where I could easily preserve a greater part of my identity.

Aside from the few pockets of community I enjoy today, I cannot say that I’ve really found a home here. Looking into eyes that reflect back an image of “different,” “foreign,” or even “repugnance” time and time again, and still maintaining a sense of "belonging to America" is quite the challenge. Despite holding the title of "naturalized" citizen, I am not sure I've ever managed to fully rid myself of the status of "alien."

Initially, I hesitated in bringing up such vulnerabilities in the workplace, but he *had* asked, and remembering our past interactions, I felt my story *deserved* to be heard. So, I responded: "Yesterday wasn't the best for me. I listened to a speech by a law professor about the implications of the most recent Muslim ban. I was pretty down for most of the day," I offered tentatively.

"What did he say?" Ron asked. "A lot of things," I began, and proceeded to summarize to the effect: "He talked about how the Muslim Ban shouldn't be mistaken for a simple travel ban, just because of the fact that two non-Muslim countries are listed on it, that including these countries in the ban is meaningless because the North Korean government doesn't allow its citizens to travel to America as it is, and that there was already legislation which pretty much banned the entry of Venezuelans into the US." Ron was listening attentively.

I continued my summation: "He mentioned how when opposition brought in the question of discrimination, the Supreme Court decided what mattered was the legal order before them, and not anything Trump had said or done. So, what this affirms is that as long as the legal language of policy is sufficiently dressed in politically correct terms, the speech and acts of discrimination conducted by the executive branch are perfectly acceptable. In its final decision, the Supreme Court decided that the order was within the jurisdiction of the executive branch and *outside* the jurisdiction of the court system. So, they stripped the moral authority of the courts in this country to interfere . . . this means the executive branch successfully consolidated its power at the expense of the judicial . . . I'm afraid this government is on shaky grounds."

Ron was visibly annoyed by this last comment. "Our government is not turning into a dictatorship, bro. I can't buy that." Frustrated that my point was not sufficiently understood, I retorted: "I'm not saying we are a dictatorship, but what I am saying is that we've taken a tragic step in that direction. It's these gradual yet pivotal steps that can cause a democracy to devolve into an autocracy."

"Trump is here for just four more years," Ron assured me. "I hope so," I muttered back. He looked incredulously at me. "Are you saying you think he's going to be around for more than four years?" "Anything's possible,"

I retorted, "America has been an imperial state for a good portion of its history. All empires fall and it's not always a pretty landing." My gloomy attitude only fueled Ron's emphatic response: "We are *not* turning into a dictatorship. You can relax about that one, bro." His response was hardly comforting.

In fact, his response made me more ill at ease, and I tried to convey the legitimacy of my fears: "The fact that you can't see the possibility of a terrible future makes me afraid that we won't see it coming when it does. If other folks assume that everything will be okay, while everything is *not*, I'm not sure how secure I should feel. Do you know what happened in this country to Japanese *citizens*? Their property was confiscated, their bank accounts were frozen, and they were thrown in internment camps." Ron continued his reassurances, even more emphatically to the effect: "There is no way internment is going to happen here! That's insane! I promise you that I will make sure it doesn't happen."

I refused to take comfort in his undeliverable promises. Giving up I finally responded, "I don't think you can guarantee me protection. Anyway, I don't think it was a good idea to bring this up. I was just trying to vent." The conversation left me more aware of our differences than our similarities. A white Christian male not being able to accept the possibility of the moral failing of a society that only affirms his place and privilege in it was not completely surprising. I could not help but feel drearier about the future than when I had initiated the conversation. I knew in my heart that if it's become acceptable to hate, fear, and effectively ban groups of Muslims from entering this country, then what's to stop this disease from deepening and being channeled toward the domestic Muslim population? Our personal experiences here certainly seem to affirm this trajectory.

Recently, my wife was followed by a driver in a pick-up truck for a few blocks in broad daylight while she walked to the store. Another day, a fellow passenger riding on the subway disembarked and started punching the train window where she was seated. What's tragic is that in both cases, my wife was traveling with our two-year-old daughter. For me, such incidents only augment a creeping awareness that we are part of a culture that accepts some people as less than human.

Since Trump's election, my wife often speaks of leaving the States for the safety of our daughter. On her father's side, my wife has Native American, Barbadian, and African American ancestral roots. On her mother's side, she has Russian and German roots. She is a native-born American citizen with deep historical ties to this land, and yet, she is more pronounced in her desire to leave than I am as a first-generation immigrant. "Whose fight are we fighting? What exactly are we trying to save if we stay? Doesn't our responsibility to our daughter outweigh all other considerations?" These are the questions that keep us up at night after our daughter falls asleep.

Truthfully, I have no clear answers. That we are approaching a definitive point in American history is not hard to see. With political and social tensions on the rise and a looming threat of economic collapse, it would be naïve to trust that everything's going to be alright, as Ron believes. This uncertainty only further complicates my struggle to find a sense of purpose and belonging here. I, for one, cannot root myself in the mythology of America being an exemplar of democracy and freedom to the world. To channel Drs. Cornell West and Noam Chomsky, what we have is a democratic experiment predicated on the murder of indigenous peoples and the slave-labor of Africans that has, more recently, mutated into a hypercapitalist military empire. Can fighting for the survival of such a deformed power structure be worth the safety of my daughter and family? This question presses me to search deeper for a more meaningful connection to this country.

If there has been a saving grace for this nation, it is the powerful voices that have risen in this country's history struggling in the name of justice for the disenfranchised and downtrodden in society. There is a reverberation of beautiful poetic resistance that can heard in the sound of Native American struggles, the civil rights struggle, the struggle for women's rights, and in the struggle of the poor and working-class peoples. It is perhaps here, by tying my intentions and efforts to this parallel tradition of justice-fighters, that I can find meaning for myself and a way forward for my family in this country.

Whether or not Muslims could be stripped of their freedom and safety belongs, at this juncture, to the domain of the unknowable future. Nonetheless, having the courage to hold such conversations, if even between colleagues from across their corporate desks, is an invaluable form of confronting the potential power of evil in our society. Having recently decided to pursue a role in religious leadership, I hope for my work to be a healing balm for the ills that increasingly surround us.

In the face of the uncertain future that lies before me, I choose to *trust*. And in the face of an evil realized, I pray for deliverance from cowardice. May God bring justice and peace to us all. Amen.

In Memoriam

KYTHE HELLER

BERT. THERE WAS HIS gaze. An incredibly gentle, suffering, wryly humorous gaze, as if barely aware of its own depth, its kindness; always seeming clearly present, yet also a bit distracted, removed.

Right now, more than a month since I last saw him, several years after meeting him, I can see that gaze he had. It has flowed into my own body. It has no sound. It was searching for something beyond what it could see, and for this reason, his gaze in my memory has an image but also no image as well.

We spoke, he spoke, of his 3-D animation scheme, of how he wanted to make a lot of money from the stock market. Of how he would like to design a website for me. Of his health, and sometimes, of his early history with the Sri Lankan Sufi teacher Bawa Muhaiyaddeen or his understanding of the Path.[1] Then he would fall silent for a while, as if searching for how to say what it was he had to tell me.

Once, we met by coincidence at Au Bon Pain, and I saw that he noticed the growing calm that came with nightfall, so deep that he looked out the window to see. Frequently, people would pass our table, glancing away from his smell and torn clothing and sometimes knocking against his

1. Cambridge, Massachusetts has, for several decades, been a place of congregation for the Boston branch of The Bawa Muhaiyaddeen Fellowship. The Fellowship belongs to a chain of transmission through the Persian mystic 'Abd al-Qādir Gīlānī (1077–1166) through to the Tamil-speaking guide known as M. R. Bawa Muhaiyaddeen (d. 1986). Bawa Muhaiyaddeen taught a diverse group of spiritual seekers in Sri Lanka prior to being invited by Americans to Philadelphia, Pennsylvania, where he resided and taught from 1971 to 1986, and where his mosque and fellowship house provide hospitality to visitors from around the world. At Fellowship meetings, participants discuss readings published in English by the Bawa Muhaiyaddeen Fellowship Press as well as listen to audio and video segments of their guide's teachings. Meetings close with the *ṣalawāt*, the Islamic prayer and salutation of blessings and peace upon the Prophet Muhammad.

wheelchair. He didn't smile, but said in a single breath: "I want to have a secret Bawa meeting, right now!" He had brought with him in his bag *The Triple Flame: Inner Secrets of Sufism* by Bawa Muhaiyaddeen.

I said that I rarely come to Au Bon Pain, that it must be because of him and his love for the teachings, and Bawa himself, that I had been brought there.

His eyes were beautiful, the most beautiful I have ever seen, so beautiful they hurt.

Part VII

STANDING WITH RESILIENCE

***The Muslim,* by Sobia Ahmad**[1]

1. *The Muslim* is the first painting in a series that Sobia Ahmad began in 2016 in response to the political climate of blatant Islamophobia and xenophobia. Each painting

From movements for immigrant rights to accompanying one another in times of loss, this section explores how we can stand together, pray together, and call together for goodness, light, and hope in our world. The standing together is not in vain; it reaffirms that our compassion is greater than any fear. The way forward requires authentic collaboration and risk-taking in order to build the necessary, durable bonds of trust. We forge these bonds by asking the difficult questions with care, by pushing the limits of our own capacity for listening, by holding ourselves accountabile, and by attending to each other's heart songs.

To begin this section, Zaynab Ansari considers the value of small interfaith efforts grounded in friendship. In preparing her reflection, she consulted academic studies on interfaith dialogue, perused journal articles, and weighed issues of theory and methodology to frame her narrative, but she quickly realized that this approach, while informative, would not necessarily provide the proper backdrop for her particular story of interfaith encounter. Hence, her reflection is not about, as she explained to me, "the theoretical underpinnings of interfaith dialogue, or interfaith work at a macrolevel," but it is instead, "about an organic unfolding of goodwill between a group of women who felt a calling at a deeply personal level, born of their faith, to start—and perpetuate—small kindnesses."

With so many injustices in the world that call out for our attention, do we have the resilience and the stamina to continue to hear and respond, to not pretend that we have not seen the silent suffering of another? Where do we find the physical power and the spiritual energy to continue to strive, even in the midst of our own fatigue? The Reverend Karen G. Johnston makes meaning from the struggles of Job, Tahirah Dean, an immigration lawyer, finds encouragement from an unexpected source, and Rabbi Michelle Dardashti takes to the streets to make an impassioned plea that is inspired as much by her commitments to justice as by her own family history. The section closes with the prayerful poetry of Madonna Arsenault, minister, artist, and spiritual healer.

---

in the series began with collaged images of Muslims in pop culture and news. The final black-and-white paintings only show hints of these sourced images, a reference to misrepresentation and obliteration of Muslim identities through the polarizing and toxic political discourse. The series of paintings is not only a product of catharsis but also a symbol of personal empowerment and resistance whereby the creative process itself becomes a sanctuary.

Small Kindnesses

Zaynab Ansari

In the Name of God, the Lord of Mercy, the Giver of Mercy[1]

"Hast thou seen the one who denies religion? That is the one who drives away the orphan, and does not urge feeding the indigent. So woe unto the praying, who are heedless of their prayers, those who strive to be seen, yet refuse small kindnesses!"[2]

THE KNOXVILLE WOMEN'S PEACE INITIATIVE

This story began with the simplest gesture of all, the small kindness of a woman named Kate Roos, who moved to Knoxville four years ago and promptly emailed the city's only mosque, Masjid Annoor. Fortunately for me, the mosque administrator decided I was just the person to respond to Kate's email as I was settling into my responsibilities as women's scholar-in-residence for the community under the auspices of Tayseer Foundation (now Tayseer Seminary), an organization established to serve the spiritual, educational, and *da'wa*[3] needs of the Muslim Community of Knoxville.

1. It is part of Muslim tradition to commence every good act, including the act of writing, with the name of God, called the *basmala*. In fact, nearly every chapter of the Qur'an begins with this utterance. This translation of the basmala is adopted from Abdel Haleem, *The Qur'an*.

2. Qur'an 107:1–7.

3. *Da'wa* is an Arabic word meaning a call or invitation. Broadly speaking, this term encompasses outreach, pastoral care, religious instruction, and spiritual guidance within

Like Kate, I was also a newcomer to Knoxville, having left my hometown of Atlanta, Georgia with family in tow and was adjusting to life in a pleasant—albeit much smaller—Southern city.

Prior to relocating to Knoxville, I had been active with the Islamic Speakers Bureau of Atlanta (ISB) under the leadership of the dynamic Soumaya Khalifa, whose commitment to bridge-building has propelled the ISB to a position of respect among Atlanta's interfaith community and beyond. Imbued with the desire to continue my interfaith work in my new city but unsure of where to start, I was happy to find myself sitting at Kate's dining table with two women who had also responded to her invitation: Karen Smith from Knoxville's Jewish community and Norma Bailey, a longtime member of a prominent Methodist congregation.

Kate initially conceived of her project—the Knoxville Women's Peace Initiative—as a short-term commitment. A group of interfaith women would meet at area churches once monthly for a period of six months for guided discussion and refreshments. Kate, utilizing what Jeannine Hill Fletcher has called a "storytelling model" of women's interfaith dialogue,[4] would assign a pair of questions for each gathering and encourage participants to write their reflections and share them with the group ahead of time. The question pairs were usually a balance of heavier topics and lighter fare to ensure that the intensity of discussion would not overshadow the entire experience and encourage the more reticent women to feel comfortable opening up to a group that was newly formed and was designed to push members out of their comfort zones. These early meetings also featured tours of members' respective houses of worship as well as a sampling of foods associated with cherished holiday traditions.

Despite the often challenging questions Kate posed, our group managed to cultivate an atmosphere of genuine solicitousness, empathy, and respect that is sorely lacking in today's climate of coarseness and incivility. Nonetheless, I confess to being nervous when I saw that Kate had chosen the following topic for our final meeting of the year:

> CONFLICT: People disagree everywhere. If you could mediate any international conflict, what steps would you propose to bring the parties together?

---

and beyond the Muslim community.

4. Hill Fletcher, "Women in Inter-Religious Dialogue."

With Jewish and Palestinian women at the meeting, where might this conversation lead? Thankfully, my concerns were allayed as Hanan Ayesh (Tante Hanan as she is affectionately called),[5] a pillar of the Muslim community of Knoxville, handled this sensitive topic with candor and grace. Recounting her own experience of dispossession as a stateless Palestinian, she was able to tell her story in a way that included the Jewish members of our group. It was precisely because of Tante Hanan's experiences as a Palestinian making a new life in the United States in the aftermath of dislocation that she was able to transcend her personal pain and reach out to women outside of the immediate Muslim community. As we all listened attentively to her story, I thought of Kate's second question:

> FRIENDSHIP: We have shared our lives for a half year now. What is the value of the friendships we have developed?

The response I had prepared was sincere but also rather generic in that I largely framed my involvement with the Knoxville Women's Peace Initiative as an extension of my professional responsibilities and my previous work in Atlanta. In my role as an *ustādha*[6] for the Muslim community, I knew I had an obligation to share information about Islam and promote religious tolerance, and the Knoxville Women's Peace Initiative checked all those boxes. I dutifully took notes when we toured various churches and temples and was all ready with my Islam 101 handout when the ladies visited the mosque. Ever the teacher, I was planning ahead to 2015 when I would teach a class on women in the Qur'an at our seminary and invite my new interfaith contacts. And even though I initially approached the class with the seriousness that is expected of an *ustādha* of traditional Islam, and I tried my best to teach a class that would appeal to the most conservative Muslim woman, I also found myself learning from my Christian students and appreciating their almost conversational rapport with the Abrahamic saga. In fact, I remember the joy we shared when we all realized the Islamic account of the family of Abraham, peace be upon him, was wonderfully similar to that of the Bible, with Sarah laughing when informed by the angels, that she, well past the age of menopause, was going to have a baby. "I'd

5. "*Tante*," the French word meaning "aunt" is still widely used across the formerly colonized parts of the Middle East and North Africa.

6. *Ustādh* is the Arabic term for professor or instructor, and hence, female teachers of the traditional Islamic sciences are often referred to in the feminine form of the word, as *ustādha*. While a woman can certainly hold the qualifications of a "sheikh" (f. sheikha), this title has traditionally been reserved for those with decades of Islamic learning.

laugh, too, if someone told me I was having a baby at ninety," one of the Christian women said drily, with her Muslim counterpart giggling beside her.

This delightfully human moment underscored several important points for all of us: (1) That our reading of our respective scriptures was enhanced by taking a comparative approach across faith traditions; (2) that as women we found camaraderie in our shared response to the biblical and Qur'anic accounts of Abraham's family; (3) that God validated the emotions of a woman by highlighting the way she laughed, making Sarah that much more relatable in how she dealt with the miracle of the gift of a child in her old age.

Teaching this class and seeing the sincere efforts of my Christian friends to learn about old stories from a new perspective taught me something about small kindnesses—those small moments of exchange when we let down our guard, listen to each other, rejoice in our commonalities, and learn to respect each other's differences. I began to view the Knoxville Women's Peace Initiative as more than an extension of the professional imperative to do interfaith work, and, instead, as a way to grow personally through small, genuine gestures of support and understanding. Our group continued to meet over lunch and book-club picks (*The Faith Club*); we even let men talk for a change when we organized an interfaith panel of clergy at a Unitarian church.[7]

And then tragedy struck.

My husband was killed in a motorcycle accident in October 2015, and suddenly, I found myself a widow in my thirties. Even though I was one of the youngest members of the Knoxville Women's Peace Initiative, I suddenly felt much, much older. In the loss of my husband, I now had a bond with several of the women in my group that transcended discussions of doctrine and ritual, that transcended our diverse religious backgrounds, that transcended our grousing over the contentious presidential election, and that placed all of us on an equal footing. We had a commonality wrought by the greatest equalizer of all: death. Although we were in different seasons of life, we had the shared experience of having lost a life partner, mourning the person whose departure changed the world as we knew it, and learning to live with a painful new normal.

Looking back at the notes, emails, cards, and prayers I received from the members of the Knoxville Women's Peace Initiative, I am still touched

7. Bales-Sherrod, "Women's Peace Initiative."

by the small kindnesses of this group of women who embraced me, the Muslim newcomer to Knoxville. A mere ten days after my husband's passing, I wrote of the fog and darkness of grief in an email to one friend, Susan Montgomery, telling her that I was still stumbling (as if anything else could have been expected). And she wrote back, "I'm sure that you are still stumbling in the fog and darkness of grief. I hope you have wonderful support right there with you, and please know that your sisters in the Women's Interfaith Peace Group love you deeply, and we hold you and your beautiful children in our hearts."

What had begun as a response to an invitation from Kate and an extension of my professional commitments now became a much-needed lifeline as I battled the loneliness, anxiety, and depression that accompanied widowhood. Norma Bailey, a native of Tennessee, whose cornbread we enjoyed right along with Tante Hanan's hummus at one of our first meetings, took me under her wing and made sure I got out of the house during my *'idda*.[8] I faithfully observed the requirements of my 'idda—these requirements were in no way burdensome and, in fact, allowed me a measure of closure in observing an official mourning period for my late husband. Yet, without a wider family network nearby, I felt somewhat isolated once I returned home after work. I had no interest in attending social gatherings, but I was lonely. I needed the time and space to process this devastating loss, but also knew I needed a distraction from the heaviness of my thoughts.

That respite thankfully came in the form of Norma's absolute insistence that she and I have lunch on a weekly basis and that lunch include a caloric dessert we would always split down the middle. I am forever indebted to Norma for the small kindness of treating a grieving young widow to a nice meal, and the invaluable gift of showing this young widow that a new life was possible.

In deciding how to tell the story of my interfaith women's group, I kept returning to the headlines of the day and the troubling developments

8. As specified in the Qur'an (2:234), this required minimum period of celibacy for a widowed Muslim woman is four months and ten days, or if she is pregnant, until the birth of the child. During this time, the widow should not adorn herself seeking to look sexually attractive, should not attend festive social functions, and should focus her attention on immediate necessities, such as going to work, attending to family, or taking care of personal needs. Post-divorce, a woman also observes a celibate waiting period of three menstrual cycles, or the approximate length thereof, which assures that she is not pregnant with the child of her former spouse. In cases of divorce, the former husband still has financial responsibilities toward his former wife throughout her period of celibacy, but there is no requirement for her to restrict social life in mourning.

on the national stage as the current administration stokes fears of immigrant "caravans," attacks the independence of the news media, traffics in pernicious stereotypes about marginalized groups, and targets political opponents by promoting debunked conspiracy theories and threatening to prosecute and arrest those who would protest these excesses. Like many of my fellow Americans, I am deeply worried about rising levels of anti-Semitism, Islamophobia, racism, misogyny, and xenophobia, and the obvious link between hateful rhetoric and acts of violence, as demonstrated in even a cursory glance at the news stories of 2018.

As important and as disturbing as these national developments are, and as imperative as it is to counter the forces of extremism with voices of tolerance, moderation, and pluralism through national campaigns of political organizing, civil disobedience, statements of interfaith solidarity, and support of independent journalism, it is really at the local level that one's own personal commitment to an ethic and praxis of interfaith encounter is fostered, tested, and sustained. In writing this essay, I chose to shine a light on local efforts to promote peace, build bridges of understanding, and bring women of faith together one email at a time, one meeting at a time, one dessert at a time, and one small kindness at a time.

Four years later, Norma, Karen, Lesli, Ginny, Mary Ellen, Naheed, Myra, Louise, Nancy, Dana, Janie, Susan, and other friends still gather over food and conversation. I pray we will continue to meet. We need these human connections now more than ever. We need these small kindnesses exchanged over lunch at Yassin's Falafel House, which incidentally was named "Nicest Place in America" by Good Morning America's Robin Roberts.[9] We need these small kindnesses in the sanctuaries of churches, mosques, and synagogues as we celebrate God's praise or as we mourn our communal tragedies, and we need these small kindnesses in our neighborhoods, communities, towns, and cities as we struggle for the soul of our nation.

The Prophet Muhammad, peace be upon him, is reported to have said, "Whoever is given his portion of kindness has been given his portion of goodness, and whoever is deprived of his portion of kindness has been deprived of his portion of goodness."[10]

May God give us all our portion of kindness!

9. See "Yassin's Falafel House."

10. This hadith is found in the collection of *al-Tirmidhī*, chapter 27. This particular translation is adapted from Elias, "Allah Loves Kindness."

REFERENCES

Abdel Haleem, M. A. S. *The Qur'an: A New Translation*. New York: Oxford University Press, 2004.

Bales-Sherrod, Lesli. "Women's Peace Initiative Reaches across Faith Backgrounds for Understanding and Respect." *Knox News Sentinel*. November 21, 2014. http://archive.knoxnews.com/entertainment/life/womens-peace-initiative-reaches-across-faith-backgrounds-for-understanding-and-respect-ep-789450203–353906281.html.

Elias, Abu Amina. "Allah Loves Kindness and Gentleness in All Things." Faith in Allah. August 6, 2014. https://abuaminaelias.com/allah-loves-gentleness-in-all-things/.

Hill Fletcher, Jeannine. "Women in Inter-Religious Dialogue." In *The Wiley-Blackwell Companion to Inter-Religious Dialogue*, ed. Catherine Cornille, 177–81. Chichester, West Sussex: Wiley-Blackwell, 2013.

Yassin's Falafel House Is Voted Your Nicest Place in America. ABC New Video. October 10, 2018. https://abcnews.go.com/GMA/Living/video/yassins-falafel-house-voted-nicest-place-america-58418220.

Hard-Won Patience

KAREN G. JOHNSTON

Naked I came from my mother's womb, and naked shall I return there; the Lord gave, and the Lord has taken away; blessed be the name of the Lord.[1]

PATIENCE, THEY SAY, IS a virtue. This may not be a universal adage, but patience is considered a virtue in many of the world's faith traditions. It is one of the ten *paramis*, or virtues, in Theravadan Buddhism and one of the six in Mahayanan Buddhism. Patience is lauded in Christian scriptures and is also considered praiseworthy in Islam. Patience, though, is not without its downside; too much patience, for instance, could lead to acquiescence, passivity, or complicity with injustice.

Job is, of course, a figure from sacred history that is the epitome of patience; yet, I find the emphasis on Job's patience to be irksome and likely revisionist, serving the empire, rather than the masses. Along these lines, liberation theologian Gustavo Gutierrez appreciates Job's engagement with God about the nature of unjust suffering. According to Gutierrez, Job teaches us that so long as there is suffering there should be protest, for in protest, our understanding of God becomes more precise and alluring.[2] Jack Miles responds satisfyingly to my sense of outrage at the injustice of God toying with poor Job.[3] He describes God's regret at having wagered on Job's piety, allowing Job to suffer. For Miles, God may be all-powerful, but God can also evolve through engagement with humankind. Elie Wiesel, a

1. Job 1:21 NRSV.
2. Gutierrez, *On Job*.
3. Miles, *God*.

Holocaust survivor, points to the history of redaction of the Bible and offers up his preference for a true ending: Job maintains his integrity and remains in relation with God while staying loyal to his truth as he knows it.[4]

My engagement with Job—like my overall engagement with sacred ancient texts—is from the margins. I am drawn to Job as someone who stands up to unjust suffering and enacts his agency in the world. I am drawn to Job, not because of his patience, but because he is a protester. I even once preached on the Book of Job through the lens of the marriage equality rap song, "Same Love,"[5] pointing out that just like Job refuses to accept the hateful theology of his friends, Mary Lambert refuses the theology of heteronormativity by refusing to cry on Sundays.

Job (Ayūb in Arabic) has a cameo appearance in the Qur'an, but in Qur'anic theology, God is all-powerful, unchanging, and has no integral need for humankind. Like so many of the characters that appear in both the Judeo-Christian tradition and in the Qur'an, the story is told somewhat differently. Job in the Qur'an is recognized as one of Islam's prophets,[6] and the story of his patience and loyalty to God is also briefly recounted.[7] But nowhere in the Qur'anic accounts does Job challenge God. In fact, the Qur'anic emphasis is on God's mercy and favor upon those who supplicate:

> And [mention] Job, when he called to his Lord, "Indeed, adversity has touched me, and you are the Most Merciful of the merciful." So We responded to him and removed what afflicted him of adversity. And We gave him [back] his family and the like thereof with them as mercy from Us and a reminder for the worshippers.[8]

This is not the depiction of Job that I am drawn to at all. This is a Job of submission. *Where is the Job of protest?*

After sitting with all of this, I have come to see that the central Qur'anic concept of patience (*ṣabr*), also carries with it a sense of being resolute, persevering, and steadfast, even in the face of injustice. Because God is understood to be all-powerful, suffering and injustice are often seen as a test to challenge us to rise to the next spiritual level. For instance, one verse of the Qur'an says: "And We [God] will indeed test you with something of fear and hunger, and loss of wealth, souls, and fruits; and give glad tidings to the

4. Wiesel, *Messengers of God*.
5. Haggerty et al., "Same Love."
6. See Qur'an 4:163 and 6:84.
7. See Qur'an 21:83–84 and 38:41–44.
8. Qur'an 21:83–84.

patient."[9] It is not my theology, but if that is the kind of patience that Job has—multidimensional, nuanced, hard-won—then I am on board.

REFERENCES

Gutierrez, Gustavo. *On Job: God-Talk and the Suffering of the Innocent*. Maryknoll, NY: Orbis Books, 1987.

Haggerty, Ben, et al. "Same Love." Performed by Macklemore and Ryan Lewis. Macklemore LLC, 2012.

Miles, Jack. *God: A Biography*. New York: Vintage, 1996.

Wiesel, Elie. *Messengers of God: Biblical Portraits and Legends*. New York: Simon & Schuster, 1985.

9. Qur'an 2:155.

Never Losing Faith

TAHIRAH DEAN

I HAD A RECENT and profound career crisis. The solo practitioner I had been employed by since my last year in law school sold his firm secretly with little regard for my job security or well-being. And so, as a newly minted lawyer, I was job hunting. During that period of unemployment, each morning I awoke to a burning sensation of pain and the overwhelming feeling of loss. I replayed over and over again how I could have been so naïve, so trusting, so oblivious to the deception of this person who had made glittery promises for my future. And just like a bad breakup, I blamed myself for staying with him for as long as I did and tried to feel whole again, to rid myself of the destructive sense of failure.

While I was job hunting, I was also finishing a pro bono asylum case that I had taken while at the firm. My client had fled Haiti after corrupt government officials tried to murder him. I had met him at an immigration clinic at city hall the previous spring when in a cramped conference room, and mostly through an interpreter, he told his story about how he had no choice but to flee to the United States to find work, earn a living, and send money back to Haiti to care for his family. Telling his story, he began to cry. His dark eyes were uninhibited by any pride or embarrassment.

Although I had some doubts as to the success of his asylum claim, seeing him in such a vulnerable state, I decided to take his case. This began an almost nine-month race to gather documents. Another attorney and I, with the help of a few interpreters, worked countless hours to help him craft his story and present it in its truest form, but with clarity and succinctness that fit well enough into the legal guidelines of asylum. While I busied myself trying to sort through the complexities of my client's case, I was also focused on trying to piece my life back together. I thought my self-worth was a direct reflection of my career success, and so I felt like I was, well, nothing. As I attempted to gain perspective—and to decide if I even still wanted to be a lawyer—a close friend counseled me with the following words:

> The optimum and most effective use of your effort, skill set, and knowledge occurs when the thing that you spend the most time on causes you to grow spiritually and intellectually. Your work must be the cause you want to invest your life in. It should make you feel it is worth fighting for. As a rule of thumb, optimum use and efficiency of your time spent in this world is met when your passion is the same as how you make money and how you serve the religion of Allah—all three must be the same or similarly situated.

At the time, I couldn't quite see the direct correlation between being an immigration lawyer and devoting myself to God. It was not until I walked into the JFK Federal Building that houses the federal immigration court, that I began to find clarity.

I had warned my client the previous week that there was a strong possibility that we would lose. I wanted him to understand that if we did not win, he was going to be ordered to be deported. I had convinced myself from a logical perspective that his claim simply was not supported by case law. Despite our expert testimony and our police reports—which are worth gold in court proceedings—I did not think that we could win in the age of Trump. And yet, with little resistance, the government attorney and judge agreed that my Haitian client's case warranted asylum. He was *saved*.

When the judge told my client he had won, he simply nodded and smiled a gentle, knowing smile—what appeared to me to be almost a smirk. You see, for months he had told me that God would take care of him. God would protect him. God would guide *us* to victory. And in return, I spent months trying to convince him that some prayers are simply not answered the way we wish and that life's trials and tribulations are not a reflection of *His* not showing favor on us.

How could *I*, a hijab-wearing, *sibḥa*-carrying[1] weekly mosque attendee, exhibit such a strong dismissal of faith? This devotion to pessimism came not from an absence of faith, but from a forgetfulness of God's con-

1. A *sibḥa* or *misbaḥa* is a string of beads, similar to a rosary, that can assist and remind a person to remember God often. The beads are made of wood, shells, stone, clay marble, and in more recent times, plastic. Often the number on the chain is ninety-nine or thirty-three, which are regarded as auspicious numbers. The term *sibḥa* comes from the Arabic root *s-b-ḥ*, a root that carries the meaning of constantly praising God. A common Muslim expression of awe, "*subḥān Allāh*," is derived from this same root.

stant mercy. Because I had been so consumed by my own anxieties and disappointments, I felt a need to bring my client into my own circle of doom and despair. As a gut reaction to the difficulties of his situation, I wanted him not to lose faith, but to be prepared for the worst scenario possible, just as I did in my day-to-day life (and mostly still do).

However, the day we won, this Haitian-Catholic man taught me an unforgettable lesson. He taught me to never lose faith. He taught me to hold on to every ounce of hope until there is absolutely no chance of victory—and even then, there is still the possibility for God's miracle to play out. The success of that case was mind-blowing. The fact pattern of his incident did not fit perfectly into the case law outlined in the First Circuit. It did not follow the pattern of the few asylum approvals that immigration judges throughout the country were granting—and yet, we won without any difficulty in the eyes of the judge who heard our case.

Now, when I reflect on the difficulties of this last year as an immigration attorney, and as a young professional fighting to find my place in the world, I try to remember the conviction that case, and that client, provided me with: life and law are constantly in flux, but love—love for our fellow human beings, and love for God—are neverending. This is the one thing I can, and will, depend on.

Let My People *In*!

MICHELLE DARDASHTI

"*Bo el Paroh.* / Go to Pharaoh."[1] These are the words from the Hebrew Bible that will be read in synagogues around the world this week—this is the command with which this week's Torah reading opens.[2] Moses is told he must go speak truth to power, to go unto Pharaoh.[3] This is a call that goes out to us again and again and ever so pressingly, so very urgently, right now. Going to Pharaoh. This is what we are doing here today.

I'm humbled and proud and despairing, outraged and heartbroken and determined as I stand with you here, in this moment.

I stand with you today as a daughter—the daughter of an immigrant from Iran. When I heard the news of the executive order banning citizens of seven Muslim-majority countries, including Iran, I trembled to think what might have become of my own family had such an edict rained down before my father had American citizenship.

1. Ex 10:1 JPS.

2. This reflection is adapted from a speech delivered on the steps of the Providence State House at the Muslim Ban protest in Providence, Rhode Island on January 29, 2017. It was later posted on the progressive Jewish website jewschool in the wake of developments regarding the ban on foreign nationals from mainly Muslim-majority countries. Dardashti, "Let My People In."

3. The story of the life of Moses is recounted in many different suras of the Qur'an. Several verses describe Moses and his brother, Aaron, confronting Pharaoh, including verse 20:24, "Go unto Pharaoh! Truly he has rebelled." A later pair of verses in the same sura elaborates: "Go, both of you to Pharaoh! Truly he has rebelled. Yet speak unto him gently, that haply he may remember or have fear [of God]." Qur'an 20:43–44. Another retelling of this episode provides Moses with further instruction, "So go to Pharaoh and say, 'Verily we are sent by the Lord of the worlds, that you may send with us the Children of Israel.'" Qur'an 26:16–17.

I stand with you today as a woman—a woman married to a man who is not a citizen of this country. I speak to you aware of our tremendous privilege that my husband is an Australian citizen and not a citizen of a Muslim-majority country.

I stand with you today as a Jew—a Jew enraged at the thought of how many Jewish lives could have been saved if this country's policies on refugees and immigration had been otherwise during the 1930s. I think about how many need not have perished in Europe during WWII, if only Roosevelt had willed it so.

I stand with you today as a rabbi—a rabbi outraged to hear the American president manipulate a Bible passage in his inaugural address, a passage that I hold dear. "The Bible tells us," he said—"How good and pleasant it is when God's people live together in unity." "God's people?!" I believe he was intending to quote Psalm 133, but his translation and application have subverted its meaning. "*Hineh ma tov umah-naim, shevet a<u>h</u>im gam ya<u>h</u>ad*"—"How good and pleasant it is that brothers [and sisters] dwell together."[4] Trump said, "God's people," rather than brothers and sisters (*a<u>h</u>im*, siblings)—I wonder, does he know that we are *all* God's people and that he dare not pick and choose? This moment demands that we think expansively of brotherhood and sisterhood, and of what it means to dwell *together*.

I stand with you today as a mother—a mother with her three children who are here today. I stand as a mother eager for this protest to serve as an opportunity for my children to see and be part of what "dwelling in unity" is really about.

I stand with you today as a proud and agitated American. An American-Iranian-Jewish mother and wife and daughter of immigrants who was taught to *remember*. On Passover, we tell the story of Israelites in bondage and say, "this year we are enslaved—next year may we be free." Egypt in Hebrew is *Mitsrayim* ("from the straits"), and the word comes to represent the places of narrowness and constriction that we perennially face on the path toward personal and collective liberation. That is why each and every year, we say *next year* may we be free, because we know well that there is always more work to do on the road to redemption.

I was raised to remember to care for the stranger because I was the stranger—and the oppressed, those seeking protection—because my people have been oppressed and in need of protection. I was taught

4. Ps 133:1 JPS.

to be ever-vigilant against pharaohs, to remember the Holocaust, and to never stand by while history threatens to repeat those horrors on anyone, anywhere.

The executive order—the Muslim Ban—is an egregious manifestation of *Mitsrayim*, and even if it is stayed or amended, it is clear we are going to need to remain awake and resilient. Egypt is upon us, friends, and we are going to need to be *brave*, to *love* bravely—across lines and despite fears. We are *all* God's people—we are all *each other's* people. We are going to need to boldly go to Pharaoh and say, "Let our people in!" And this is what Emma Lazarus—the Jewish immigrant whose words grace the Statue of Liberty—meant when she famously said that "until we are all free, we are none of us free."[5] *Until we are free, we are none of us free.*

I am humbled and proud and despairing, outraged and heartbroken and determined as I stand with you here in this moment—as we declare together to our Muslim neighbors, friends, and students—to refugees and immigrants and international students from Syria, Iraq, Libya, Iran, Somalia, Sudan, Yemen, and more, *know this and hear this: you are our brothers and sisters; we will dwell with you in unity—we will fight for you.*

We will go to Pharaoh. This is our pledge.

REFERENCES

Dardashti, Michelle. "'Let Our People IN': An Iranian-Jewish-Mother-Wife-and-Rabbi Speaking Truth to Power on the Steps of the State House." jewschool. July 14, 2017. https://jewschool.com/2017/07/79873/let-people-american-iranian-jewish-mother-wife-rabbi-speaking-truth-power-steps-state-house/.

Lazarus, Emma. "A Quote from Epistle to the Hebrews." *Jewish Women's Archive: Sharing Stories, Inspiring Change.* https://jwa.org/media/quote-from-epistle-to-hebrews.

5. Lazarus, "A Quote."

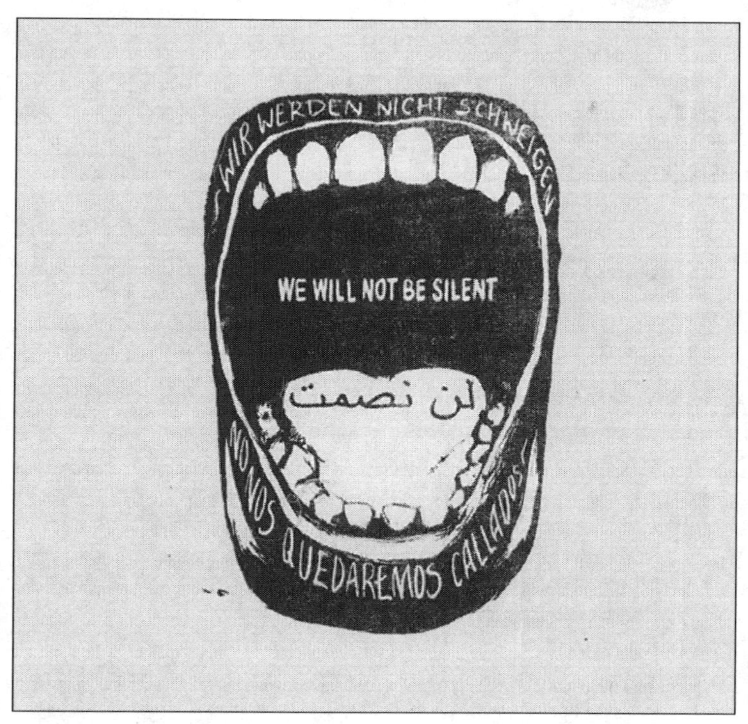

***We Will Not Be Silent*, by Erik W. Martinez Resly**[1]

1. Screenprint on fabric (2018) by Erik W. Martinez Resly in collaboration with Bakht Arif, as designed for street theater actions and trainings at The Sanctuaries in Washington, DC.

Shajara[1]

Madonna J. C. Arsenault

I

I am a Tree.
This birch of breath and bone is strong,
because of Your unfailing Kindness and Mercy.

My children climb me still.
You are the Womb Who carries them forever,
and the Breasts Who nurture their souls.
My bark is curled back in beauty.
Only You can see.
Do what You will.

My bark will kindle what You desire.
The surest canoes come from the birch.
I am carved to carry prayer.
Yā Khāliq, yā Barī'[2]

1. *Shajara* means "tree" in Arabic.
2. O Creator, O Fashioner.

II

Divine Compassion,
this willow is falling
into Your purest water.
My tendrils are whirling
into You.
I know You see.

They soak into Your currents.
You are the All-Encompassing,
the tide my soul understands,
the path among my curves.
Yā Baṣīr, yā Wāsiʿ.[3]

III

I remember
the guidance of the hours,
the purifying direction.
Your Love,
inward and outward,
embracing me forever.

Breath of the Compassionate,
You have created the sun and waters;
You sustain all beings.
You know all things.
Yā Hādī, yā ʿAlīm.[4]

3. O Possessor of Sight, O All-Encompassing One.
4. O Guide, O Knower.

Epilogue

Celene Ibrahim

This Project That Is America

As I have compiled this anthology, the future of the Trump-era legislation widely known as the Muslim ban is being debated within the American judicial system and in the public sphere. Protections for women asylum seekers fleeing abuse have been rolled back, protests of policies promoting family separation for asylum seekers are continuing in the face of unmet promises for reunification, a new denaturalization task force has been announced, and the ongoing uncertainty for undocumented people is leaving families who have been in the United States for decades vulnerable, without recourse to a basic sense of safety and security. As if that were not enough to rend our hearts and our communities, heinous mass shootings continue to tear through our society with mind-numbing regularity.

Our problems are symptomatic of collective moral failings, our insatiable greed, our quests for power and recognition at any cost. Some would point to religion as part of the problem; but our arrogance, ignorance, and under-probed ideologies are the construction material for dividing walls. Yet our highest moral values—civic and religious alike—call us to build together, to create bonds of trust, and to give generously out of a profound sense of compassion for one another. How do we actually achieve these ideals in the midst of all of life's messiness and amidst all of our human failings?

YEARNING FOR LIBERTY

The life of the spirit—whether within institutional contexts or at their fringes—is where liberation from egoism is to be found. We must attempt to transcend our baser tendencies by cultivating our capacities for generosity, empathy, and humility. The struggle against ignorance and egoism is what the Prophet Muhammad, may peace and blessings be upon him, described as "the greater jihad," the struggle that ultimately transcends every other life struggle. This was the cause that I was initially drawn to within Islam, and this is the cause that continues to be a driving motivation of my work, whether as a chaplain or as an academic.

In the process of struggling to be faithfully Muslim in America, I have had to dispel a lot of ignorance, including my own, but I have also witnessed a good share of light and hope. Never could I have imagined that this religion, as misunderstood and denigrated as it was in post-9/11 America, could nonetheless draw coalitions of tens of thousands of allies turning out and standing up at airports and town squares across the country in what will, no doubt, be remembered as watershed moments for American Muslims, as people from all walks of life affirmed their solidarity with their neighbors, colleagues, and friends in the face of blatantly anti-Muslim legislation. Never could I imagine that in the course of my training as a Muslim theologian I would be invited to preach in more Sunday pulpits than there are Sundays in the month.

We are living in unpredictable times, and we must continue to show up, speak up, and stand up for and with one another. Sure, it is harder to build than it is to destroy, harder to trust than to fear, easier to be preoccupied with our self-centered whims than to give freely of what we most love. It may be easier to sidestep moral responsibility than to hold ourselves accountable; still, we must struggle to build, to trust, to give, to love with abandon, and to hold ourselves to a higher standard.

Human beings do not come into the world accompanied by an operational manual for how to treat other human beings. Our manuals must be assembled from our life experiences, from the texts and traditions that inspire us, and from the people who have influenced and shaped us. Through encounters with and across human differences, we are challenged to become yet more compassionate beings, beings better equipped to struggle against the vanities of our egos. In short, as my colleague and friend Basma so aptly captured it: "our experiences change who we are."[1] Even as we celebrate our own identities and experiences, we must never stop growing. Having a sense of identity and belonging is a beautiful aspect of being human; however, in our convictions and our alliances, we must not lose sight of our interdependences and the fundamentally porous nature of our beings on the deepest of levels.

Can we care for one another with the ideals of civility, dignity, honesty, truth, commitment, and generosity that undergird our great wisdom traditions? Can we bolster the version of robust pluralism for which these wisdom traditions, and the American polity, can stand? Can we be greater together? Can we still dare to dream?

REFERENCES

Peace, Jennifer Howe, and Or Rose. "The Value of Interreligious Education for Religious Leaders." In *Interreligious/Interfaith Studies: Defining a New Field*, edited by Eboo Patel, Jennifer Howe Peace, and Noah Silverman, 172–82. Boston: Beacon, 2018.

1. See Peace and Rose, "The Value of Interreligious Education," 173–76.

Index of Scripture